Theorising Desire

Also by Kristyn Gorton

PSYCHOANALYSIS AND THE PORTRAYAL OF DESIRE IN TWENTIETH-CENTURY
FICTION: A Feminist Critique

Theorising Desire
From Freud to Feminism to Film

Kristyn Gorton
*Lecturer, Department of Theatre, Film and Television,
University of York*

First published 2008 by
PALGRAVE MACMILLAN
Houndmills, Basingstoke, Hampshire RG21 6XS and
175 Fifth Avenue, New York, N.Y. 10010
Companies and representatives throughout the world

PALGRAVE MACMILLAN is the global academic imprint of the Palgrave Macmillan division of St. Martin's Press, LLC and of Palgrave Macmillan Ltd. Macmillan® is a registered trademark in the United States, United Kingdom and other countries. Palgrave is a registered trademark in the European Union and other countries.

ISBN-13: 978–1–4039–8960–4   hardback
ISBN-10: 1–4039–8960–5   hardback

This book is printed on paper suitable for recycling and made from fully managed and sustained forest sources. Logging, pulping and manufacturing processes are expected to conform to the environmental regulations of the country of origin.

A catalogue record for this book is available from the British Library.

Library of Congress Cataloging-in-Publication Data

Gorton, Kristyn, 1972–
    Theorising desire: from Freud to feminism to film / Kristyn Gorton.
        p. cm.
    Includes index.
    ISBN 1–4039–8960–5 (alk. paper)
1. Desire in motion pictures. I. Title.

PN1995.9.D39G67 2008
792.43'653—dc22   2007048686

10   9   8   7   6   5   4   3   2   1
17   16   15   14   13   12   11   10   09   08

Printed and bound in Great Britain by
CPI Antony Rowe, Chippenham and Eastbourne

For Paul

Contents

Figures

Acknowledgements

This book was written in part due to a grant from HEFCE which not only allowed me time to write sections of the book, but also gave me the opportunity to work with Sara Ahmed, whose work on emotion has influenced my approach to desire. Research for this book developed from work I did for *Psychoanalysis and the Portrayal of Desire in Twentieth-Century Fiction: A Feminist Critique* (Edwin Mellen, 2007); it is informed also by articles I have had accepted for publication in the journals *Feminist Review, Studies in European Cinema and Feminist Theory*.

My gratitude goes to my former colleagues at Leeds Metropolitan University, in particular: Lance Pettitt, Mary Eagleton, Simon Gunn, Valerie Alia, Melanie Chan, Neil Washbourne, Michael Bailey, Dan Laughey, Dario Llinares, Claire Chambers, Steve Wright, Dave Webb, Pat Cook, Elaine Newsome and Sue Chaplin, who have supported, inspired and nurtured me along the way. Lisa Taylor deserves special mention for not only being a wonderful colleague but also a most treasured friend. Although by the time this book is in print I will have taken up a position in the Department of Theatre, Film & Television at the University of York, I will not forget the pleasure of working with them.

I am fortunate to have a large and supportive family who continue to love me from across the Atlantic: Margie and John Wheeler, Meggan and Andrew Watterson, Elizabeth Wheeler, Tracy and Kirk Ritari, Cathy and David Watterson, Jane and Maier Driver, Sally and John Garber, Charles Seelbach, Betty Boyd, Heather Flett and Chad Gibbs— thank you for being the kind of family that is there for every celebration and crisis. My friends and family here and elsewhere are invaluable: Joanne, Connor and Leon Blackledge, Belinda Johns, Jamie Murphy, Catherine Porter, Brigie de Courcy, Kevin McGee, Louisa Tamplin, Esther Wohlgemut, Kamila Shamsie, Krissy and John Ancher, Claire Higson, Allyn Pazienza, Brian McCook and Jenny Wheeldon deserve exceptional recognition, along with Johnny and Matthew Marsden, my gorgeous step-sons, who although relatively uninterested in my work, always want their own copies. Many thanks to Zoe Beloff, for inspiring conversations and for making the brilliant film

Charming Augustine. Patricia O'Neill deserves special recognition, not only for her careful attention to the manuscript but also for her never-ending friendship. She is the kind of teacher who inspires you to be one.

Finally, and as always, I want to thank Paul Blackledge. This book is dedicated to him, for without him this book would have just been a conversation we had in the pub a long time ago. He continues to inspire me to write about desire and emotion—things he always brings out in me.

Introduction

The concept of desire maintains a strong influence on the narratives we read, the stories we hear and the images we see. Desire is a fluid, multiple and dynamic force that is transformative, destructive and life-changing. It is a difficult and perhaps an impossible concept to pin down, explain or 'solve'. Desire's abstract nature is part of its power; its elusive quality is what draws us in and invites us to 'make sense' of its energy.

In this book I examine the concept of desire through its expressions in film, television and popular culture, and attempt to synthesise interpretations of desire from psychoanalytic, feminist and film theoretical perspectives, in order to demonstrate how the concept of desire offers us a powerful way of understanding ourselves, the society we live in and the limitations and possibilities we have for self-expression. I suggest that desire is a progressive force that underlines movement—whether of a narrative, a gaze or analysis and that it resists interpretation and any final closure.

In her excellent study 'Metaphors of Desire' (1997), Alice Deignan traces the various ways in which desire is used as metaphor using the Bank of English, a 211-million word resource which draws on naturally occurring, current English, such as is found in magazines, letters, conversation and radio journalism. Through this resource, Deignan offers a catalogue of the ways in which desire is used as metaphor—such as 'desire as an external force', 'desire as an awakening', 'desire as appetite' and 'desire as fire' (1997, 25–33). Her work outlines the ways in which desire is used to explain life-altering situations and to catalogue its consequences and manifestations.

As this book will argue, one of the most potent metaphors of desire used within film and television is desire as an awakening, as a force or movement that draws the subject from her position and transforms

1

her life. Part of the reason I draw on contemporary examples as illustrations of how we can theorise desire is because it is possible to cut across genres and expectations and yet still find similar expressions of the concept of desire. We can take examples as disparate as the classic Hollywood film *A Streetcar Named Desire* (1951), the British television series *Blackpool* (2004) and the Indian film *Fire* (1996), for instance, and find very similar references to the way in which desire changes lives.

Deepa Mehta's moving film *Fire*, for example, is a story of two women who fall in love with each other. Within the film, desire is figured as something transformative and life-changing. The film focuses on the lives of Radha (Shabana Azmi) and Sita (Nandita Das), who live with their husbands and mother-in-law above the restaurant/video store in which they both work. Sita is disappointed with her arranged marriage to Jatin, who is really in love with another woman. She is seen as more progressive than Radha, as she will not passively accept her situation and instead wants more from her life. She draws Radha into her world and into the possibility that there is more to life than subservience to one's husband. As their relationship develops, the women become concerned that the family will discover their secret. Radha begins to feel selfish for the desires she feels and tells Sita that she really is not much different from Mundo, who has been caught masturbating to pornography in front of the family's elderly mother. She asks Sita: 'Is it so bad to be that selfish? I'm not so different from him. It scares me.' 'This is unfamiliar for me—this awareness of needs, of desires ...' (Mehta 1996). No longer simply the object of her husband's repressed desires, Radha begins to experience desire herself and at first sees this as a frightening and threatening feeling—something that could possibly destroy the safety and security of her home. As her feelings develop she gains strength from her desire for Sita and finally confronts her husband with her feelings. He tells her that 'desire brings ruin' and she replies: 'you know that without desire I was dead. Without desire there is no point in living. And you know what else? I desire to live. I desire Sita. I desire her warmth, her compassion, her body. I desire to live again' (Mehta 1996). Her admission of desire and rejection of his advances enrages her husband and in the midst of their argument, her sari catches fire. Her husband watches without helping, and instead carries his mother to safety. In his eyes, the fire that engulfs Radha is her punishment and evidence that 'desire ruins'. However, fire is used in Mehta's film not as a destructive element, but as one, like desire, that is liberating and transformative. In the final scene we see the two women hold each other in their arms. Although changed by the fire, Radha is also freed from the life she has been leading and open to the new desire that embraces her.

Moving from an independent and highly evocative film on the screen to a television series that plays with the musical genre, the notion that desire is transformative and life-changing is presented and explored in Peter Bowker's *Blackpool*. The series begins with a murder in a Blackpool casino owned by Ripley Holden (David Morrissey). DI Peter Carlisle (David Tennant) is hired to investigate the case and instead falls in love with Holden's wife, Natalie (Sarah Parish). She feels undesirable to her husband and finds Carlisle's attention exciting and intriguing. They spend the night together and for once in a long time, she experiences desire. The next day they meet on the seaside in order to discuss both what happened and the fact that Carlisle is investigating her husband. When asked what the night meant to her, Natalie tells Carlisle it was 'like when someone turns on the lights and you realise you've been sat in the dark for hours' (Bowker 2004). This metaphor, of turning the light on in a dark room, is used to convey the way desire opens new possibilities and initiates change in the characters' lives whether they wish for it or not. Indeed, Natalie tries to return to her husband feeling that she is obliged to support him, but in the end, he encourages her to follow her desires and not to miss the opportunity because of her feelings of loyalty to him. The series usefully explores two desires: Ripley's desire to open a Las Vegas-like Casino in Blackpool and the desire between Natalie and Carlisle. Ultimately, the series suggests that Ripley is able to let go of Natalie because he understands the true importance of desire to living one's life. He never compromises on his desire even though his expectations are not fulfilled, and he expects and allows the same for his wife, even though it means losing her.

The likening of desire to a light turned on can be found in *A Streetcar Named Desire*, a film that I feel needs to have some mention for its relentless presentation of desire on screen. Adapted from Tennessee Williams's 1951 play, many will remember the plot, but for those who do not, the film centres on Blanche DuBois's (Vivien Leigh) visit to her sister Stella's (Kim Hunter) house. Stella's husband, Stanley Kowalski (Marlon Brando), is reticent to welcome Stella's sister in the house, particularly as he believes she has unfairly squandered the family inheritance. Blanche's demand for aesthetic beauty and extravagance is an affront to Stanley's working-class values and he sees her as a frivolous and pretentious woman. The close confines of their small apartment and the heat of New Orleans leads to dramatic confrontations between Stanley and Blanche and ultimately to her unwilling departure. Blanche initially seduces one of Stanley's card-playing buddies, Harold Mitchell (Karl Malden). They go out together to dance and in the moonlit night; Blanche confides in 'Mitch' about the untimely loss of her first love. She recounts her first experience of desire: 'He was a boy, just a boy when I was a very young girl. When I was 16 I made the discovery—love—all at once and much, much too completely. It was like you suddenly turned a blinding light on something that had always been half in shadow; that's how it struck the world for me' (Kazan 1951). Blanche's reference to 'turning a light onto darkness' anticipates the later television series where the same metaphor is used to describe a moment of desire and self-awakening. In both cases, desire is posited as something positive and productive—as a force that renders the world as different and as more intense.

These examples, however disparate and brief, highlight the way in which desire does something to the characters and the narrative to move them along, to change the path they have been on, to transform the way they see the world. They highlight the transformative movement of desire, and at the same time exemplify desire as something that is always 'in progress' and therefore difficult to pin down. Part of what this book aims to do is to consider where psychoanalysis, feminist theory and film theory can be useful in terms of theorising the concept of desire: to map out their lines of intersection and difference and to consider new ways of bringing them together in terms of theorising desire. The point in doing this is not only to appreciate where a theorisation of desire might fall in current work within cultural studies, but also because desire needs to be understood both in terms of an abstraction and in terms of an everyday presence.

Recent literature on desire (Irvine 2006; McGowan 2004; Verhaeghe 1999b) illustrates a shift from a society that would understand the concept of desire in relation to sexuality to one that would more likely figure the concept in terms of material acquisition. It is more common, in other words, that someone would think about the desire for chocolate or the latest ipod than about their feelings for the girl next door. Part of this shift is blamed on the progressive effects of capitalism, while others, particularly those influenced by psychoanalytic thought, see it as a result of the destruction of the big 'Other'; or in more colloquial terms: the death of the master figure. Another noted shift is from a society that prohibited enjoyment to one that encourages and, as some argue, demands enjoyment. The result is that desire has come to be figured in very different ways and through diverse representations. And yet, desire maintains very stringent boundaries, particularly in terms of female desire.

'From Freud to Feminism to Film' marks out the intellectual contributions from psychoanalytic, feminist and film theory to a theorisation of desire. The concept of desire can be traced back before Freud and the birth of psychoanalysis, but Freud's understanding of desire maintains its dominance in both feminist and cinematic interpretations and in current perspectives of desire in contemporary culture. It is for these reasons that I limit the origins of this theorisation to Freud. The 'from' is not intended to reflect a point of departure or to refer to a historical development, rather it is used to emphasise the ways in which each school of thought has added to a conceptual development of desire. The 'to' signs for the ways in which these intellectual influences both resonate with and resist each other. Concepts such as risk, hysteria, the gaze, shame and melancholia, which structure the book, are used to explore moments of convergence between psychoanalysis, feminism and film. Cinematic and televisual examples both compliment my theorisation of desire and offer their own contribution. In other words, the use of film and television in this project is not simply a matter of applying theory to text but evidence of the ways in which these mediums deepened, enrich and provide an understanding of desire.

The first three chapters are more heavily weighted towards a theorisation of desire; the final two chapters consider more specifically how desire can be theorised through cinematic and televisual examples. Chapter 1, for instance, traces the concept of desire from Freud to feminism to film in order to provide the reader with the necessary theoretical background to appreciate the practical applications of the concept of desire to contemporary film, television and popular culture. This chapter does not presume to be comprehensive in its scope, instead it offers a focused and accessible introduction to the concept in order to best explore desire in subsequent chapters. In exploring some of the models of desire, this chapter also considers the relationship between desire and risk through an analysis of Michael Winterbottom's film *Code 46* (2003). The film illustrates what could be referred to as a contemporary Oedipal drama, and in so doing, helps to consider the ways in which desire is mediated by risk.

The second chapter draws on the figure of the hysteric, and on the theorisation of hysteria, often thought to be the beginning of psychoanalytic thought, particularly given Freud's and Lacan's early work on hysteria and paranoia. Freud's well-known case of Dora serves as a background to contemporary articulations of hysteria in Todd Haynes's *Safe* (2003) and through a reading of *Bridget Jones's Diary* (2001) and the popular American television series *Ally McBeal* (1997–2002).

Chapter 3 examines the concept of the gaze, from Freud's work on scopophilia, to Lacan's 'mirror theory' and cinematic and feminist appropriations of this concept and its theorisations. I then consider, in particular, how the gaze functions within melodrama. Drawing on a comparison of Douglas Sirk's *All That Heaven Allows*, Rainer Werner Fassbinder's *Ali: Fear Eats the Soul* and Todd Haynes's *Far From Heaven*, I argue that desire is constructed, through the gaze, as something that transforms people's lives and as something that draws in the viewer and encourages the viewer to 'have a good cry'. This 'good cry' marks the viewer's participation in the film and in the construction of desire.

In Chapter 4, I consider the implicit link between female desire and shame. French film director Catherine Breillat argues that part of what her work offers is a vision of shame. Referring to her films *Romance* (1999) and *Anatomy of Hell* (2004), this chapter explores the difference between submission and surrender and the affect of shame within presentations of female desire. The chapter also examines the popular American television series *Sex and the City* (1998–2004) as a means of exploring how the issue of shame is handled in a mainstream and widely viewed programme.

Finally, Chapter 5 considers how melancholia is linked to desire through an examination of memory, repetition and loss. Through discussions of *Hiroshima Mon Amour* (1959) and *In the Mood for Love* (2000), this chapter argues that repetition moves desire along a register of affect and decentralises its place within psychoanalytic constructions of desire: it underlines desire as *movement*.

Throughout the book there is an emphasis on a theorisation of desire that does not fall neatly into any one model of the concept of desire. Instead, this book aims to draw on a number of ways in which desire has been understood in order to fully explore its potential within contemporary culture and through contemporary texts. In order to do so, this book both draws on recent work on emotion and affect as well as from psychoanalysis, feminism and film studies.

1
Theorising Desire

> Desire is an attitude aiming at enchantment.
> (Sartre 1956, 394)

In her work on the 'cultural politics of emotion' Sara Ahmed poses the question, 'what do emotions do?' (2004) rather than asking what emotions are. As she suggests, 'emotions are not simply something "I" or "we" have. Rather, it is through emotions, or how we respond to objects and others, that surfaces or boundaries are made: the "I" and the "we" are shaped by, and even take the shape of, contact with others' (2004, 10). The distinction Ahmed makes is an important one, one that can be extended to thinking about desire and its affects. Instead of asking what desire is, it is more productive to ask, what does desire do?[1] How does it create surfaces and boundaries? How are 'we' shaped by its affects? And how is desire presented to us on screen? This book will rely on examples from film, television and contemporary culture to consider both how we theorise desire, and what desire does.

Another reason to take this approach, instead of a more historically orientated or definition-based project, is because the applications I will draw upon largely come from popular culture. It is important therefore to think about what desire *does* rather than to consider what it *is*. As Joke Hermes points out in her re-reading of popular culture: 'The value of popular culture, whatever its textual qualities, is in what audiences *do* with it' (2005, 13). Audiences do things with what they see or read; they respond both emotionally and physically to events on screen. It is for this reason, and others, that I will focus my attention on what desire does rather than attempt to define what it is or to map out its parameters. In order to understand what desire does, it is also necessary to consider how it is theorised, particularly how it has been interpreted within cultural studies.

How do we theorise desire? Desire has been understood as both an emotion and an affect, as a drive, and as the essence of human subjectivity (Spinoza).[2] Psychoanalytic interpretations position desire as lack (Freud and Lacan); Deleuze and Guattari challenge this conception and figure desire as production; feminist theory addresses the gendered nature of desire (Irigaray, Braidotti and Grosz); and in contemporary criticism desire is linked with materialism and alienation. This chapter will explore ways in which desire is theorised in order to provide a conceptual background to allow us to theorise how desire is presented on screen, and how desire works in culture.

In order to theorise desire it is necessary to consider psychoanalytic models. However, in so doing, I am at risk both of alienating some readers who consider psychoanalysis passé and of frustrating other readers for not following psychoanalytic interpretations to the letter. In taking this risk, I hope to demonstrate the importance of an engagement with psychoanalysis and, at the same time, the necessity to challenge its interpretations through an engagement with other theoretical models. In *The Metastases of Enjoyment*, Slavoj Žižek comments on the way the academic community ritually announces the death of psychoanalysis: 'One of the seasonal rituals of our intellectual life is that every couple years, psychoanalysis is pronounced *démodé*, surpassed, finally dead and buried' (1994, 7). The viability of psychoanalysis as a critical tool within cultural studies remains a contested issue, and yet it is a critical tool we cannot do without in a theorisation of desire.

In their work on 'rethinking psychoanalysis in the postmodern era' Elliott and Spezzano argue that what is emerging today is a kind of 'psychoanalysis of psychoanalysis' (1999, 28). One of the consequences of this development is a reconsideration of the relation between self and other. In traditional psychoanalysis the movement between unconscious fantasies and rational understanding is considered to be the foundation of the analytic process. Postmodern interventions, however, emphasise the centrality of desire, affect and imagination as essential to the creation of 'personal meaning and intersubjective understanding' (Elliott and Spezzano 1999, 28). In other words, one of the central issues within psychoanalysis concerns that which can 'be psychically processed and thus transformed' (Elliott and Spezzano 1999, 29). Focus on transformation places emphasis on a connection between remembering and forgetting: in order to cure the patient it is necessary to excavate the psyche. This process establishes a model whereby remembering and talking through or 'working through' these memories (therapeutic cure) allows the subject to 'let go' of past traumas. The postmodern turn calls this model into question, drawing attention to the 'heterogeneity and polyvalence of psychic representations'; it embraces the 'fragmentation and dislocation inherent in human experience' (Elliott and Spezzano 1999, 31–32) which demand rethinking of central concepts such as narcissism, hysteria and melancholia, concepts which will be explored in subsequent chapters. The influence of postmodernism on psychoanalysis, Elliott and Spezzano argue, demands a more 'open and creative approach', one that understands 'meaning as also rooted in non-verbal or pre-symbolic modes of generating experience' (1999, 32).

In rethinking psychoanalysis, Elliott and Spezzano also suggest that the problem of the scientific status of psychoanalysis, a problem addressed specifically in Lacan's *The Four Fundamental Concepts of Psychoanalysis* (1977), is replaced by problems of 'internal critique, cross-linking and fusion of existing paradigms' (1999, 29)—in other words, psychoanalysis must update itself in order to remain a vital theory. In identifying some of the problems, questions and new formations that emerge within psychoanalysis after the postmodern turn, Elliott and Spezzano validate psychoanalysis as a theoretical framework that continues to have relevance and usefulness to scholars despite the challenges it faces in light of new theoretical developments.

However, Elliott and Spezzano's approach also poses some new questions and problems. What happens, for example, to central concepts within psychoanalysis, such as desire, when we 'psychoanalyse psychoanalysis'? How does the appropriation of psychoanalysis by critical theorists into other paradigms such as postmodernism, feminist theory and film studies effect our understanding and use of concepts such as desire?

If there has been an 'affective turn', as theorists such as Woodward (1996), Berlant (1997) and Nicholson (1999) suggest, is this a turn away from psychoanalysis? And if so, how do we theorise the concept of desire? Part of what this chapter will argue is that while psychoanalytic models are still viable, they are made more vital through the influence of feminist theory, particularly in work on affect and emotion, and in cinema studies. Instead of turning away from psychoanalysis, it is useful to consider how psychoanalysis can be revitalised in conjunction with other theoretical models within feminist and film theory.

Theorising desire

One of the most useful definitions of desire can be found in Jean-Paul Sartre's *Being and Nothingness* (1956). Sartre describes desire as *trouble* (1956, 387) and draws an analogy between troubled water and the desiring consciousness as troubled. According to Sartre's analogy, desire stirs things up from below, muddying the surface, and clouding our perspective. And yet, as Sartre points out, this 'troubled water' maintains its essential characteristics: its fluidity and viscosity. In this way Sartre draws attention to the physical transformations desire affects: most of us will know that when we are 'in love' we see, feel, taste, smell and experience things differently (and usually more acutely). Our bodies feel different to us; we can literally feel the affect desire has on us. Sartre writes:

> Desire is defined as *trouble*. The notion of 'trouble' can help us better to determine the nature of desire. We contrast troubled water with transparent water, a troubled look with a clear look. Troubled water remains water; it preserves the fluidity and the essential characteristics of water; but its translucency is 'troubled' by an inapprehensible presence which makes one with it, which is everywhere and nowhere, and which is given as a clogging of the water by itself. [...] If the desiring consciousness is *troubled*, it is because it is analogous to the troubled water.
>
> (1956, 387)

The conceptualisation of desire offered by Sartre in *Being and Nothingness* reminds us to consider desire as something that affects not simply the body, but consciousness. Desire, for Sartre, is 'not only *longing* ... which directs itself through our body toward a certain object' (1956, 387), but *trouble*.[3] In other words, desire clogs, obstructs and arrests consciousness. Referring to the expressions often associated with desire, that 'it takes hold of you' or 'overwhelms' or 'paralyzes', Sartre draws attention to desire's specificity and the distinction that can be drawn between desire and other drives such as hunger. Sartre's understanding of desire draws attention to the way desire positions, anchors or fixes the individual in the world and in its relation to an Other. He also points to the impossibility of desire in its desire to possess the Other: 'Such is the impossible ideal of desire: to possess the Other's transcendence as pure transcendence and at the same time as *body*, to reduce the Other to his simple *facticity* because he is then in the midst of my world but to bring it about that this facticity is a perpetual appresentation of his nihilating transcendence' (1956, 394). Part of desire's pull is towards an impossible transcendence; this impossibility creates a lack and, at the same time, a draw. Freud, as I will go on to discuss, defines desire in terms of movement, and this emphasises the connection between desire and drive that is formulated in his theories. He also conceives of a lack, which is developed further in Lacan's work on desire.

Freud's legacy

Freud's legacy continues to have a strong grip over critical theory, as Peter Brooks points out: 'Freud, the *Times Literary Supplement* reported three years ago, remains the most frequently cited writer of our time— cited, I think, a bit like Jean-Jacques Rousseau two centuries ago: as the presiding genius of our culture and the author of its symptomatic ill-nesses' (Brooks 2000, 2). Jerry Aline Flieger argues that 'even when his speculations are outlandish, Freud is never *simply* wrong: many of the cutting-edge works that purport to be anti- or post-Freud are in fact deeply indebted to Freud's insights' (2005, 9). She goes on to stress that 'more important than the rightness or wrongness of any of Freud's the-oretical speculations is the fact that his thought encourages us to ques-tion rigidly held truths as inherently suspect in their motivation, thus opening a field for debate and revision' (Flieger 2005, 9), a belief that echoes Peter Gay's assertion in the introduction to his *Freud reader*: 'No matter: ignorant or well-informed, our culture has found Freud's vision of mind compelling enough to live with it, whether comfortably or not' (Gay 1995 [1989], xiii). In discussing his recent experience re-reading Freud, Paul Robinson claims that 'It's like falling in love all over again [...] There's a quality about these texts which is incredibly seductive' (2000, 168–169). The seductive nature of Freud's work is particularly relevant to a critique of his understanding of the concept of desire.

Of course there is a great and growing body of literature that would disagree with the positive tenor of these comments, works such as Richard Webster's *Why Freud Was Wrong* (1995), John Forrester's *Dispatches from the Freud Wars* (1998) or Frederick Crews's *The Memory Wars: Freud's Legacy in Dispute* (1995) attest to recent discussions that Freud is no longer relevant or 'right'.[4] The stress in this chapter is on Freud's intel-lectual conceptualisation of desire and the ways in which this interpre-tation is presented and debated within cultural studies.

Freud's Oedipal complex is the cornerstone of psychoanalytic theory, and, as such, functions as the primary narrative for our understanding of the concept of desire. 'Having finally brought to fruition the concept of the superego, Freud realised that the Oedipus complex was with good reason the cornerstone of psychoanalysis—its overcoming was the single most momentous sign of human culture' (Mitchell 2000 [1974], 73). Kaja Silverman in *Whose Freud?* argues that 'to say "My desire has nothing to do with the Oedipus complex," would be to essentialise and detem-poralise what is finally nothing but a structural imperative. It would be to make something closed out of the very thing whose function is to open us up to the multiplicity and multifariousness of the world'

(2000, 153).[5] The central narrative that runs throughout psychoanalytic theory, from Freud to Lacan, is the Oedipal drama: 'It is not just another complex: it is the structure of relations by which we come to be the men and women that we are' (Eagleton, 1983, 156).

The myth of Oedipus is one of the most influential in the twentieth century, and the appearance of Oedipus in recent articles and books (Eagleton 2003; Madison, 2000; Flieger, 2005) attests to its continuing relevance. Arising from a combination of self-analysis and his case studies on infantile neuroses, the Oedipus complex emerges as a unifying theory in Freudian psychoanalysis. In a letter to Wilhelm Fliess on 15 October 1897, Freud writes: 'the Greek legend seizes on a compulsion which everyone recognises because he feels its existence within himself. Each member of the audience was once, in germ and in phantasy, just such an Oedipus, and each one recoils in horror from the dream-fulfilment here transplanted into reality, with the whole quota of repression which separates his infantile state from his present one' (Freud 2001 [1966], vol. 1, 265).

Freud's reading of *Oedipus the King* draws together his theories on dream interpretation, wish fulfilment, repression and subjectivity into a master discourse on human sexuality.[6] In Sophocles' *Oedipus the King*, Oedipus is the 'solver of riddles' who unwinds the tangled string of his own fate (1972, 9). Oedipus's insistence on interpretation, on a cure or solution to the woes of his kingdom brings about his downfall. For in so doing, he not only reveals answers, but uncovers truths about his identity and sexuality: that he has killed his father, Laius, and married his mother, Jocasta. Sophocles' text introduces the potentially destructive relationship between mother, father and son as well as the dangers of answering the unanswerable.[7]

Oedipus the King dramatises the primal scene of desire for Freud, and as such, the Oedipus complex becomes the underlying foundation of psychoanalytic interpretation.[8] The Oedipal complex ultimately concerns the socialisation of the individual—the passage from desiring child to desiring adult, mastered by transferring desires and establishing identification with the 'right' parent. Freud's theorisation of the Oedipal complex and its dissolution known as the 'castration complex' is fundamental to the way psychoanalysis locates sexual difference in the operation of the genitals. Woman becomes lack because the little boy does not see anything where the penis should be. This 'missing' penis characterises her as 'lack'. For Freud, this difference is a result of biology or anatomy and it is a 'truth' that factors within his theorisation of the Oedipal and castration complexes.

The fact that the little girl must realise, through her awareness that she does not have a penis, that she is *lacking* is crucial to understanding both Freud's and Lacan's conception of desire. Following Freud, we can see that a girl learns to desire in terms of being desirable, whereas a boy learns to change his desire from his mother to another woman. This is a fundamental difference in terms of the position each gender takes in psychoanalytical terms of desire: one learns to desire, the other learns to be desirable.

Feminist interventions (Part One)

The distinction Freud makes in terms of anatomy is taken up in a feminist engagement with psychoanalytic models. French feminists, such as Hélène Cixous and Luce Irigaray in particular, have argued against Freud's and Lacan's conceptualisation of desire and of the primacy of the Oedipal complex. In *This Sex Which is Not One* (1985), for instance, Irigaray addresses the lack that psychoanalysis equates with woman. She asks, 'So woman does not have a sex organ?' (Irigaray 1985b, 28) and answers that they have at least two: two lips that touch each other without any external help. Using the metaphor of 'two lips', or as a metaphor for metonyme, as one critic suggests,[9] Irigaray stresses that woman's sexuality is not only double, but *plural* (1985b, 28). Irigaray's 'another look' at psychoanalysis draws her reader's attention to the 'truth' psychoanalysis gives to anatomy insofar as it determines sexual difference. Offering another reading of woman's genitals as two lips instead of as lack, she offers an alternative to the psychoanalytic interpretation.[10] In so doing, Irigaray challenges the psychoanalytic claim of 'anatomy as an irrefutable criterion of truth' (1985b, 70–71) and offers an image to replace the lack assigned to women in psychoanalytic readings.

However, in order to posit this alternative image she draws attention to the importance of the genitals in desire and sexual difference. Offering 'two lips' instead of a lack does not necessarily refigure the importance psychoanalysis gives to the operation of the genitals; it just replaces one image with another. The fact that psychoanalytic theory sees lack and Irigaray's second look finds plurality still means that the genitals are determining women's relation to desire. In other words, Irigaray does not suggest that psychoanalysis is mistaken or 'wrong'; rather she implies that they have missed what *is* there.

Oedipus also motivates Cixous's critique of myths, in 'Sorties'; although she does not directly deal with the Oedipal myth, she does deal with the castration complex, which is the dissolution of the Oedipal complex. She challenges the importance of myths by suggesting that we, as feminists, should be able to laugh at their ridiculousness, although she acknowledges that their continuing presence makes it difficult to do so: 'We have been frozen in our place between two terrifying myths: between the Medusa and the abyss. It would be enough to make half the world break out laughing, if it were not still going on' (Cixous and Clément, 1986, 68).

For Irigaray and Cixous, woman is cosmic, open, multiple and without boundaries. Feminine language is also understood in these terms: without limits, multi-layered, and essentially different from man's. Irigaray argues in *This Sex Which is Not One* that '[Woman's] desire is often interpreted, and feared, as a sort of insatiable hunger, a voracity that will swallow you whole. Whereas it really involves a different economy more than anything else, one that upsets the linearity of a project, undermines the goal-object of a desire, diffuses the polarization toward a single pleasure, disconcerts fidelity to a single discourse' (1985b, 29–30). Although many feminists agree with Irigaray's interpretation, the implication in this statement is that there is an essential female desire that psychoanalysis has misunderstood.

The projects Cixous and Irigaray construct suggest the dominance psychoanalysis continues to have in the narrative understanding of desire. They rely on the structures Freud constructs and Lacan revises— to 'upset', 'undermine' and 'diffuse'—in order to build the foundations for their own interpretations of female desire.

Contemporary Freud

The existence of the unconscious is crucial to the understanding of the psychoanalytic process and to Freud's conceptualisation of desire. In 'The Unconscious' Freud argues that there must be an unconscious because there are thoughts we have, moments we spend, when we are not conscious of what we are thinking. He also catalogues acts such as slips of the tongue (popularly known as 'Freudian slips') as proof that there must be an unconscious. 'Repression' works to keep things from the conscious mind; once something has been repressed it no longer is part of our everyday knowledge. However, as Freud argues, as long as something remains repressed, things will emerge into consciousness. This is why the myth of Oedipus is so fundamental to Freud: if Oedipus had not repressed his desire to kill his father and marry his mother he may have been able to avoid his destructive future. Lacan argues that 'Freud's unconscious is not at all the romantic unconscious of imaginative creation' (1994 [1977], 24). Instead, as Lacan argues, Freud is interested in

'Impediment, failure, split. In a spoken or written sentence something stumbles. Freud is attracted by these phenomena, and it is there that he seeks the unconscious' (1994 [1977], 25).[11]

The resonance of Freud's interpretation of Oedipus and the unconscious is apparent in Western culture. The terms 'repression' and 'denial' are commonplace, and to a certain degree most accept that the 'talking cure' really is effective. Television talk shows such as *Oprah* and *Ricki Lake*, in many ways, can be understood as the cultural legacy of Freudian/psychoanalytic theory. Cinema and television also emphasise the need for us not to repress our desire, unless we want disastrous consequences. In *Love in a Time of Loneliness: Three Essays on Drive and Desire* (1999), Paul Verhaeghe discusses some problems with Freud's use of *Oedipus* to formulate his understanding of human sexuality. He also points out that in contemporary society Freud's modernist understanding of identity has been replaced by Lacanian alienation: 'Television produces a never-ending stream of images ensuring that virtual reality is more real than real reality, which in turn, is not merely a pale reflection of this, but in many cases even becomes a product of it. A modern identity can no longer be described in terms of the Freudian divided duality. Instead the *division* has a central place […] The early Freudian identification has now been replaced by Lacanian alienation, in which the subject is turning on a wheel of a never-ending succession of reference figures, constantly divided by different desires' (Verhaeghe 1999b, 118). Verhaeghe suggests that the effect of multiple desires and reference points on an individual leads them to a sense of increasing anxiety and insecurity, and a desperate search for something to identify with.

Recent sociological literature on the concept of individualism, for instance the work of Anthony Giddens (1990, 1991), Ulrich Beck and Beck-Gernsheim (2001) and Zygmunt Bauman (2001), highlights the demand on the individual to be self-reflexive and to self-monitor and yet, to be aware of the risks posed by modern society. Beck suggests that 'individualisation is a compulsion, albeit a paradoxical one, to create, to stage manage, not only one's own biography but the bonds and networks surrounding it and to do this amid changing preferences and at successive stages of life, while constantly adapting to the conditions of the labour market, the education system, the welfare state and so on' (2001, 4). Following the work of these authors, it is clear that we have moved into a culture that values and reiterates the position and privilege of the individual.

This culture of individualism has given way to what Elliott and Lemert refer to as 'privatized worlds'. In *The New Individualism: The Emotional*

Costs of Globalization (2006) Anthony Elliott and Charles Lemert chart a shift from a politicised culture to a privatised culture. Drawing on work by Ulrich Beck, among others, they consider the impact of 'reflexive individualism' and the way in which it places emphasis on 'choosing, changing and transforming' (Elliott and Lemert 2006, 97). Important to this book, they also consider how the emphasis on the individual and private worlds has led to a 'confessional therapeutic culture', found in TV talk shows such as *Oprah* and *Dr Phil*, and, increasingly, as I will go on to argue in Chapter 2, in contemporary culture.

The shift that Elliott and Lemert identify has also been the subject of work by Lauren Berlant, who argues that we increasingly live in 'an intimate public sphere'. According to Berlant the shift from a political public sphere to an intimate public sphere has led to a national politics that does not figure the nation in terms of the racial, economic and sexual inequalities that separate and divide the public; instead 'the dominant idea marketed by patriotic traditionalists is of a core nation whose survival depends on personal acts and identities performed in the intimate domains of the quotidian' (1997, 4). And what better place to perform these acts and identities than on television? Indeed, more recently, Berlant highlights the way in which intimacy has increasingly been moved into the public domain and negotiated on our television screens. She argues, for instance, that 'in the U.S. therapy saturates the scene of intimacy, from psychoanalysis and twelve-step groups to girl talk, talk shows, and other witnessing genres' (Berlant 2000, 1).[12]

'Witnessing genres', as Berlant refers to them, underline an individual's ability to self-regulate, make choices, compete, monitor his/her performance and transform: televisual examples might include *Big Brother's* 'diary room', 'healthy competition' in *Survivor* and transformation in *What Not to Wear*. These programmes highlight the emphasis placed on 'choosing, changing and transforming' that Elliott and Lemert identify as part of a self-reflexive individualist society. As they argue: 'The main legacy of this cultural trend is that individuals are increasingly expected to produce context for themselves. The designing of a life, of a self-project, is deeply rooted as both social norm and cultural obligation' (Elliott and Lemert 2006, 13). As Elliott and Lemert suggest, individual choice and self-transformation have become a cultural imperative and this constructs the multiple desires and reference points that Verhaeghe identifies.

Lacanian revisions

One of the most significant developments that Jacques Lacan brings to his return to Freud is the fact that he situates the actions of the unconscious in language. The idea that 'the unconscious is structured as a language' might seem a given to us now, but as Moustafa Safouan points out, 'before Lacan analysts analyzed other things, for example personality or the dynamics of the unconscious [...] Before Lacan no one thought of locating the subject *within the very act of talking*' (2004, 3, author's italics). Lacan's incorporation of language and discourse into the fundamental concepts of psychoanalysis was crucial to psychoanalysis but also to the way feminism and film later utilized psychoanalytic concepts.

Lacan engages with Freud's Oedipus complex in a way that makes it difficult to understand exactly how he understands the myth of Oedipus and how he uses it to privilege his own theorisation of the castration complex. Shoshana Felman notes this ambiguity in her analysis of Lacan's use of Oedipus. She claims: 'Nowhere in Lacan's writing is there any systematic exposition of his specific understanding of the significance of Oedipus' (Felman 1987, 102). In *The Four Fundamental Concepts of Psychoanalysis* Lacan argues that 'no one is any longer concerned, with certain rare exceptions to be found amongst my pupils, with the ternary structure of the Oedipus complex or with the castration complex' (1994 [1977], 11). Here Lacan refers to the developments that have taken place in psychoanalysis and he expresses his disappointment that analysts are not interested in understanding the fundamental concepts such as Oedipal repression and castration complex. Instead they ignore them and have developed instead concepts which are, for Lacan, 'clearly retrograde and pre-conceptual' (1994 [1977], 11). His statement falls in line with a paradox Malcolm Bowie (1991) points to: on the one hand, Lacan does want to be true to the letter of Freud, but on the other, imagines himself as the only one capable of carrying on those traditions (in the face of always feeling excluded from the psychoanalytic community). Indeed, Lacan frames his exclusion as an indication of his influence.

Lacan's 'Desire and the Interpretation of Desire in *Hamlet*' exemplifies the way he revises Freud in order to dismantle the primacy of Oedipus, to assert the importance of the castration complex and to propose the phallus as the prime signifier. Lacan privileges his reading of castration over Freud's Oedipal complex, and in so doing he situates punishment or lack at the forefront of the exchange in desire. Lacan maintains that Hamlet's lack of ability to act on his own desires is at the root of Shakespeare's tragedy. He suggests that Hamlet loses his way in desire because he does not know what he wants.

The narrative structure of *Hamlet* serves as a loose framework for Lacan to explicate some of the most fundamental concepts in psychoanalysis, particularly those that directly effect the movement of desire, such as the 'Other', *objet a* and the role of the Phallus. Lacan broadly argues that

Hamlet is caught between avenging his father's murder and envying Claudius. At the centre of this tension is Hamlet's desire for his mother. Lacan reads Gertrude as Hamlet's 'Other', the 'primordial subject of the demand' (1982, 12). Because Hamlet desires his mother he cannot choose between his feelings of revenge and jealousy. However, unlike Freud's interpretation of Sophocles' *Oedipus*, Lacan does not 'blame' Hamlet for his repressed feeling; rather he suggests that Gertrude's own desires for Claudius keep Hamlet from going through the castration complex and subsequently from knowing what he wants.[13]

Lacan's reading of *Hamlet* ultimately situates woman as the cause of Hamlet's confusion and of his inability to rise to his rightful seat. Although Lacan may move away from Freud's understanding of anatomy as destiny in terms of sexual difference, he still concludes that woman is lacking or rather, she must be lacking in the movement of desire.[14] As Jacqueline Rose argues in *Feminine Sexuality* (1982, 42), for Lacan it is 'not that anatomical difference *is* sexual difference (the one as strictly deducible from the other), but that anatomical difference comes to *figure* sexual difference, that is, become the sole representative of what that difference is allowed to be' (2005, 42). Lacan's positioning of Gertrude and Ophelia as 'Other' and 'objet a' to the subject Hamlet supports the paradigm Freud raises in his theorisation of the 'castration complex'. The girl must want to *be* the phallus, that is, she must strive to be like the phallus, whereas the boy must want to *have* the phallus, in other words, he must try to possess his object of desire. Although Lacan moves away from the 'truth' of anatomy, he only does so in order to situate it in language.

Feminist interventions (Part Two)

In her excellent study of Lacan and feminist epistemology, Kirsten Campbell poses the very relevant question: 'should feminists know better than to read Lacan?' (2004, 25). Campbell's question can just as easily be applied to Freud and the whole of psychoanalysis, and indeed feminists who have taken up this question since the 1970s, such as Germaine Greer (1971), Kate Millet (1970), Betty Friedan (1976 [1963]) and Shulamith Firestone (1979 [1971]), have questioned and refuted psychoanalysis's conceptualisation of desire. Following Juliet Mitchell and Jacqueline Rose's (1982) re-examination of feminism and psychoanalysis however, many feminists began to consider the productive possibilities in an engagement with psychoanalysis. Feminists such as Jane Gallop (1982), Kaja Silverman (1988), Elizabeth Grosz (1990a) and Judith Butler (1987) offered critiques that engaged with psychoanalysis without becoming 'dutiful daughters' to it. Campbell suggests that this engagement can be termed 'productive appropriation' (2004). This term characterises a relationship with psychoanalysis that recognises its influence and centrality, but at the same time, its specificity. This encounter does not assume a union, rather a useful way forward in terms of theorisations of concepts such as desire. However, this approach is similar to Spezzano and Elliott's configuration in that psychoanalysis is being appropriated, in this case by feminist theorists, for its own problems. Campbell acknowledges that she 'asks what this particular psychoanalytic account does, or fails to do, *for* a specific feminist problematic' (2004, 27, author's italics). She places psychoanalysis in the field of feminist theory in order to use it for feminist politics. Although this sounds like a new way out of the impasse between psychoanalysis and feminism, it is one that has been considered in other feminist work on psychoanalysis. In the 1999 introduction to her work, for example, Juliet Mitchell praises Mari Jo Buhle's recent work on psychoanalysis and feminism[15] because it demands that the 'phallocentric model be remedied to understand female sexuality'.[16] The term 'remedies' suggests that Buhle 'cures' the ailing phallocentric model of its symptoms by giving it a dose of good old feminism. In this example, feminism becomes the healing analyst of the poor, ailing psychoanalysis: she is in the position of psychoanalysing psychoanalysis, curing it of its phallocentric symptoms. In terms of a theorisation of desire, I would argue that it is more useful to acknowledge the points of convergence and departure between feminism and psychoanalysis in order to consider how each paradigm handles the concept of desire. In other words, I am arguing that no one paradigm is capable of offering a complete theorisation of desire; instead, we must rely on a combination of models in order to understand its potential.

Desire graphs

In the 'Subversion of the subject and the dialectic of desire in the Freudian unconscious', Lacan offers four graphs to explain the signification of desire and the way in which meaning is constructed retroactively. In *The Sublime Object of Ideology* Slavoj Žižek draws attention to the way in which these graphs present the relation between signifier and signified and demonstrate how meaning is constructed (1989, 100–101). The 'button tie', 'anchoring point' or 'rigid designator' (*point de caption*)[17], what Žižek also refers to as a 'knot of meanings', becomes an 'impossible-real kernel', 'the surplus produced by the signifying operation' (1989, 95–97).

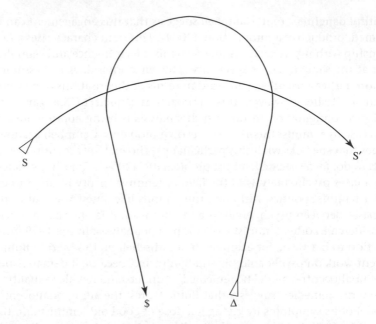

Figure 1.1 Graph 1, from p. 681 of ECRITS: THE COMPLETE EDITION by Jacques Lacan, translated by Bruce Fink. Copyright 1996, 1970, 1971, 1999 by Editions du Seuil, English translation copyright 2006, 2002 by W.W. Norton & Company Inc. Used by permission of W.W. Norton & Company, Inc.

Desire Graph I (Figure 1.1) is what Lacan calls 'the elementary cell' (2006, 681) because it contains the basic elements of the unconscious structuring of meaning in language. The line moving up and down in an arc represents the movement from the pre-symbolic intention, or pre-conscious intention to the subject—in less complicated terms, from your unconscious thoughts to your conscious awareness. The two points at which the line meets stands for what Lacan terms as 'button tie [*point de caption*]' (2006, 681). These 'button ties' fix or fasten meaning. The point on the right stands for the Other and the point on the left stands for the big Other, the point which governs meaning. This graph demonstrates for Lacan the way meaning is fixed retroactively. That is, the point of exit comes before the point of entrance; it steps out of the signifying chain at a point preceding the point at which it has pierced it. This means that meaning precedes signification. It also helps us to understand why we might believe we know the meaning of something before we actually do or why we think we recognise something familiar in those we fall in love with.

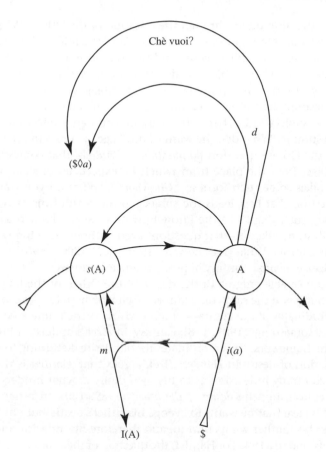

Figure 1.2 Graph 3, from p. 690 of ECRITS: THE COMPLETE EDITION by Jacques Lacan, translated by Bruce Fink. Copyright 1996, 1970, 1971, 1999 by Editions du Seuil, English translation copyright 2006, 2002 by W.W. Norton & Company Inc. Used by permission of W.W. Norton & Company, Inc.

In the second graph (Figure 1.2), we can see the upper graph which articulates the question of desire and demonstrates the way desire stands in relationship to both the Other and to fantasy, which is on the far end of the question posed by the Other in desire. The question posed by the Other is *Che Vuoi* or 'What do you want?' Desire resides in the gap that opens between the demand ('What do you want from me?') and the imaginary response answered in fantasy. In this way, fantasy functions as a construction or as an imaginary scenario filling out the void by giving us a definite answer to the question 'What does the Other want?'

Lacan theorises desire through the question of the Other, 'What does the Other want?' and, in so doing, emphasises the role of the analyst to find meaning, to establish a cure and to 'attempt to reintroduce a form of transcendence, the object of desire, instead of conceptualising the positivity of desire as a production of assemblages' (Khalfa 1999, 78). This question, according to Lacan, is part of the analytic process, and leads the subject to his/her path of desire through a reformulation of the question to 'What does he want of me?' Lacan argues in *Écrits*: 'That is why the Other's question [*la question de l'Autre*]—that comes back to the subject from the place from which he expects an oracular reply— which takes some such form as "*Chè vuoi?*," "What do you want?," is the question that best leads the subject to the path of his own desire, assuming that, thanks to the know-how of a partner known as a psychoanalyst, he takes up that question, even without knowing it, in the following form: "What does he want from me?"' (2006, 690).

As Žižek explains: 'Fantasy appears, then, as an answer to "*Che Vuoi?*", to the unbearable enigma of the desire of the Other, of the lack in the Other; but it is at the same time fantasy itself which, so to speak, provides the co-ordinates of our desire—which constructs the frame enabling us to desire something' (1989, 118). Fantasy, in Žižek's understanding, provides the framework, the co-ordinates for our desire. Returning to Lacan's theorisation of desire in *Hamlet*, Žižek argues that 'Hamlet is therefore hindered not by indecision as to his own desire ... what hinders him is doubt concerning the *desire of the other*' (1989, 120). In other words, Hamlet is clear that he wants to avenge his father's death, but not as clear whether his mother wants him to, and therefore his indecision leads to inactivity and to a lack. For Hamlet, the question of the other's (Gertrude's) desire comes back and opens up an uncomfortable possibility of enjoyment. Žižek suggests that 'If the Name-of-the-Father functions as the agency of interpellation, of symbolic identification, the mother's desire, with its fathomless "*Che vuoi?*", marks a certain limit at which every interpellation necessarily fails' (1989, 121). *Hamlet* serves to illustrate the way in which desire allows for identification and at the same time establishes barriers against interpretation and understanding.

Deleuze and Guattari

Moving away from lack and from the primacy of the Oedipal complex, Deleuze and Guattari define desire in terms of production. Desire takes a central role in their assessment of capitalism and schizophrenia—and it becomes both life and death; as Claire Colebrook writes: 'the death of this or that body is not at all negative. Without the death of organisms there would be no change, evolution or life in its radical sense' (2006, 2). To read desire in discourse with Deleuze and Guattari's theories in mind encourages readers to make connections, to follow movements, to create new possibilities instead of closing them down with interpretative solutions. One of the most important moves Deleuze and Guattari make, particularly for feminists, is to rethink desire outside of lack and outside a negative framework. In her early work on desire and Hegel, Judith Butler argues that Deleuze's theory moves desire from a negative interpretation towards a productive one. She writes: 'Deleuze's theory prescribes a move from negative to productive desire which requires that we accept an emancipatory model of desire' (1987, 213).

In *Anti-Oedipus*, the first of their two-volume series on 'capitalism and schizophrenia', Deleuze and Guattari argue that 'the traditional logic of desire is all wrong from the outset' (1983 [1972]), 25). They argue that the Platonic logic of desire demands a choice between production and acquisition, a choice that Deleuze and Guattari problematise because it situates lack at the centre of the movement of desire: 'From the moment that we place desire on the side of acquisition, we make desire an idealistic (dialectical, nihilistic) conception, which causes us to look upon it as primarily a lack: a lack of an object, a lack of the real object' (1983 [1972], 25). Conceptualising desire in terms of acquisition forces a lack within the subject that can only be fulfilled by the object of desire, an object that will never actually be acquired.

Deleuze and Guattari acknowledge that psychoanalysis does not *simply* choose acquisition in its theorisation of an object of desire (or *objet petit a* in Lacanian terms); they are not unaware of the link psychoanalysis makes between desire and production, as they write: 'Desire thus conceived as production, though merely the production of fantasies, has been explained perfectly by psychoanalysis' (1983 [1972], 25). The key phrase here is 'the production of fantasies'; with this distinction Deleuze and Guattari isolate the difference between their project and that of psychoanalysis. Instead of understanding desire as only a production in fantasy, or in the imaginary or symbolic domains, Deleuze and Guattari want to understand desire in the real, the social, or even within the splitting between the real and the imaginary. In so doing, they do not simply promote production instead of lack; rather they problematise the psychoanalytic usage both of lack and of production and locate that problem in the use of the imaginary and symbolic to structure desire.

Deleuze and Guattari locate lack in the subject not in desire itself: 'Desire does not lack anything; it does not lack its object. It is, rather, the *subject* that is missing in desire, or desire that lacks a fixed subject' (1983 [1972], 26).[18] In this way, they shift the emphasis in the movement of desire towards an in-between territory; or, to use their terminology, a 'deterritorialized' space (1983 [1972], 35). Lack in Deleuze and Guattari's refiguration becomes an *effect* of desire, rather than an origin (1983 [1972], 27). The shift they make in emphasising lack in the subject rather than in desire have important bearings on feminist revisions of desire, as will be discussed.

In Deleuze and Guattari's rethinking, desire moves along deterritorialized lines. Their model of desire does not rely on lack to structure and motivate desire as does a psychoanalytical interpretation. As Rosi Braidotti argues: 'In their appeal to a more positive theory of desire, Deleuze and Guattari argue that the idea of desire as lack reflects the specific historicity and the socio-economic conditions of a moment of capitalist domination. It is historically located and consequently dated' (2003, 57). Deleuze and Guattari's alternative model opens up new ways to think about desire as well as about subjectivity, as I will explore in later chapters.

Feminist interventions (Part Three)

It is necessary to note that the relationship between Deleuze and Guattari and feminist theory has not always been an amicable one. Although there is less contestation between feminists and Deleuze and Guattari than there is between feminism and psychoanalysis, many feminists, notably Rosi Braidotti, Elizabeth Grosz and Alice Jardine, have warned feminists against allying themselves too quickly with Deleuze and Guattari's work, in particular Deleuze and Guattari's model of the 'Body without Organs'. And yet, there has been a significant shift towards a greater acceptance of work by Deleuze and Guattari, most notably from the same theorists originally cautious about them: Elizabeth Grosz and Rosi Braidotti.[19] Indeed, Braidotti points out that although most of 'the uses that Deleuzian philosophy is put to are still polemical and ambivalent towards feminist theory [...] a growing corpus of Deleuzian feminism is taking shape with remarkable rigour' (2002, 65). She argues that 'the most fruitful starting point for an alliance between feminist concerns and Deleuze's thought is precisely the effort to imagine the activity of thinking differently' (2002, 70).

It is also important to note that this movement towards Deleuze has been made before, particularly within feminist theory. In 'refiguring lesbian desire', for instance, Elizabeth Grosz attempts to move beyond a psychoanalytic 'ontology of lack' towards the productive potential in

Deleuze's understanding of becoming (1994b). Grosz's work has been key to initiating a move within feminist theory, which arguably influenced scholars such as Barbara M. Kennedy and Laura U. Marks, towards a reconsideration of Deleuze's work and its productive potential to refigure concepts such as desire. As Grosz explains:

> As production, desire does not provide blueprints, models, ideals, or goals. Rather, it experiments, it makes: it is fundamentally aleatory, inventive. Such a theory cannot but be of interest for feminist theory insofar as women are the traditional repositories of the lack consti-tutive of desire and insofar as the oppositions between presence and absence, between reality and fantasy, have conventionally constrained women to occupy the place of men's other.
>
> (1994b, 76)

Not only does Grosz establish a rationale for the move from psychoan-alytic lack to Deleuzian production, but it is also possible to detect the move towards affect in her use of Deleuze. Her attention to desire as a movement, to something that causes bodies to move or 'to do', sets the scene for later work that concentrates more specifically on this move-ment, this becoming.

Elspeth Probyn, for example, draws on Grosz's work to think more specifically about what desire does, how desire 'moves us at different times and in different ways to engage' (1996, 151). In her figuration of 'becoming-horse', for instance, she considers desire as movement in an attempt to construct a queer use of desire. Instead of conceiving desire as pointing towards one object (person, place or thing), and therefore falling into the negative polemics of lack, Probyn wants to consider the movement inherent to desire. Like Grosz, she turns to Deleuze, more specifically to his notion of 'becoming', in order to figure this movement. Drawing on images of 'girls and girls and horses' and work from Colette and Radclyffe Hall, she is interested in the 'lines of desire' that run through these intermingled images and how this way of approaching desire frees us from situating it in one object or reducing it to lack. As she argues: 'Turning away from the game of matching signifiers to sig-nifieds, we can begin to focus on the movement of images as effecting and affecting movement' (1996, 59).

What is clear in both Grosz's and Probyn's Deleuzian refigurings is an emphasis on understanding desire as movement. And this becomes very useful to scholars who want to think of alternative ways to theorise desire. Their figurations, as mentioned earlier, also work to inform projects on

Deleuze in cinema studies insofar as they emphasise movement and intensity. However, although these models are useful, both for feminist theory and cinema studies, they are still caught up in an intellectual stalemate between psychoanalysis and Deleuze, an impasse which is familiar to many by now. The other problem is that movement is just as much a part of the psychoanalytic conceptualisation of desire as it is a part of Deleuzian production. As Grosz points out in her feminist introduction to Lacan: 'Desire desires the desire of an other. Desire is thus a movement, an energy that is always transpersonal, directed to others' (1990a, 65). In psychoanalysis, desire is a movement, but one with a focal point, whereas in Deleuze's conceptualisation this movement is more fluid and open-ended—however, what underlines both theories of desire is movement and therefore, instead of counterpoising these theoretical models, it seems more useful to examine the ways in which this movement functions and how it can be connected more specifically to recent work on affect. Indeed, as I will go on to argue in Chapter 5, one of the possibilities work on affect offers is a way out of the impasse between psychoanalytic lack and Deleuzian production.

Freud's, Lacan's and Deleuze and Guattari's models of desire construct contrasting and opposing interpretations. One could say there is a contrast here between a negative conceptualisation of desire and a positive or productive one and also a contrast between a (modern) search for meaning and a (postmodern) recognition of multiple interpretations. However, to call one 'negative' and the other 'positive' only leads us to circular (and endless) debates. Feminist interventions into these debates have drawn attention to the gendered nature of theorisations of desire and have challenged interpretations which posit woman as lack or as a 'symptom' of male desire.

Contemporary theorisations

In *On Desire*, William B. Irvine suggests that we are living through 'an auspicious time for a re-examination of desire' (2006, 4). Recent advances in psychology and neuroscience have brought us closer than ever to understanding 'why we want what we want' (Irvine 2006). And yet, in terms of theorising desire, outdated models such as those discussed, from psychoanalysis and philosophy, are still the most prevalent and influential in cultural theory. Desire is associated with lack, production, intensity, sensation and force. An object of desire can be a person, place, thing or an ideal; it can refer to something in the past, present or future. Like shame, compassion, hate or loss—emotions and affects that have been the subject of study recently (Probyn, 2005; Berlant, 2004; Ahmed, 2004; Eng and Kanzanjian, 2003)—desire is something that everyone will have experienced or is familiar with. And yet many will think that their feelings of desire are unique and personal, which is why someone might say, 'I love you more than she does' or 'I love you more than anyone else in the world'.

The internalisation of desire has been taken up in recent work, both in psychoanalytic circles and in those concerned with emotion and affect. The paradox that comes after the postmodern turn, as some theorists suggest, is that instead of freeing up our relationship to desire, it has alienated and commodified it. We can see this paradox reflected in the demands for enjoyment popularised by corporate America: Nike's ('Just do It!'), Coke's ('Enjoy!') and McDonald's ('I'm loving it!') suggest that it is up to us to enjoy; the demand is there, we need only to give in. In Todd McGowan's recent work on 'Lacan and the emerging society of enjoyment', he argues that the paradox is that 'there is less pleasure now than there ever was' (2003, 133), and as Žižek argues: 'the direct injunction "Enjoy!" is a much more effective way to hinder the subject's access to enjoyment than the explicit Prohibition which sustains the space for its transgression' (1999, 367). Interestingly, Claire Colebrook reaches a similar conclusion in her work on Deleuze, stating that 'the power of capitalism does not lie in its repression of our pleasures, but in its coding of all those pleasures into money *and* in producing a surplus value of that code: for we are now enslaved, not by being *denied what we want*, but by being manufactured *to want*. My desire must be *for* this or that purchasable pleasure' (2006, 133). Instead of being more accessible, desire has become more inaccessible. Lauren Berlant gestures towards this failure in her work on intimacy; she argues that 'virtually no one knows how to do intimacy; that everyone feels expert about it (at least about other people's disasters); and that mass fascination with the aggression, incoherence, vulnerability, and ambivalence at the scene of desire somehow escalates the demand for the traditional promise of intimate happiness to be fulfilled in everyone's everyday life' (Berlant 2000, 2).

Indeed, the 'promise' of happiness and its attendant disappointment is central to Paul Verhaeghe's (1999) work. Verhaeghe argues that

> Every desire can be stilled with an object that is for sale: all you have to do is make the decision and carry it out. This is the new alienating myth that seeps in everywhere nowadays, and is replacing the previous equally alienating myth. The previous myth was the Hollywood version of the couple who live happily ever after. I would call the

present myth 'the junkie ideology'—buy the right stuff and pleasure
follows. Meanwhile the fact that this is not the case has become
increasingly unclear. The main result is boredom and a search for
new boundaries.

(1999b, 134)

Boredom, and the many ways to escape from it, has come to characterise
popular culture, more than desire and passion. Mobile phones, ipods,
gameboys and personal televisions all attest to the need to have
something 'on hand' to distract us from the banality of everyday life.
As Žižek argues: 'the utopia of a new post-psychoanalytic subjectivity
engaged in the pursuit of new idiosyncratic bodily pleasures beyond
sexuality has reverted to its opposite: what we are getting instead is
disinterested boredom' (1999, 367).

Unlike the Hollywood myth of 'happily ever after', the emphasis in
contemporary narratives is often on material gain and satisfaction
through having the right house, car, handbag, shoes, etc. Although I
agree with the emphasis Verhaeghe places on boredom and materialism,
within the anti-capitalist movement and in 'fringe' film there is a growing
emphasis on dismantling and challenging this conceptualisation of desire.
There is a sense that we need to return to desire in order to motivate
those who have become too bored to do anything else but buy more
things. Indeed, many films are beginning to challenge this ideology and
have gone a long way to *trouble* the relationship between consumer and
corporation.[20]

Another shift worth highlighting is the movement of porn from the
fringe to the centre.[21] An industry which in 2002 made over $57 billion,
porn can no longer be regarded as a sideline and as such, has been theorised as signifying 'new socio-spatial sexual relations' (Simpson and
Reading cited in Ruddock 2006, 124). Porn is no longer in the closet but
available on every shelf and across the Internet. On the one hand, our
society codifies sex as an intimate activity and then, on the other, gives
us porn—there is an inherent contradiction/paradox that the viewer is
forced to reconcile. Linda Williams thoughtfully considers the contradictions inherent to our understanding of porn in *Hard Core: Power,
Pleasure, and the "Frenzy of the Visible"*, arguing that one of 'the most
important of these conflicts was the difficulty hard-core films have in
figuring the visual "knowledge" of women's pleasure' (1999, xvi).

There has also been a change in terms of desire and nationality. As
many critics have argued, America is characterised more by its fear and
self-loathing (Moore 2004; McGowan 2004) than by its virulence and

pride. As Elaine Showalter writes: 'It's a standing joke that Americans no longer view themselves as sinners struggling with the guilt of lust, avarice, or greed but rather as sick people addicted to sex, shopping, or sweets' (1997, 8). A quick trip to 'google' reveals the wide range of understandings about desire: an entry for 'Desire' Magazine, 'publishers of erotica for women and men'; 'Insurgent desire'—the online Green Anarchy Archive; Dictionary Definition: Desire: 'A how to self help knowledge base to answer questions on control, management and understanding self, helping one deal, learn, know and master self'; 'Pure Desire', Christian help for sexual addiction: 'Christian-based help for sexual addiction with books, seminars, and assistance to local churches' (www.google.co.uk , search 'desire', 9 February 2006). Two of the four definitions offer advice on how *not* to desire or how to *manage* desire. One of the implications in the media, particularly in the press and on the Internet, is that desire is 'out of control', but recent studies suggest that this is far from the truth (Ruddock 2007).

It is clear that desire has been called into question by psychoanalytic, Deleuzian and affect theorists—and yet what is not clear is how we are to theorise it and what it does. So what does desire do? I want to suggest that desire creates recognition (through identification and the gaze); it marks the narrative; it highlights the moment when lovers' eyes meet; it affects the lives of characters; it marks their bodies, forcing them to move, act or react differently; and it transforms people—radically alters their being-in-the-world. I want to suggest, moreover, that we consider desire as a way of thinking and as a kind of intelligence (Thrift 2004); as something that supports connections and relations and that produces an expression that is impossible to contain or categorise.

Theorising desire in film

From more general ideas about desire, and theorising desire, I will locate a theorisation of desire more specifically in film. As in feminist theory and postmodernism, psychoanalysis has been appropriated by film scholars to explain and describe cinematic apparatus. Theorists such as Christian Metz (1975), Laura Mulvey (1975) and Jean-Louis Baudry (1974–75 [1970]) brought psychoanalytic tools to cinema studies and considered how concepts such as the gaze, identification and desire functioned within cinema and its audience. However, as a number of theorists have since commented, many of these psychoanalytic concepts were used in ways that misunderstood or misconstrued their interpretation within psychoanalysis. Joan Copjec, for instance, explains the way

Lacan's theorisation of the 'mirror stage' is misappropriated in the context of his later work on the 'gaze' (1994). Copjec's work illustrates some of the problems that occur with the appropriation of psychoanalytic concepts into other paradigms, which will be explored in more detail in Chapter 3.

The presence of psychoanalysis and the use of psychoanalytic concepts in cinema studies is contested and challenged, in particular, in Bordwell and Carroll's *Post-Theory* (1996).[22] They argue that psychoanalysis became a dominating and restrictive presence within film studies, even though, as Žižek argues in the introduction to his work on Krzysztof Kieślowski: 'except for Joan Copjec, myself and some of my Slovene colleagues, I know of no cinema theorist who effectively accepts Lacan as his or her ultimate background' (1994, 2). The result, as Todd McGowan and Sheila Kunkle argue in *Lacan and Contemporary Film* (2004), is that 'Lacanian psychoanalysis has disappeared from film studies' and, consequently, has become 'post-theoretical' as Bordwell and Carroll prophesied (2004, xii, footnote 1). The other consequence of this change is a renewed interest and use of work by Gilles Deleuze.

When 'theorising desire' within film it is important, I would argue, not to fall into constrictive and contained readings of film (whether psychoanalytic, feminist or Deleuzian), but rather, to leave room for the ineffable. Desire comes through most potently when it is not closed down; equally, theorising desire must involve leaving room for not understanding. Jeffrey Pence does a magnificent job of explaining what this involves and demands from film theory in his reading of the 'spiritual film', which, in many ways, anticipates the procedures necessary for theorising desire in cinema. Pence argues that '[a] criticism that evades an open engagement with the limits of the knowable becomes instrumental; a criticism geared exclusively toward demystification ultimately produces reification. A more proper analytic response is to attend to the ways in which such films produce experiences, and call for responses, at the edge of the knowable' (Pence 2004, 29). This approach, alongside an understanding of the need to remain at the 'edge of the knowable', is particularly apt for an exploration of desire in film. It is also one that draws on Deleuze's understanding of the radical potential in cinema. In her analysis of his cinema books, Colebrook writes that for Deleuze 'cinema is only cinema in its revolutionary potential, a potential to transform the ways in which perception orders its images, and thinking is only thinking when it is creative, when it does not repeat the already formed and recognised' (2006, 15). Deleuze's understanding of cinema's 'revolutionary potential' leads to a different way of exploring film. We are encouraged to think differently about the images presented to us and to challenge our relationship to these images. As Deleuze argues: 'we must no longer ask ourselves, "What is cinema?" but "What is philosophy?" Cinema itself is a new practice of images and signs, whose theory philosophy must produce as conceptual practice' (1989, 280). And this call from Deleuze for a new approach to cinema has been embraced by scholars such as Barbara M. Kennedy and Laura U. Marks precisely because Deleuze attends to the material. His suggestion that we might look for what a text *does* instead of what it *means* liberates interpretation within cinema studies to a certain extent.

In *Deleuze and Cinema* (2000), for instance, Kennedy attempts to map out an aesthetics of 'force and of sensation' (2000, 5), arguing that Deleuzian interpretations of desire show up psychoanalysis as ineffective in terms of explaining the 'materiality of the filmic experience' (2000, 27). She argues that psychoanalysis's emphasis on lack and negativity 'cannot account for the viscerality and vitality of film as a processual experience, encapsulated through movement and duration, which is why we need to look for more complex accounts of cinematic desire' (2000, 42). One of the limitations in Kennedy's approach, however, is that her use and indeed celebration of Deleuze overlooks a more nuanced approach to desire which does not simply counterpoise psychoanalytic approaches with Deleuzian models.

In contrast, Mark's (2000) recent work on 'inter-cultural cinema, embodiment and the senses' uses Deleuze to theorise the materiality and vitality of the film, but also connects her theorisation with work on affect which allows us to think of the ways in which filmmakers use cinema to transmit a physical sensation of home and culture. Marks uses the term 'haptic cinema' to describe a bodily relationship between the viewer and the image. Instead of inviting an identification with a figure, 'haptic cinema' describes a 'dynamic subjectivity between looker and image' (Marks 2000, 164). An example of a haptic image, offered by Marks, is the opening of *The English Patient* (Anthony Minghella, 1996) 'in which the camera moves over a skin-like surface that turns out to be a close-up of rough watercolour paper' (Marks 2000, 177).

There are two things I want to draw attention to here: first, the use of Deleuze and Guattari to theorise affect and the materiality or 'skin' of the film; second, the way psychoanalysis and Deleuze and Guattari are held in opposition to each other and signified as negativity or lack and as positivity or production, respectively (from making meaning or creating a singular meaning) to multiple meanings—production (reading for what the text does). Although work on affect and emotion allows us to reconsider the material and physical experience of the film (opens up interpretation), in terms of theorising desire, the use of Deleuze returns us to the debate between desire as negative and desire as productive. Although psychoanalysis may have disappeared from cinema studies, as McGowan and Kunkle suggest, it is still often held in opposition to other models. Effectively psychoanalysis remains as a haunting spectre. Instead of playing one paradigm off the other, it is useful to consider how they each elucidate specific aspects of the filmic experience.

Do not compromise your desire!

Code 46 (2003), directed by Michael Winterbottom and written by Frank Cottrell Boyce, offers an opportunity to think through the theorisations of desire presented within this chapter and the stress within psychoanalytic theory on the Oedipus complex. *Code 46* takes place sometime in the future, a future where genetic cloning and IVF has developed to such an extent that couples must be screened in advance in order to determine whether or not they are allowed to reproduce. 'Code 46' is the term given to anyone who violates the mandate not to reproduce with someone who has similar genetic coding: to do so is to transgress the laws and codes of society and technological advancement. The film begins with the definition of 'Code 46' and its various articles; it states that 'any human being who shares the same nuclear gene set as another human being is deemed to be genetically identical. The relations of one are the relations of all' (Winterbottom 2003).

William Geld (Tim Robbins) goes to Shanghai in order to investigate theft at an insurance company, appropriately called 'The Sphinx'. Insurance 'covers' are now issued in order to allow people to travel into different parts of the world. Those who are denied cover are denied for a reason (or so the director implies)—the motto of the insurance company is 'The Sphinx knows best'. With the help of an 'empathy virus', William is able to intuit the truth from those he interviews. In the process of his investigation he falls in love with Maria Gonzalez (Samantha Morton). Despite knowing that she is the person he is looking for, he does not turn her in to the authorities; instead he spends the night with her.

In meeting Maria, William loses the co-ordinates of his desire[23]—he is no longer sure of himself or of his actions, instead he finds himself drawn to her almost hypnotically. When they got to a club together, Winterbottom films Morton dancing under a strobe light. The effect is that we can see Morton's face and body highlighted at slow intervals: first her eyes, then darkness, then her mouth, then darkness, then her hips. The slow hypnotic quality of the filming matches the pace in which William is falling for Maria. The suggestion is that his desire is almost out of his control and not in his conscious mind. When he returns home to his wife and son, he is unable to stop thinking about Maria; indeed, as he walks into his home he imagines being passionately greeted by her (while his 'real' wife remains in the kitchen).

When a man dies after travelling on a 'false cover', William is sent back to Shanghai to re-investigate the fraud. The sequence from the beginning of the film is repeated upon his return (the sequence takes us back through the drive into town and past border controls, through the long corridor of his hotel, and then into the insurance company), except this time Maria is missing. She has been dismissed for 'body issues' and has been sent to a clinic on the 'outside'. There William discovers that Maria has violated 'code 46' and has been given a termination and had the memory of him, their night together and the abortion removed from her mind. They also install a virus which makes her body physically repulse at William's touch.

William insists on taking Maria from the clinic and takes her home. There he collects a sample of her hair and takes it to a genetic testing centre—a place designed for people to find out whether they can marry and reproduce together. A couple next to William are told that they are allowed, and indeed are encouraged, to reproduce since they are a good gene match. William however is told that he cannot have relations with the woman whose hair he has brought in. He discovers that she is a 50% genetic match with his own genetic coding, and a 100% genetically identical match to his mother. In other words, she is a 'genetic twin' to his mother. Upon hearing this news, he heads straight for the airport, desperate to return to his family; however, his cover is now expired and he is not allowed to leave. He must return to Maria and ask her to get him 'false cover'. When she meets him in the airport with the cover, Maria tells William that she remembers him from her birthday dream (part of her memories that were not erased). At this point, he is unable to leave her and they escape to Jebel Ali, a Freeport city.

Because Maria's body has been programmed (by the virus) to physically reject William, he must tie her down in order to make love to her. The scene is very uncomfortable for the viewer. Maria's body is physically rejecting him and indeed, at many times, she screams out against what he is doing, but then there are moments, which we are expected to recognise as her 'true' feelings, when she smiles at him and tells him she loves him. What the scene implies is that the desire between them is real, but the taboos against such a union keep both body and mind in discomfort and rejection. After Maria has called the authorities to report her violation of 'code 46', William attempts to save them both by driving away, but they crash and it is at this point that the romance is ended. Following the accident, Maria is banished to 'al fuera' (outside), the undesirable outskirts of civilisation, whereas William is taken home and has the memory of her erased from his mind. He is 'cured' and able to return to his wife, son and their life together.

The film raises many important issues, not all of which can be explored here. Jackie Stacey, for instance, has argued persuasively how the film demonstrates societal concerns about genetic and racial purity and how these anxieties are mapped out cinematically (2006). Throughout the film, characters use a hybrid language, mixing English, Japanese, French, Italian and Spanish randomly and intermittently—using phrases and words such as 'lo siento', 'hombre', 'te amo' and 'palabra'. This hybrid language gestures towards some of the consequences of globalisation that have taken place in the future and to the mixing of cultures that exists. And yet, despite the fluidity of language, it is clear that the movement between borders and countries has become more restricted. The notion of borders and crossings is portrayed as more severe and less forgiving— a commentary on the future of migration as well as miscegenation.

Although the film lends itself to many interpretations and comments on a futuristic society, I would like to draw attention to the way in which Winterbottom presents a contemporary Oedipal myth and refigures the consequences of this desire. There are two fundamental differences to note in the fates of the two main characters of both Sophocles' myth and Winterbottom's film: the mother, Jocasta, in Sophocles' myth kills herself, whereas Morton's character is left in the marginal space of the undesirables. Oedipus blinds himself, whereas William is 'restored' to his original life. However it could be argued that he is now blinded to the truth of his past and of his desires.

The film is narrated throughout by Maria, who tells the story as a love story. She wonders at the end of the film whether William remembers her, for she is the only one left with the memory of their transgression. One of the fundamental questions the film raises, as voiced by Maria, is 'If we had enough information we could predict the consequences of our actions [...] If we knew what would happen in the end would we ever be able to take the first step to make the first move?' (Winterbottom 2003) The film questions the relations of fate, belief and desire in our lives. At one level, the film suggests that our future selves are not in control of their own desires, and yet on another, the suggestion is that there is still room for freedom and rebellion.

Winterbottom's film resonates with many of the contemporary readings of desire—intimacy as an increasingly public phenomenon, the regulation or even colonialisation of desire, and the primacy of emotion as a social tool, something that is accepted as a valuable skill, and not gendered as feminine and therefore culturally dismissed. The presentation of desire in *Code 46* emphasises intimacy through slow camera movements, through the attention to Maria and William (very few other characters are introduced), through music and slow camera panning, and through the use of landscape (desert versus the cityscape). The film suggests that in the future sunlight becomes so dangerous that people must work during the night and sleep during the day, thus giving the film a different dimension of sense deprivation. Life is lived during the night, during the time normally reserved for dreaming. This adds to the myth-like quality of the film and to the link between *Code 46* and Sophocles' *Oedipus Rex*.

What does desire do in the film? It moves us through the story of William and Maria; it moves them to pursue their desires for each other, even though there are many barriers against such a pursuit. It reminds us of how potent desire can be and how it initiates even the most conservative and cautious person to risk everything. It causes new beginnings, new memories and ultimately new stories. Desire moves us to challenge everything we believe in, to re-evaluate our ethical and moral relationship to ourselves and the world and to position ourselves accordingly.

In Winterbottom's version of the Oedipal complex, desire is ultimately about taking a risk, not simply about following one's destiny. Oedipus was able to kill his father because he did not know it was his father. He was blind to the truth. Shakespeare's Hamlet was not able to kill his (step)father because he does not know what he wants and so fails in his desire. In *Code 46* William gives way to his desire. He does not compromise his desire even after finding out that the object of his desire is a genetic clone to his mother. The fundamental difference in this myth is that there is no father to kill. The only 'father figure' is the state, which 'corrects' the risk William has taken by erasing his memory and placing Maria on the 'outside' of civilisation.[24]

In his assessment of risk, Žižek argues that 'the sad reality of our late capitalist tolerant liberal society: [is that] the very capacity to *act* is brutally medicalized, treated as a manic outburst within the pattern of "bipolar disorder", and as such to be submitted to biochemical treatment' (1999, 387). Žižek is referring here to the case of Mary Kay Letourneau, a schoolteacher who began a passionate relationship with one of her students, 13-year-old Vili Fualaau, and served a seven-and-a-half-year sentence for statutory rape.[25] The question that Mary Kay's case raises for Žižek is how could she put everything (family, job, reputation) at risk? How could she risk everything she had for one person, knowing that a relationship with this person was impossible? A similar ethical dilemma is posed within *Code 46*: why would William risk losing everything (family, job, reputation) in order to have a sexual relationship with his mother's genetic clone? In the case of *Code 46*, one could argue that the stakes are even higher, considering William takes the risk of violating the ultimate social taboo. And yet, as viewers, we are convinced by and even supportive of William's decision. The risk seems worth taking. But how do we judge this decision ethically?

With regard to Mary Kay, Žižek believes that the most depressing moment of the case was when Mary Kay began to 'compromise' her desire—that is, under the pressure of media and public scorn, she began to feel guilty and to repent for her feelings. When Mary Kay gave way to her desires, the medical establishment was given space to come in and attribute her passion to 'bipolar disorder' and to medicalise what, according to Žižek, was an act of passion. In the end, Mary Kay did not compromise her desires, and is now married to Vili and has two children with him. This case illustrates for Žižek the power and dangers in compromising one's desire. It also allows us to think about how we ethically judge passionate encounters. Instead of trying to apply general rules to this case, Žižek argues that we must make room for the 'uniqueness' of desire: 'On a more radical level, one should insist on the uniqueness, the absolute idiosyncrasy, of the ethical act proper—such an act involves its own inherent normativity which "makes it right"; there is no neutral external standard that would enable us to decide in advance, by a simple application to a single case, on its ethical status' (1999, 388). As Žižek points out, there is no textbook case to throw at a situation such as Mary Kay's, and so perhaps, we need to be more allowing of desires we cannot understand.

In the case of *Code 46* this decision is not left to us as viewers. Despite their attempts to escape, William and Maria are captured and punished for their crimes. William is found guilty, but considered to have a momentary lapse of reason, and medicalised insofar as he has all memory of Maria and their time together erased from his mind. He is able to fully return to his wife and son and their life together. William's 'full' recovery is made evident in a final scene where he is making passionate love to his wife—we, as viewers, are convinced that he no longer has any memory of Maria—he has been blinded to his desire for her. In contrast, Maria is left fully aware of their time together and the fact that she is now alone.

Žižek argues that 'Lacan's maxim "Do not compromise your desire!" fully endorses the pragmatic paradox of ordering you to be free: it exhorts you to dare' (1999, 392). Winterbottom's film compels us to dare, but reminds us of the consequences and, indeed, the realities of a society that is increasingly in control of our intimate lives: a contemporary Oedipal drama that suggests that men can pursue their ultimate desires and be forgiven for losing their way—their slates can be wiped clean. However, the film also suggests that women are not as free to make these choices, and ultimately run the risk of being left 'outside' if they transgress.

The rise of an individualistic society with 'privatised worlds' means that desire is increasingly negotiated in the public sphere and that the individual is expected to respond to the demand to 'enjoy', 'take pleasure', *desire*, but also to self-monitor and self-discipline—the demand not to compromise your desire is mediated to some extent by the demand that you do not allow your desires to compromise you.

2
Hysterical Desire

> The hysterical body is of course typically, from Hippocrates through Freud, a woman's body, and indeed a victimized woman's body, on which desire has inscribed an impossible history, a story of desire in an impasse.
>
> (Peter Brooks 1995, xi–xii)

> The hysteric's question, then, is related to how we all position ourselves in, and are positioned by, the forces of our culture.
>
> (Patrick Fuery 1994, 129)

The rise of an individualistic society also means an increase in the expectations placed on individuals to know what they want, to know their desires and to seek answers in everything from horoscopes, to TV talk shows to new age therapies. Beck points out that

> The overtaxed individual 'seeks, finds and produces countless authorities intervening in social and psychic life, which, as his professional representatives, relieve him of the question: "Who am I and what do I want?" and thus reduce his fear of freedom.' This creates the market for the answer factories, the psycho-boom, the advice literature—that mixture of the esoteric cult, the primal scream, mysticism, yoga and Freud which is supposed to drown out the tyranny of possibilities but in fact reinforces it with its changing fashion.
>
> (2001, 7)

Questions such as 'Who am I?' and 'What do I want?' are those voiced by the hysteric and are answered in a hysterical fashion through the 'psycho-boom' which, instead of relieving a sense of anxiety, works to create new problems, questions and hysterical symptoms. It is important here to separate out the different forms individualism takes, as Foucault does so well in *The Care of the Self* (1986). He reminds us that individualism involves an attitude of independence towards a group of people, a valuation of private life and 'an intensity of the relations to self, that is, of the forms in which one is called upon to take oneself as an object of knowledge and a field of action, so as to transform, correct, and purify oneself, and find salvation' (1986, 42). Although these aspects of individualism are often interconnected—it is the last form of individualism, that of the intense relation to self and self-transformation, which becomes central to a theorisation of desire.

The last chapter argued for desire's radical potential in theory and in terms of self-transformation. Not compromising on desire necessitates a risk and a refusal to give way to fear and self-doubt. In order to pursue their desire for each other, Maria and William have to transgress the law, and risk being punished. Winterbottom's contemporary Oedipal drama highlights the ways in which intimacy can be regulated and controlled by society through strict codes, monitoring techniques and surveillance.[1] The film also considers the consequences that follow any challenge to a society that monitors forms of intimacy. As the film's ending implies, these consequences are often gendered and involve different levels of retribution.

If when theorising desire the narrative of Oedipus is the central story within psychoanalysis, then the hysteric is its central figure; as one theorist has suggested: 'psychoanalysis can historically be called the child of the hysterical woman' (Smith-Rosenberg 1985, 197). Or, as Jan Campbell argues: 'Oedipus and hysteria are simply two sides of the same coin' (2005, 7). In light of these claims, and in lieu of the intense relation to self imagined in theorisations of hysteria, this chapter will explore the way hysteria has been theorised and consider the way it is presented in contemporary film.

In the prefatory remarks to his infamous 'fragment of an analysis of a case of hysteria', commonly known as the Case of Dora, Freud tells his readers that the 'causes of hysterical disorders are to be found in the intimacies of the patients' psycho-sexual life, and that hysterical symptoms are the expression of their most secret and repressed wishes' (2001 [1953], vol. 7, 8). So, from the beginning of our journey into understanding hysteria we are made aware of its intimate, repressed and secret nature. We are also introduced to readers of hysteria who may not be reading as a means of contributing to the psychopathology of the neuroses, but, as Freud warns, may use the narrative information as a '*roman à clef* designed for their private delectation' (2001 [1953], vol. 7, 9). Freud's prefatory remarks establish three main characters in the study of hysteria: the analyst, the patient and the reader. Each character works towards establishing the intimate world of the hysteric, whose secret desires always and forever remain just out of reach. The 'truth' of the hysteric's desire, her voice, often remains the greatest enigma—sought in particular by the analyst and the reader. It is not only the analyst who performs an anatomy of the hysteric but also her reader, who hopes to discover something overlooked or to unlock a secret truth previously dismissed.

Hysteria continues to have a relevance and explanatory power within contemporary culture. However, it also continues to be associated with woman, and in particular with either a celebration of her hysterical agency or a condemnation of her inability to 'fit in' with societal expectations (Leavy 2006). It has been argued that the hysteric is the voice of the highly individualised and atomised consumer (Verhaeghe 1999a), who looks for escape or uses a hysterical response as a form of rebellion or resistance. Hysteria continues to express the difficulties therefore in articulating desire and of our relation to desire. But is hysteria repressed desire, unspeakable desire or the inabilty to satisfy desire? Part of what this chapter will explore is hysteria's intimate relationship to desire and the ways in which hysteria continues to be used to explain female desire in particular.

Hysteria has been linked with woman since its inception, and was originally understood as an illness that originates in the womb. Freud's work on hysteria, specifically in his case on Dora, highlights his use of dreams to interpret symptoms, and is the foundation for his work on repression and the unconscious. Feminist theory has often characterised the hysteric as either a victim of patriarchal control or as a heroine. In this chapter I discuss hysteria as it appears in psychoanalysis, feminist theory and film, in order to demonstrate how hysteria and the study of hysteria are intimately linked to a theorisation of desire. I argue that hysteria, as a concept, exposes the difficulties in articulating desire: both in terms of the hysteric and the analyst/theorist who wants to explain her malady. I also argue that hysteria can be read as a contemporary articulation of the 'crisis' that marks texts such as Todd Haynes's *Safe* (2003) and Sharon Maguire's *Bridget Jones's Diary* (2001) around societal expectations of women.

Contemporary hysteria

Hysteria, as a diagnosis, is still used in contemporary discourse. A recent *New York Times* article regarding a case of mass hysteria in a school near Mexico City, for example, suggests that hysteria is still very much an existing issue. As the article details: 'Mexico's public health authorities have concluded that the girls at the Children's Village School are suffering from a mass psychogenic disorder. In layman's language, they have a collective hysteria' (Malkin, 2007, A4). In his excellent study *Approaching Hysteria* (1995), Mark S. Micale draws attention to hysteria's 'obscene interpretability' (1995, 285). He argues that hysteria has been understood as 'a manifestation of everything from divine poetic inspiration and satanic possession to female unreason, racial degeneration, and unconscious psychosexual conflict ... It has been construed as a physical disease, a mental disorder, a spiritual malady, a behavioural maladjustment, a sociological communication, and as no illness at all' (1995, 285). Hysteria's 'obscene interpretability' thus lends itself both to characterising and explaining social and cultural experiences simultaneously.

Within the last decade, there has been a renewed critical and cultural interest in the concept of hysteria and its relevance to social theory (Wilson 2004; Mitchell 2000; Bollas 2000; Verhaeghe 1999a, 1999b; Bronfen 1998; Kirby 1997; and Showalter 1997). Although much of the literature questions whether or not hysteria still exists,[2] most accounts argue that it is not only still present in contemporary society, but that it is now more contagious and more prevalent than before. For instance, Paul Verhaeghe argues that 'hysteria is not disappearing, it only changes its appearance and, if need be, its partner' (1999a, 92). In *Mad Men and Medusas* (2000), Juliet Mitchell argues that 'Hysteria has not [...] disappeared from the twentieth-century Western world; it is rather that this world manifests a hidden hysteria and is not recognising it' (2000, 134). In an article titled 'Is Hysteria Real? Brain Images Say Yes', Erika Kinetz of *The New York Times* argues that 'despite its period of invisibility, hysteria never vanished—or at least that is what many doctors say' (26 Sept. 2006, D1). Elaine Showalter goes even further in *Hystories* (1997) and maintains that 'Hysteria not only survives in the 1990s, it is more contagious than in the past' (1997, 5). What is clear throughout these accounts of hysteria is that its explanatory power lies in its ability to characterise contemporary issues.

Micale takes up the issue of hysteria's disappearance and its re-emergence within recent critical and cultural studies; he argues that 'The termination of an entire disease form, especially one that appears to have such a long and venerable history, is surely a noteworthy event' (1995, 169). Micale suggests, as do others,[3] that hysteria did not go away, rather it was called something else. Because of the negative associations with hysteria, it was referred to more often as 'conversion disorder'. Micale also adds that hysteria as a diagnosis may have lost ground to other diagnoses such as epilepsy, syphilis and melancholia (1995, 171–174) and given rise to contemporary illnesses such as chronic fatigue syndrome and anorexia, which share many similarities with hysteria, in that they affect women, have links to sexual trauma and have been widely publicised within the media (1995, 289–291). Finally, Micale suggests that part of the reason for hysteria's disappearance is because it is inextricably linked to psychoanalysis—so getting rid of hysteria is part of the project of getting rid of psychoanalysis (1995, 292). Whatever the reasons for its 'disappearance', hysteria has 're-appeared' over the last two decades as a subject of study, evidenced by the wide range of literary, social and cinematic interest.

Although there appears to be consensus among critics that hysteria exists, there is little agreement about what it means, does or stands for in contemporary culture. Theorists have exploited hysteria's 'obscene interpretability' and used it to refer to a wide range of societal ills and transformations such as the breakdown of patriarchal culture, the rise of anxiety-related illnesses, the desire for paternal authority and a need to return to the body and the biological.

In *Love in a Time of Loneliness* (1999b), for instance, Paul Verhaeghe[4] argues that, following fundamental changes in society, people have become hysterical in their desire for security. He suggests that 'the desire for a secure anchor has resulted in the fact that people today can be described as being hysterical by definition' (1999b, 119). Conflicting desires such as those to succeed in one's career, to maintain a 'happy' marriage, to raise 'healthy' kids, to look great no matter what age, to have a beautiful home, car, etc. put pressure on the individual to such an extent that one is caught in a position of feeling unhappy with everything. No matter what you achieve, there is still something further to be achieved, or someone else who has achieved more. He argues that 'modern hysteria is looking for an Other as a place of safety, looking for something or someone in whom to *believe*' (1999b, 119). In other words, Verhaeghe suggests that the loss of a master figure and the breakdown of patriarchal culture has created a society that is desperate to find someone or something who will lessen the burden of these conflicting desires—someone who can guarantee the right answers (1999b, 122).

Verhaeghe's argument comes from a psychoanalytic mourning over the loss of the father, an argument that others,[5] such as Slavoj Žižek, pose in their reading of the contemporary hysteric. Žižek argues that 'beneath the hysteric's rebellion and challenge to paternal authority, there is thus a hidden call for a renewed paternal authority, for a father who would really be a "true father" and adequately embody his symbolic mandate' (1999, 334). One of the problems that Žižek foresees in the narrative that leads from the patriarchal Oedipus to postmodern and multiple identities is that it 'fails to account for the new forms of domination emerging from postmodern subjectivity itself (1999, 360). 'Is not the "culture of complaint," Žižek asks, 'today's version of hysteria, of the hysterical impossible demand addressed to the Other, a demand that actually *wants to be rejected*, since the subject grounds his/her existence in his/her complaint' (1999, 361). Or does Žižek's reading simply mask a desire to find a need for paternal authority behind the resistance to it?

Hysteria has also been elided with a kind of cultural malaise that is typified by an endless desire to have access to an inner world of the other. As psychoanalyst Christopher Bollas explains so adeptly in his work on hysteria:

> To identify with and represent the other's internal objects is the hysteric's passion, easily satisfied with reading books or watching films, where the self enjoys the illusion of secret access to the other's imaginary ... In intimate relations the hysteric demands endless access to the other's internal world. 'What are you thinking about?' 'You must tell me what you thought about the film ... in great detail!' These demands become the daily territorial song of the hysteric, who enters the other's imaginary, trying out the other's introjects for garments, intended to mirror the other to himself or herself.
>
> (2000, 162)

In Bollas's interpretive hands, the hysteric becomes a wistful, daydreaming, slightly bonkers but loveable child-like creature, who yearns to talk and talk all day long about his/her feelings and desires, but fears actually doing anything about them. In his rhetorical description of hysterical lovers-to-be, Bollas suggests that they would talk and talk and talk some more, bumping into each other and giggling, eventually spending whatever sexual energy they may have on the experience of talking about it (2000, 168). If they were ever to consummate their feelings for each other it would have to take both of them by surprise.

The act of interpreting and re-interpreting hysteria, or using it to stand in for a range of different cultural meanings is not a new phenomenon. Indeed, the concept of hysteria has a long and venerable history, both in the medical and clinical literature and in socio-cultural literature. The word 'hysteria' is derived from the Greek word, 'hysteria' meaning 'uterus'. One of the oldest surviving documents of medical history, an Egyptian papyrus dating from around 1900 BC, records a series of strange behaviours in women. This document is thought to be the earliest record of hysteria and to represent early thought that hysteria was caused by a 'travelling womb'. The suggestion was that if the womb was barren for too long, it would begin to migrate and move towards the throat, thus cutting off the breath of the woman affected. The most effective 'cure' for this condition was 'immediate marriage' or 'marital *fornicatio*' (Micale 1995, 20). In the seventeenth century, the belief that the womb was the cause of hysteria was challenged by Charles Lepois, who, very importantly, argued that hysterical pathology did not originate in the womb or soul, but in the head (Micale 1995, 21). This shift paved the way for work by Jean-Martin Charcôt, the most important figure in the nineteenth century on hysteria and perhaps the most well known outside of Freud. In Charcôt's estimation, hysteria was a neurological defect, an illness that came from a combination of hereditary disposition and nervous degeneration. Charcôt did not believe there was any 'cure' for his patients, unlike Freud and Breuer, whose *Studies on Hysteria* paved the way for the 'talking cure' and the birth of psychoanalysis.[6] As Foucault has remarked, Charcôt's work not only illustrated a desire to observe, measure and categorise hysteria, but his work also served as an incitement to a discourse on the 'truth' of sexuality; as he argues: 'the important thing, in this affair [that of Charcôt and his presentations], is not that these men shut their eyes or stopped their ears, or that they were mistaken; it is rather that they constructed around and apropos of sex an immense apparatus for producing truth, even if this truth was to be masked at the last moment' (1978, 56). Charcôt's work on hysteria and his elaborate hysterical presentations led to an 'interplay of truth and sex' (1978, 57), which as Foucault argues, remains in place today.[7]

It is important to note, however, that there are significant differences between the medical model of hysteria and the socio-cultural model of hysteria. There are also several different interpretive strategies that make up the historiography of hysteria. However, Micale argues, it is less important in an exploration of hysteria in contemporary culture to decide conclusively what hysteria *means* nor do we need to decide whether it is a *real* disease. Rather, Micale, as an historian, is more interested in asking questions such as 'What were the popular and cultural meanings and associations of the concept? And how did these associations operate socially and culturally within their own time?' (1995, 115). In this chapter I want to take a similar approach, in that I am not asking what hysteria *means* nor whether it is *real*, instead I want to consider how the study of hysteria is linked to a theorisation of desire within psychoanalysis and feminist theory. I also want to consider how hysteria continues to be used as a metaphor or expression of repressed or inarticulate desire within popular culture.

Within psychoanalytic theory, particularly within works by Freud and Lacan, the hysteric is characterised as a figure of fragmented and disjointed thoughts, silent, sexually repressed, prone to convulsive physical behaviour and, for the most part, as female. She can be understood as representing the enigma of female desire at the heart of Freud's search for an answer to the question, 'What does Woman want?' Analysis is designed to use desire to uncover the secret knowledge the hysteric keeps from the analyst. The analyst's job is to construct a coherent history of the analysand in order that she might identify herself. Fundamentally hysteria represents the inability to articulate desire—the crisis that comes from being unable or unwilling to accept one's own desires. Hysteria also presents us with the desire of the analyst who desperately tries to enable the patient to articulate her desires.

Freud and hysteria

Freud's encounter with Charcôt and his work on hysteria formed the basis of his theories on repression and the unconscious.[8] Similarly, Lacan's early work on paranoid women helped him to formulate the 'mirror theory' which was influential in his understanding of desire and identification.[9] Ultimately psychoanalysis is a search for meaning, as Lacan states: 'We are always looking for meaning. That is what makes us different' (1993 [1981], 196). Meaning is derived from the analytic sessions which aim to discover the analysand's desires. In a sense then desire is used as a tool to unlock and uncover hidden truths about the subject. The most important reason to return to the figure of the hysteric is to mark out the way analysts seek to 'cure' or 'solve' her enigma. Elisabeth Bronfen argues in her critique of hysteria that the hysteric becomes a patient because her story is irregular and fragmented; 'leaving out, distorting, and rearranging information—the analyst faces an elusive and enigmatic version and his responsibility becomes the reconstructing of a complete and logical narrative' (1998, 53).

In his influential work on melodrama, Peter Brooks argues that 'hysteria offers a problem in representation: Freud's task, from the *Studies of Hysteria* onwards, is learning to read the messages inscribed on the hysterical body—a reading that is inaugural of psychoanalysis as a discipline' (1995 [1976], xi). Indeed, as French psychoanalyst Juan-David Nasio argues: 'the hysteria of those early years did not only give birth to psychoanalysis; it left an indelible stamp on the theory and practice of the discipline today' (1998, xxi), a claim that is validated by the continued interest in hysteria in contemporary psychoanalytic practice and cultural theory.

Freud's early work on hysteria in *Studies in Hysteria* (1893–1895, co-authored with Josef Breuer) contains Freud and Breuer's case studies (including Breuer's infamous study of 'Anna O'). However, it is not until the publication of *Three Essays on Sexuality and Other Works* (1901–1905) that his analysis of Dora appears.[10] Freud's 'fragment of an analysis'[11] refers to the interpretations he makes of his three-month session with Dora,[12] a name he gives to eighteen-year-old Ida Bauer. The case highlights Freud's use of dreams to interpret symptoms and follows the publication of *The Interpretation of Dreams*: 'The dream, in short, is one of the *détours by which repression can be* evaded' (2001 [1953], vol. 7, 15, author's italics). Freud sees dreams as more reliable since the patient is often 'consciously and intentionally' (2001 [1953], vol. 7, 17) keeping things from the analyst because of their feelings. Dora's case also becomes a way for Freud to explain the workings of the unconscious and repression. Throughout his analysis, Freud emphasises sexuality as the key to the problem of neuroses and psychoneuroses. He writes in the postscript to the case: 'I was further anxious to show that sexuality does not simply intervene, like a *deus ex machina*, on one single occasion, at some point in the working of the processes which characterize hysteria, but that it provides the motive power for every single symptom, and for every single manifestation of a symptom' (2001 [1953], vol. 7, 115). However, as Jacqueline Rose suggests, it is Freud's failure to analyse Dora in terms of a 'normative concept of what a woman should be' that led him to 'recognise the fragmented and aberrant nature of sexuality itself' (1982, 28).

Dora's case has been the subject of numerous essays, articles, books and collections, from psychoanalytic and feminist approaches and those that combine the two. Claire Kahane and Charles Bernheimer subtitle their definitive collection of essays on Dora: 'Freud—Hysteria—Feminism' for, as Kahane argues, Dora stands in the middle of contemporary questioning of the relation between interpretation and sexual difference (1990 [1985], 20). The various readings and interpretations offered *In Dora's Case* testify to the way in which Freud's 'fragment of analysis' opens itself up to interpretation and re-readings. Steven Marcus goes as far as to suggest that 'Freud's case histories are a new form of literature; they are creative narratives that include their own analysis and interpretation' (1990 [1985], 90). In the majority of work on Dora, theorists identify two central concerns, which Jacqueline Rose calls the 'vanishing points' of Dora's case: 'the theory of feminine sexuality and the concept of transference' (1990 [1985], 141). In terms of a feminist response to Dora, which will be discussed in more detail later, the primary concern is whether Dora can be recuperated as a heroine, or whether she is ultimately a victim.

In order to make sense of Dora's place within work on hysteria, and in particular in work by Freud and Lacan, it is necessary to offer some background on the case itself. Following the discovery of a possible suicide letter and after Dora suffered from a 'fainting spell', she was brought to Freud by her parents who were concerned by her increasing disinterest in social affairs and her 'low spirits' (2001 [1953], vol. 7, 23). Freud had treated Dora's father years before for syphilis—so a previous link is established by Freud, and indeed, he sees Dora as having inherited many of her problems from her father. Freud never met Dora's mother, and she is the most invisible figure within his analysis. 'I never made her mother's acquaintance. From the accounts given by the girl and her father I was led to imagine her as an uncultivated woman and above all as a foolish one, who had concentrated all her interests upon domestic affairs [...] She presented the picture, in fact, of what might be called the "housewive's psychosis"' (2001 [1953], vol. 7, 20).[13] It is very telling, not only that the mother is not consulted in terms of her daughter's illness, but also that Freud decides to dismiss her on the grounds of her position as a housewife. She is considered by Freud to be irrelevant and unable to understand her own illness.[14]

Freud makes a point in his prefatory remarks to explain that in this case history 'sexual questions will be discussed with all possible frankness, the organs and functions of sexual life will be called by their proper names, and the pure-minded reader can convince himself from my description that I have not hesitated to converse upon such subjects in such language even with a young woman' (2001 [1953], vol. 7, 9). Freud then goes on to explain himself in light of the role of the gynaecologist that must see a woman 'uncovered' but does not become excited by the examination. He is very careful to argue that his frank discussions of sexuality with Dora are not a 'good means of exciting or of gratifying sexual desires' (2001 [1953], vol. 7, 9). Freud's defence of his straightforward manner re-appear throughout his analysis of Dora.[15]

At the same time he is developing his theoretical ideas of the unconscious and of repression, he does not seem to notice the way his justifications keep returning to his analysis.[16] Freud assures us that 'there is never any danger of corrupting an inexperienced girl. For where there is no knowledge of sexual processes even in the unconscious, no hysterical symptom will arise; and where hysteria is found there can no longer be any question of "innocence of mind" in the sense in which parents and educators use the phrase' (2001 [1953], vol. 7, 49).

It is important here to recognise the way in which Freud attributes knowledge to hysteria: an unconscious justification? Do his latent desires lie beneath this claim? One of the most important developments that Freud achieves through his analysis of Dora is the theoretical argument that conscious thoughts are often contrary to our unconscious ones. In other words, the thoughts we are able to express are generally the exact opposite of the ones we hold true in our unconscious. It is possible to use Freud's own analysis to suggest or argue that he is both uncomfortable with the manner of the questions he asks Dora but also that they excite him.

Indeed, although he is careful to convince us that Dora must know about these sexual acts and does not have an 'innocent' mind, it is also clear through his own recollections of the sessions that he leads her into some analyses that she herself does not understand nor agree with. He believes in his analysis of her first dream, for instance, that the jewel-case her mother wants to save from the fire is symbolic of 'female genitals'. When he offers this analysis to Dora she tells him: 'I knew you would say that' (2001 [1953], vol. 7, 69) which Freud believes to be 'a very common way of putting aside a piece of knowledge that emerges from the repressed' (2001 [1953], vol. 7, 69, ftne 4). He tells her that what she means in saying 'I knew you would say that' is that she 'knew that it *was* so' thus reminding Dora that everything is 'turned into its opposite' (2001 [1953], vol. 7, 69) in the analysis of dreams. This also serves to merge Freud's analysis with Dora's unconscious.

It is also important to note the way Dora analyses Freud—she *knew* he would say 'that'. She knew that he would fill in the missing signifier of her dream with a sexual reference? Even in Freud's analysis, it appears that Dora is aware of the way in which he is reading/analysing her dreams. Bronfen in *The Knotted Subject* argues that 'Whereas Freud's investigation questions Dora's desire and the source of her sexual knowledge, Dora, by her negations and her sudden silence, turns the text back on the narrator, forcing it to also question Freud's desire and the source he is willing to ascribe to his knowledge of hysteria' (1998, 341).

I would argue that it is not so much that Dora causes the text to 'turn back on its narrator' although it is clear that Dora questions Freud's approach. Instead, it is Freud's narration of events that exposes his desire to find an origin for Dora's hysteria and to 'solve' the mystery of her malady.

Dora's case is fundamentally about sexual desire. At various points, Freud reads Dora's dreams and admissions as proof that she desires her father, Herr K, Frau K, her governess, and even himself.[17] She is also accused of wanting to be or to replace her mother. The only character she is not shown as having sexual feelings for is her brother. At the same time, Freud accuses Dora of not having 'normal' responses to 'normal' offers of sexual desire. In his analysis of her first traumatic sexual incidence with Herr K, for example, he is confused why Dora did not enjoy the sexual advances of an older man. Freud does not accept Dora's reactions to Herr K's advances and cannot understand why she is not aroused by him. He adds in a footnote that he knows Herr K because he accompanied Dora's father when he came to visit; Freud remarks that Herr K was 'still quite young and of prepossessing appearance' (2001 [1953], vol. 7, 29, fine 3). Freud is so determined that Dora should desire Herr K that he constructs a secondary analysis and decides that Dora does not desire Herr K because he has already had a relationship with his children's governess.

In his work on hysteria, Paul Verhaeghe argues that at the centre of Freud's early work is a belief that something is *displaced* into a kind of expression that is not intrinsic to it and this something amounts to desire—not just desire but 'psychosexual desire' and a resistance to it (1999a, 15). For Verhaeghe, this central idea was the real 'starting-point' for psychoanalysis; 'hysteria was no longer determined by some mysterious trauma, but by an inarticuable desire that kept on being displaced' (1999a, 15).

Desire of the analyst

Lacan argues that Freud's work on hysteria demonstrates the illusion of mastery in the scene of analysis. He returns to Freud's work on Dora in order to suggest that the analyst must be aware of his own desires before he is able to interpret the desires of the analysand: 'So hysteria places us, I would say, on the track of some kind of original sin in analysis. There has to be one. The truth is perhaps simply one thing, namely, the desire of Freud himself, the fact that something, in Freud, was never analysed' (Lacan 1977, 12). Lacan implies that the 'original sin' in psychoanalysis lies with Freud's inability to articulate his own desires in the scene of analysis.[18]

Lacan's interest in surrealism, 'madwomen' and their writings shaped his approach to his doctoral work and to his case studies. His earlier work, 'Ecrits 'inspirés': Schizographie', 'Le probléme du style et les formes paranoïques de l'expérience', and 'The case of Aimée, or self-punitive paranoia', develops a theoretical framework that becomes central to the interpretation of his influential 'mirror theory'. As I have argued elsewhere, Lacan's early work illustrates a desire to uncover 'secret truths' regarding the sexual nature of the crimes he analyses, particularly those involving women.[19] Perhaps aware of desire's function within his own work, Lacan returns to Freud's case with Dora and criticises Freud for projecting his own desire onto Dora. While Lacan does this in part to revise Freud's interpretation, he also wants to assert his own approach to the analytic scene. Lacan poses the question: 'what is the analyst's desire?' (1977, 9) and argues that the 'analyst's desire can in no way be left outside our question' (1977, 10). In other words, Lacan argues that the analyst must be aware of his own desire before he can begin to understand the desires of the analysand. Lacan argues that psychoanalysis must concern itself with desire: 'It is absolutely essential that we should go back to this origin if we wish to put analysis on its feet' (1977, 12).

For Lacan, the emphasis on desire differentiates psychoanalysis from other disciplines. Lacan tries to conceive of psychoanalysis as a science, but points out that most sciences are not founded on the views of one man (i.e. Freud) (1977, 10). Lacan understands Freud as establishing psychoanalysis through the relation between desire and language (and the unconscious) (1977, 12). He criticises Freud regarding his case with Dora arguing that because Freud did not analyse his own desire well enough he transferred his desire to Dora ('[Freud] allowed himself to be overwhelmed') (1977, 12, 38). Lacan re-reads Dora's case believing that he is clearer than Freud regarding desire, and argues that the law of the father governs desire: 'Freud could not yet see ... that the hysteric's desire—which is legible in the most obvious way in the case—is to sustain the desire of the father—and, in the case of Dora, to sustain it by procuring it' (1977, 38).

Desire, in Lacan's figuration, is crucial to the subject's sense of self and her relation to others; it is fundamental in terms of creating a social being. As Bowie suggests: 'Desire is the subject-matter of psychoanalysis, but something is always left out when the analyst writes about it [...] However hard he tries to "articulate desire"—by constructing a theory of it, say – desire will always spill out from his sentences, diagrams or equations' (1991, 1). Lacan's return to Freud emphasises the difficulty and perhaps the impossibility of articulating desire, whether in terms of the scene of analysis or in terms of the act of theorisation.

Feminism and hysteria

As Micale points out, the 'largest, most active, and most transformative interpretive tradition within the new hysteria studies' comes from the feminist tradition (1995, 66). For this reason, it is impossible to comment on all the feminist work that has been done on hysteria.[20] Instead, I focus on some keys texts within new hysteria studies and the question of whether to read the hysteric as a figure that resists patriarchal authority or as an unfortunate victim of patriarchal control, a question that characterises the feminist approach to hysteria. Freud himself suggested that hysteria, as a medical condition, may be understood as an effort to receive attention, to break from the confines of a patriarchal society, as a rebellion against the expectations placed on women, or as a revolt against the limitations imposed. According to Freud, hysterical women were not just 'ill', they were outwardly rejecting the position they were being put in. Freud discusses 'motives of illness' and suggests that 'ill health will be her one weapon for maintaining her position' (2001 [1953], vol. 7, 42, 44). In other words, illness is one way that women can escape their position and force men to do as they would want. In Freud's words: 'It will procure her the care she longs for; it will force her husband to make pecuniary sacrifices for her and to show her consideration, as he would never have done while she was well' (2001 [1953], vol. 7, 44). Judith Feher Gurewich argues that Dora's case piqued Freud's interest in solving the enigma of female desire, a quest that he would never realise. As she writes: 'Freud discovered psychoanalysis by following the path of hysterical desire [...] However, Freud made one mistake: he wanted to stay ahead of the hysterical game. He thought he could give his hysterical patients the answer to their question, "What does a woman want?" He believed they wanted a master who held the secret of their most unknown wishes' (1999, vii). Part of the failing within Freud's project, as articulated both in Lacan's work and in feminist theory, is that his desire to uncover a secret, inner knowledge led him towards his desires, not Dora's.

Elaine Showalter suggests in her 'hystory' of hysteria that 'Feminist academic interest in hysteria first emerged through the writing of women's history. Early in the women's liberation movement, reclaiming the hostile labels attached to rebellious or deviant women became a popular feminist strategy' (1997, 54). In her earlier work on feminism

and hysteria, Showalter refers to hysteria as the 'daughter's disease', suggesting that hysteria might have been a 'mode of protest for women
deprived of other social or intellectual outlets' (1985, 147).[21] Anna O.
(Bertha Pappenheim) analysed by Breuer was the first case history of
hysteria in *Studies on Hysteria* (1895). She 'was the inventor of the "talking cure"' (1985, 155) and later became prominent as a feminist activist,
social worker, translator of Mary Wollstonecraft's *Vindication* and play-
wright (1985, 155). As Showalter argues: 'hysteria and feminism do exist
on a kind of continuum [...] If we see the hysterical woman as one end
of the spectrum of a female avant-garde struggling to redefine women's
place in the social order, then we can also see feminism as the other end
of the spectrum, the alternative to hysterical silence, and the determi-
nation to speak and act for women in the public world' (1985, 161).
Showalter positions hysteria as the alter ego of feminism: one is silent
and yet still actively challenging patriarchal order and the other is vocal
and public. Her model is very much in line with other feminist work on
hysteria which positions the hysteric as a passive aggressive force against
social order.

Carroll Smith-Rosenberg, for instance, reads hysteria as a strategy that
offered women in the nineteenth century an opportunity to reposition
their place within the confines of the family structure (1985, 200).
Hysteria as a 'flight to illness', as I have discussed earlier, allowed women
power they would not otherwise have if healthy, as Smith-Rosenberg
argues: 'through her illness, the bedridden woman came to dominate her
family to an extent that would have been considered inappropriate ... in
a healthy woman' (1985, 208). This new position, however, was heavily
mediated by the physician, who could either validate the woman's illness, and thereby support her influence over her family, or dismiss her
behaviour as childish and indulgent. Indeed, as Smith-Rosenberg points
out, 'emotional indulgence, moral weakness, and lack of willpower characterised the hysteric in both lay and medical thought' (1985, 205). It is
not surprising therefore that contemporary articulations of hysteria
often represent the hysteric as emotionally selfish and undisciplined.

In their influential *Freud's Women* Lisa Appignanesi and John Forrester
argue that 'the label "hysteric" legitimized the increasingly endangered
status quo in a period of rising demands for equality and independence'
(1992, 68). Bronfen refers to Appignanesi and Forrester's work on 'Freud's
women' by drawing attention to the fact that Dora (Ida Bauer) emerges
later in life as a highly successful teacher and player of bridge. For
Bronfen, this 'ending' symbolises a kind of triumph for Bauer: 'At this
point in her life at least, Dora seems to have been successful at juggling

the contradictions in her hysteria—playing a game with her female partner that she had learned from identifying with her analyst' (Bronfen 1998, 343). Bronfen's celebration of Dora, which carries similarities to many of the essays in Kahane's collection, *In Dora's Case*, stands in contrast with Showalter's point in *Hystories* that 'claiming hysteria and admiring its victims may have had inspirational functions in the 1970s [...] But Saint Dora's days are over. Today's feminists need models rather than martyrs; we need the courage to think as well as the courage to heal' (1997, 61). Showalter's point deserves further consideration and gestures towards the way criticism has evaded the 'real' of Dora's life in favour of creating a martyr of her.[22]

So far, the terrain I have mapped out focuses on ideational reasons for hysteria and, according to theorists such as Elizabeth A. Wilson (2004) and Vicki Kirby (1997), these interpretations of hysteria overlook biology. Indeed, as Teresa Brennan points out: 'misapprehensions about hysteria are themselves instances of the tendency to split biological or physical inquiry (real things) from psychosocial explanation (not real things)' (2004, 3). However, recent work on hysteria has started to address this split.[23] Wilson's work, for instance, encourages feminism to embrace neurological accounts of the emotions in that they may offer a more grounded approach to feminist theories of affectivity and embodiment (2004, 83). Elizabeth Grosz's *In the Nick of Time* (2004) and attention to affect theory attests to a renewed focus on Darwin and biology (a return to the body). However, in terms of theorising hysteria, is there not a danger of returning to the biological model of the 'travelling womb' that once defined hysteria? Wilson answers this question with reference to male hysteria and concludes that 'all matter wanders', 'compliance' she argues 'is matter's most rudimentary character, and the proclivity to conversion is its most natural operation' (2004, 16). Wilson's reading of hysteria, in particular of conversion hysteria, also questions the idea of self-transformation, popularised in particular in 1970s consciousness raising narratives, as I will go on to explore.

Safe

Instead of tracing the constitutive links between early cinema, hysteria and Charcôt's *Iconographie photographique de la Salpêtrière*, as others such as Georges Didi-Huberman (2003) and Jan Campbell (2005) have done so convincingly, I want to locate my critique of hysteria and its relation to desire in contemporary film. If, as Verhaghe and others argue, hysteria is part of a wider anxiety within society over a loss of control and a desire for safety, then Todd Haynes's *Safe* is a perfect illustration of this interpretation. As Mary Ann Doane suggests: '*Safe* is a response to a pervasive media-generated discourse about risk' (2004, 6). Set in San Fernando Valley in 1987, *Safe* reflects the alienation and desire for security that Verhaghe uses to define contemporary hysteria. Indeed, Haynes's use of 'environmental illness' can be linked to contemporary illnesses such as 'Gulf War syndrome' or 'chronic fatigue'.

The opening scene of Todd Haynes's *Safe* is shot from the inside of a car as it drives through the deserted suburban streets of the San Fernando Valley. With an original music score by Brendan Dolan, the effect is ominous and enclosing. The camera takes us through a wrought iron gate and into the 'safety' of the garage. In the scene that immediately follows we witness the two main characters, Carol (Julianne Moore) and Greg (Xander Berkeley), having sex. All we can see, however, is Greg's back and Carol's disinterested face as she lies underneath him, accepting and even comforting her husband into orgasm. What these scenes immediately establish is the enclosed and monotonous space of the wealthy suburban life and Carol's position within it. She is a 'homemaker', whose limited responsibilities include pruning roses, choosing furniture and going to the dry cleaners. Carol is a woman with very few attachments—she does not have a job or career, she has housemaids to do the cooking and cleaning, she has a detached relationship with her stepson and husband, and very few friends. Haynes spends the first half of the film emphasising the monotony and isolation of Carol's life, so much so that we, as viewers, feel very little warmth towards her character or feel sympathy when she begins to experience hysterical symptoms.

Following a 'fruit diet' Carol begins to feel unwell and seeks advice from her physcian who assures her that she is very healthy—indeed her only 'vice' is milk, which he tells her to avoid for a while. When Carol's condition deteriorates, despite assurances from the physician that she is more than healthy, she takes interest in a self-help group designed for people 'who smell fumes'. Carol attends one of the workshops and begins to believe that she has an 'environmental illness'—an illness that is described as a 'disease you catch from your environment'. After a hysterical attack at one of her friend's baby showers, Carol undergoes a series of 'allergen' tests and creates a 'safe room' in the house that is free from any toxins or fumes. As the workshop assures her: 'safe bodies need safe environments to live'. As viewers we begin to witness a change in Carol, she is more self-aware, she has a purpose, something more than domestic responsibility.

However, when Carol goes to pick up the dry-cleaning, this time carrying her oxygen tank with her, she is exposed to pesticide (which they are spraying in the store) and collapses into a convulsive fit. Following this incident she is put in the hospital. However, as her physician points out, there is no medical explanation for her condition. While in the hospital Carol sees a commercial for Wrenwood, a centre designed for those suffering from 'environmental illness'. As its director, Peter Denning explains, like chronic fatigue syndrome and AIDS, 'environmental illness' is a condition that attacks the immune system, and at Wrenwood, there is help. Wrenwood is situated in the outskirts of Alberquerque, New Mexico. A series of small cabins and a 'centre' are designed to keep toxins to a minimum. The house rules, as Carol learns on her first evening, are silent and gender segregated meals, no drugs, smoking or alcohol, moderation in dress and sexual restraint. All vices are removed in the hope that the patients will focus their energy towards personal growth. Each night the members meet for an inspirational lecture from their leader, and close with the mantra: 'We are one with the power that created us, we are safe and all is well in our world.' Carol thrives in this new environment and makes friends with the other patients. She finally belongs and is resistant to her husband's affections and desires for her to come home when he visits. The film closes with Carol entering her new cabin, which resembles an igloo on the outside and a miltary bunker on the inside. She walks to the mirror and says: 'I love you, I really love you.'

Haynes presents a critique of self-transformation through Carol's journey from the suburbs of San Fernando Valley to the outskirts of New Mexico. Leaving viewers with her admission of self-love inside the protected and removed interior of her 'safe house'. Carol has transformed, but as the film asks: into what? Carol's journey is implictly contrasted with the consciousness raising narratives of 1970s feminism. In 1970s novels such as Erica Jong's *Fear of Flying* (1973) and Lisa Alther's *Kinflicks* (1976), the narrative moves from the domestic and therefore oppressed to a constructed notion of liberation.[24] Imelda Whelehan writes:

> The heroines of the [consciousness raising] novels realize that there is something wrong in their lives and the plot of the novel often follows their quest to fix it. Relationships with men are primarily seen as fraught with complexities and unexamined repressive structures, which often prevent the happy resolution of the women's emotional and sexual desires. The burden of the narrative turns on their analysis of these wrongs and the action they propose as a result—leaving the

marital home, [...] determining to put their own aspirations first, and so on.

(2005, 175)

Haynes's narrative turns around the notion of self-discovery, as do the consciousness raising novels of the 1970s. Carol leaves the marital home, determined to look after her own needs and desires. In both cases we are left with the image of a woman alone, but filled with self-love. In other words, Haynes ask us to question what it means to be liberated in the late 1980s as well as what it means to be 'sane' or 'healthy'. He plays with the notion of self-healing by using the language and yet he contrasts this language with the patients' isolation.

Unlike the 1970s narratives of liberation which linked empowerment with sexual freedom, Haynes's version of self-transformation leaves Carol with nothing but platonic and superficial love. One of the men in the group accompanies Carol back to her 'safe' house, and it is clear that although there is some affection between them, neither will pursue this sexually—not only because Wrenwood promotes sexual restraint, but also because Carol wants an escape from sexual desire. The film plays with Carol's lack of sexual desire throughout—beginning with the opening scene in which Carol lies dispassionately underneath her husband's body while he makes love to her. This is the only time we, as viewers, witness them having sex. In another scene Carol's husband, Greg, gets angry with her when she tells him she still has a headache: 'No one has a fucking headache every night of the fucking week' (Haynes 2003). When Greg comes to visit her at Wrenwood and tries to hold her she starts to cough and violently pulls away from him, explaining that 'it must be his cologne', although as he tells her, he is not wearing any. In these moments we witness a physical reaction to any suggestion of sexual desire. Carol becomes 'safe' from the risk of sexual desire. And perhaps this is Haynes's strongest critique of late-1980s America, which became increasingly afraid of the risk posed by AIDS.[25] Carol's 'flight to illness' also removes her from her position of housewife, which is represented as a deadening and soulless position.

In the first part of the film, Haynes positions Carol as someone who is relatively free of attachment, despite being married and having a stepson. She does not engage with these relationships, nor with any others, such as friends or family. She is presented as someone whose daily routine involves nothing more than taking in the dry cleaning, pruning the roses and drinking milk. She is bland and uncomplicated. And yet she also complains to both her doctor and husband of being stressed. The shift in her persona is noticeable as she begins to attend to what she believes to be an environmental illness. What little pleasure she takes before in her mundane, everyday rituals she now seems to feel in her efforts to 'cure' herself.

The reference to an environmental illness introduces a biological component to Carol's hysteria. She is convinced that her symptoms can be explained by a chemical overdose in her system, although both her medical doctor and her husband can find no rational understanding for this diagnosis. In this way, Haynes presents a biological aspect of hysteria—the fumes or chemicals cause a hysteric reaction. And yet, when Carol arrives at Wrenwood, one of the focuses within the group is on self-blame and the mind's power to 'make one ill'. Although the camp is designed to keep its patients from the biological contaminants that make them sick, the camp's 'leader' conducts group sessions that are designed for each patient to come clean with the ways in which they self-harm. He wants them to learn to love themselves, and therefore the world. He stresses the importance of 'positive thinking' which, in part, seems to overshadow the role of biological contaminants.

In 'Things to Come: A Hysteric's Guide to the Future Female Subject', (1994)[26] Juliet Flower MacCannell argues that the feminist celebration of the silent expression of hysteria (passive-aggressive agency) fails to offer a model for feminine desire that would enable a woman to voice her jouissance.[27] MacCannell considers the claim that there is not a female subject because there is not yet a female desire through an analysis of Margaret Atwood's *The Handmaid's Tale*. Arguing that it raises the two questions posed by hysteria: that of 'what does a woman want?' and 'am I a man or woman?' (1994, 110), MacCannell reads *The Handmaid's Tale* as an anatomy of hysteria. She also sees *The Handmaid's Tale* as a way of re-interpreting the rebellion in hysteria as opposed to its silence. In each case where Offred experiences jouissance in her hysteria, 'a little fragment of the discourse of the master falls away' (1994, 126). MacCannell argues that Offred 'gropes sidelong towards a recounting of her "own" history, her time for understanding: it will never come, of course, be in time, in her time, or her discourse. But it will be in her reconstructed voice' (1994, 128). MacCannell understands hysteria as offering a special 'voicing' that allows the return of jouissance (1994, 128).

Safe performs a similar anatomy of hysteria and even takes us through Carol's breakdown into hysteria. Carol moves sideways towards her own self-understanding. In the final moment when she 'voices' her jouissance with 'I love you, I really love you' she reaches the truth through her hysteria. I am suggesting that we can read the film as reconciling the conflicting desires that Verhaeghe discusses in the beginning of this chapter. At Wrenwood, Carol is free from questions such as 'Who am I?' 'What do I want?' She finds solace and freedom in Wrenwood because of its determined rules and the presence of a 'master' who answers the questions. As Verhaeghe suggests 'Constantly torn and full of inner doubt, the hysteric is fascinated by a figure with a massive sense of self-assurance who knows it all, and who pronounces this knowledge like an oracle, without the slightest sign of inner doubt' (1999b, 121). Haynes represents the leader of Wrenwood, Alan Dunning, as someone who has taken on the position of authority, who acts like a father figure to all his patients—someone who is full of both self-assurance and knowl-edge. He does not live on the site of Wrenwood, instead he has a very grand house high on the Cliffside—as if to watch over and protect his followers. We can read Haynes's film as a desire for a master figure, as Verhaeghe suggests, although this necessitates accepting the argument, which he puts forward, that feminism has dismantled patriarchy to such an extent that we now desire its return. In wondering 'where all the fathers have gone' Verhaeghe cites Germaine Greer, Doris Lessing and Camille Paglia as evidence that even feminism wants the 'fathers of yes-teryear' (1999b, 77) to reassert their patriarchal control.

MacCannell on the other hand, still following psychoanalysis, argues that someone like Carol (following her reading of *The Handmaid's Tale*) finds her own jouissance in slowly dismantling patriarchal order (so Carol takes her own steps, goes against her husband's and doctor's wishes, and chooses her own path which enables her to tell herself: 'I love you'). Another reading can be established through work by Wilson and Kirby. We can read the way biological elements affect the body to such an extent that it is transformed, and this has less to do with the ideological models posed above. Yet this is also contradicted by the presence within the camp on psycho-babble, self-healing and the guru's belief that you need to be able to think positively to keep the immune system functioning.

What if instead we read Carol's hysteria as voicing the need for inti-macy and belonging? She is devoid of any real attachments, confined to a life of taking the dry cleaning, pruning her roses—Haynes's emphases her confinement, isolation, alienation from her own life. She is always inside, safe from any risk posed outside. And yet the outside starts to enter (literally) into her system. Even milk, her only vice, become a threat to her well-being. Until she starts to become aware and goes to Wrenwood—she finally belongs, she is finally safe. Instead of reading this desire as a desire for the return of the patriarchal father, or even as capable of dismantling patriarchal order, it seems more likely that this is a desire borne from alienation and self-doubt. Desire for safety is the product of a society that continually emphasises fear—that reminds us that everything around us—from the food we eat, to the water we drink, to the people we live next to, are potential threats against our lives. This culture of fear produces people full of self-doubt, self-loathing and questions—such as 'who am I' 'what do I want' and what do I desire?' The ability to answer these questions, as Haynes poignantly suggests in the closing scene, can only come from oneself.

The rebellious hysteric

'Confusion and contradiction mark understandings of feminism in US popular culture at the turn of the 21st century' (2001, 105) argues Amanda Lotz in her article on postfeminist television criticism. In *Television and Sexuality* (2004) Jane Arthurs believes that 'the widespread popular success of *Sex and the City* and *Ally McBeal* suggests that contradictory and unstable texts steeped in melodramatic and comedic excess are usable precisely because they allow people to explore the contradictions and instablities of their own subjectivity' (2004, 133–134). Charlotte Brunsdon refers to the use of these texts by theorists in their pursuit of writing the feminist 'ur' article: the one that sets up a television programme or film with a central female character, proposes an obvious feminist reading of the text in which both text and heroine fail, and then saves it on the grounds that it reveals, with sympathy, humour and realism, the complexities of being a woman today (2006, 44). Whether looking at texts such as *Sex and the City*, *Ally McBeal* or *Bridget Jones* from the position of their popularity, their presence within feminist theory or their appeal to viewers, theorists note the ambivalence and contradiction that mark them. In the final section of this chapter, I will read the contradiction and instability that is recognised within these texts as an expression of hysteria over the question of what it means to be a woman in contemporary Western society.

Throughout Helen Fielding's *Bridget Jones's Diary* (1997), the basis for Maguire's 2001 film, there are references to Jane Austen's *Pride and Prejudice* and an inversion of her infamous and ironic opening line: 'It is a truth universally acknowledged, that a single man in possession of a good fortune, must be in want of a wife' (1996 [1813], 5). Contemporary women, endowed with more financial independence and lifestyle choices than the previous generation, are thought to want a husband once they reach thirty. Although there are many comparisons to be made, I think

the important thing here is to remember that *Pride and Prejudice* is a contemporary fantasy—particularly with the BBC production starring Colin
Firth. Part of that fantasy involves believing that there is a 'Darcy' for
every Elizabeth. And yet, Bridget Jones is not like Elizabeth Bennet. If a
comparison was to be drawn, Bridget is more like the youngest and most
'foolish' sister, Lydia, than Elizabeth.[28]

Instead of reading Bridget Jones as a pathetic hero or hysterical victim,
I want to think about her as a rebellious figure,[29] a woman who fails *in
spite* of societal expectations, not because of them. It is possible to read
moments in the film as illustrating Bridget's rebellions, although it must
be noted that they are set within the context of the clichéd happy ending.
The moments I am referring to are moments when Bridget fails to live up
to expectations set by those external to her, specifically her mother, her
colleagues and her friends. In these moments she represents a woman
who pushes back societal norms because there really *is* something else—
and that in failing, she is rejecting the framework set by masculine parameters. These moments are often marked by a hysterical reaction by Bridget
and gesture towards thinking about how hysteria is used in this film to
mark out a rejection of societal demands or expectations.

For instance, when Bridget is asked to introduce a new author at a
book launch event she does anything but live up to the expectations of
those around her, including herself. When she asks her friends for
advice, Jude tells her: 'Right, no pressure Bridg but your whole future
happiness now depends on how you behave at this one social occasion'
(Maguire 2001). As viewers we recognise the set-up: we have no false
expectations that Bridget will sail through the event and impress the
audience. And indeed, she fails to 'behave' and instead begins her introduction by shouting 'oy!' to get everyone's attention. The scene is
designed to make viewers laugh, even cringe with embarrassment for
Bridget, and also to make her more endearing. Her failure to 'behave'
and therefore to achieve future happiness can be read as an act of rebellion, as a denial to comply with the expectations demanded of her. It
also throws the notion of happiness into question. Does this one social
occasion really determine Bridget's happiness? No, most likely it will not.
But how many times have people put this kind of expectation on one
event; how often do people demand themselves or those close to them
to perform perfectly in order that they may achieve an elusive notion of
happiness. The point here is that Bridget succeeds even though she fails,
and continues to take risks even when she 'loses'.

If Bridget's inabilities are hinted at in the first film, the sequel, *Bridget
Jones 2: The Edge of Reason* (Beeban Kidron 2004), focuses entirely on

these moments. The cover photograph with Bridget between the two men in her life 'Mark Darcy' (Colin Firth) and 'Daniel Cleaver' (Hugh Grant) has her looking distinctly confused and incapable (whereas the first film's cover has her peeking up from her diary). Spying on Darcy through the skylight of his flat, appearing at the opera with orange dye on her face, these 'moments' of inability are grossly exaggerated, presumably with the intention of inviting viewers to laugh at how idiotic Bridget can be and yet still be loved. If the ending is happy and romantic, Bridget only succeeds in getting there through failure and mishap. She continually 'messes up' but does not see these failures as indications of her overall inability to succeed. Instead she consistently 'tries again', takes another risk, and in the end is rewarded with a happy ending.

There is something to take from Bridget's failures, that goes beyond the majority of feminist readings which bemoan the way in which *Bridget Jones* perpetuates the myth that single women need a man. Instead of reading the text this way, it is possible to understand this text, and those like them, as illustrating a woman who succeeds despite failure. She does not conform to anyone's expectations of her, she behaves hysterically and cannot self-discipline or self-regulate as illustrated in her diary entries. In other words, Bridget is not a successful individual or a super-woman, she is 'a fallible heroine [who] makes her readers feel so much better about their own attempts at self-improvement' (Whelehan 2005, 180).

In order to expand on this point further, I want to briefly reference the popular television series *Ally McBeal*, starring Calista Flockhart. It seems impossible not to mention Ally McBeal and her hysterical dreams in the context of this argument. I want to refer in particular to Series One of *Ally McBeal*, and even more specifically to the 'dancing baby' that first appears in Episode 11, 'Cro-Magnon'. In this episode Ally and one of her managing partners, John Cage, are defending a nineteen-year-old boy who has punched another man in his girlfriend's defence. The central premise of the episode is that humans possess innate and primal qualities. Cage defends the boy's actions on the basis that he is a man and therefore 'part warrior'. He speaks to the 'truth' of man's nature as needing to defend himself and a woman's chastity (in that order). Cage's defence is implicitly contrasted with Ally's 'primal' dancing baby who he suggests is a metaphor for her ticking maternal clock. Cage advises Ally to confront her hallucination/fantasy and the episode closes with Ally and the 'baby' dancing together.

Fantasy is often used in the series to suggest Ally's unconscious desires. However these moments are dealt with satirically—not through the cliché of romance as in *Bridget Jones*; satire does not allow the same scope for interpretation.[30] Ally's body is by no means silent—like *Bridget Jones* she is portrayed as bumbling, always tripping and falling, prone to outrageous spectacles. Although the series as a whole raises interesting issues concerning the representation of feminism in contemporary culture, as I have explored elsewhere (Gorton 2004), this episode is essentialist in its suggestion that there are primal forces within men and women that compel them, indeed necessitate them to follow their desires. The episode explicity suggests that woman's real role in life (far from being a successful lawyer) is to be a mother. And that, although a woman can choose another path, these 'primal' instincts will haunt her and even run the risk of exposing her professional capabilities if she does not confront them. In short, what the episode constructs is an image of a hysterical woman— one who is ignoring her sexual instincts to procreate and reproduce and because of this has hysterical projections and hallucinations.

In her reading of Ally McBeal as a hysteric, Patricia Leavy argues that 'Ally McBeal created a public spectacle out of the silenced hysteric which created a space where the ritualized execution of gendered social power could be subversively resisted. Ally McBeal was not a neurotic in the popular negative sense but rather she challenged normative conceptions of what a "together woman" is' (2006, 34). Following a feminist approach to the question of hysteria, as discussed before, leads Leavy to position Ally McBeal as a revolutionary, not a neurotic. However, Leavy takes this reading a step further, in light of the contemporary nature of the programme, and sees Ally as a challenge to the 'together woman' or 'superwoman' propogated within popular culture.

Safe, *Bridget Jones* and *Ally McBeal* all illustrate a desire to escape the demands and expectations placed upon individual women. They either use illness, incompetency or emotion to avoid the pressure of being what Leavy refers to as a 'together woman'. Hysteria, in these instances, can be read as an expression of resistance and rebellion to conformity, however, in most cases, such as in *Bridget Jones* and *Ally McBeal*, the rebellion is short-lived and the 'crisis' of marriage and motherhood is remedied within the context of a conventional happy ending.

If we return to the image Bollas creates of the hysteric—a bumbling, giddy and day-dreaming sort—then it is possible to read both Ally McBeal and Bridget Jones as contemporary hysterics. They spend a great deal of time in their fantasy lives, are constantly making spectacles of themselves, and yet in spite of this, as Bollas points out, their slightly mad characters are loveable and have attracted devoted audiences. It is also worth noting that Bollas's description of the hysteric is a very bodily one—of someone bumping into things, giggling and talking—and we can see this in both characters. Their bodies are illustrated as extreme—Ally is absurdly thin, Bridget Jones, in contrast, is always shown spilling out of her clothes. As a consequence, celebrity magazines have devoted a great deal of attention to both actresses' bodies: to Renee Zellweiger's need to gain weight for the part of Bridget Jones and to Calista Flockhart's need to gain weight in general.

Instead of rendering the hysterical body as excessive or as a repository for inexpressible desires, it is possible to read the hysterical figure as marking out the conflicts that emerge within contemporary society around the contradictory demands for enjoyment and self-discipline. The hysterical figure as performed in films such as *Safe* and *Bridget Jones* is an individual who expresses a desire for self-transformation but also for acceptance. Whereas the last chapter considered how desire can be theorised as movement through the risks people take or do not take, this chapter has demonstrated the ways in which desire can be theorised as a force against the acceptance of pre-existing expectations, such as marriage or motherhood. It also suggests that hysteria represents a physical confrontation with these expectations and provides individuals with an expression for what are often inarticulable or unacceptable desires.

3
Gaze and Melodrama

> If I wish to look at you but you do not wish me to, I
> may feel ashamed. If I wish you to look at me but you
> do not, I may feel ashamed. If I wish to look at you and
> at the same time wish that you look at me, I can be
> shamed
>
> (Silvan Tompkins 1995, 152)

In his seminal work on melodrama, Peter Brooks figures the hystericised body as a key emblem of the convergence in the concerns of melodrama and psychoanalysis: 'a body that has become the place for the inscription of highly emotional messages that cannot be written elsewhere, and cannot be articulated verbally' (1995 [1976] preface, xi). He understands the hystericised body to represent a story of 'desire in an impasse' which the last chapter explored through contemporary examples in *Safe*, *Bridget Jones* and *Ally McBeal*. However, instead of figuring the hysterical body as a reservoir for inexpressible desires, the body, in the texts mentioned, becomes a site of a complex negotiation between desire, fear and agency. The previous chapter also focused on the excessive interpretability of hysteria and its relation to desire. Questions such as 'What do I want?' or 'Who am I?', voiced by the hysteric's body, come through in representations of the hysteric, whether in theory or on film, as well as in literature regarding the concept of individualism and its increasing influence on the way we negotiate emotion in our 'privatised worlds'.

If the last chapter's concern was on the difficulties in expressing desire, this chapter considers the excessiveness of desire's articulation, and what better genre to focus on than the melodrama? As Brooks argues: 'the desire to express all seems a fundamental characteristic of the melodramatic mode. Nothing is spared because nothing is left unsaid' (1995 [1976], 4).

In her work on desire in the women's film, and more specifically on Max Olphüs's *Letter from an Unknown Woman* (1948), Tania Modleski argues that 'it seems fair to say that many of the classic film melodramas from the 30s through the 50s are peopled by great, or near-great, hysterics— women possessed by an overwhelming desire to express themselves, to make themselves known, but continually confronting the difficulty, if not the impossibility of realising this desire' (1987, 327). However, by the close of her essay, Modleski's revises her argument, noting the inadequacy of this model to an interpretation of the woman's position within melodrama. Instead of linking reminiscences within the text to hysteria, Modleski understands these returns and repetitions as establishing a different relationship to time and desire and as she argues, 'it is of this difference that the text speaks' (1987, 336).

One of the primary ways desire is established in cinema is through the gaze and we if take *Letter from an Unknown Woman* as example, then we can think of the many moments in which the camera focuses on Lisa Berndle (Joan Fontaine) gazing at Stefan Brand (Louis Jordan) in unrequited desire. The 'look' that is constructed between two people in a film is often meant to represent desirous feelings and is usually held between actors long enough to establish this form of intimacy for viewers and to establish 'a different relationship to time and desire'. In describing desire between people, many will refer to the 'look' they share or when their eyes 'first' meet. The cliché 'love at first sight' reflects the importance Western culture places on the gaze and the moment when lovers first 'lay eyes' on each other. This chapter will explore the concept of the gaze, as theorised in psychoanalytic, feminist and film theory, and consider how this concept is related to the presentation of desire in cinema. It will also trace the way the gaze and shame are linked within psychoanalysis and in recent work on emotion and affect.

Freud

Freud's theorisation of scopophilia, the pleasure of looking and being looked at, is contextualised within his understanding of deviation and perversion. It is also part of his interpretation of drives and on primary motivational forms. Given this, we understand the gaze as crucial to the exchange between people, particularly an intimate one. American psychologist Silvan Tompkins's work draws out the link between looking and shame and crucially, he draws attention to the fact that the gaze is transmitted through the eyes.

In his chapter on 'the sexual aberrations', Freud makes a distinction between the person 'from whom sexual attraction proceeds', known by Freud as the 'sexual object' and 'the act towards which the instinct tends', known as the 'sexual aim' (2001 [1953], vol. 7, 135, 136). He then further catalogues the deviations in respect of both the object and the aim. Scopophilia, taking pleasure in looking, is a 'deviation in respect of the sexual aim' and must be understood in the context of Freud's interpretation of this and other 'perversions'. Freud outlines three ways in which scopophilia becomes a perversion: (a) if it is focused exclusively on the genitals; (b) if it is related to overcoming disgust (he offers the example of the voyeur); (c) if taking pleasure in looking is seen as a sexual act in and of itself, instead of being part of foreplay and thus leading to the sexual aim of intercourse (Freud offers the example of exhibitionists who take pleasure in exposing themselves and watching others expose themselves) (2001 [1953], vol. 7, 157). Following the example of the exhibitionist, Freud notes how scopophilia, like sadism and masochism, involves both active and passive forms. Looking and being looked at necessitates taking up both the active and passive position, which for Freud is a 'remarkable' characteristic of this perversion: the only force which opposes scopophilia, according to Freud, is shame (2001 [1953], vol. 7, 157).

Freud clarifies his understanding of the active/passive form of scopophilia in 'instincts and their vicissitudes' in which he points out that the active aim (that of looking) precedes the passive (being looked at). However, he argues that there is an earlier stage to scopophilia that differentiates it from sadism and masochism. Although both involve taking up different active/passive positions, scopophilia begins as an auto-erotic instinct (2001 [1957], vol. 14, 130). Freud argues that the first stage in scopophilia involves a person looking at his/her own sexual organ in a mirror. This self-exhibitionism and auto-eroticism is then transformed into looking at an external sexual object and being looked at by someone else. For Freud, 'scopophilia—exhibitionism' and 'sadism—masochism' are opposite instincts: 'These are the best –known sexual instincts that appear in an ambivalent manner' (2001 [1957], vol. 14, 132). Freud further explains these instincts by referring to the 'three polarities' that govern our mental life: 'Subject (ego)—Object (external world)', 'Pleasure—Unpleasure', and 'Active—Passive' (2001 [1957], vol. 14, 133). Freud uses these polarities to help think through the several opposites of loving ('loving—hating', 'loving—being loved', loving and hating simultaneously, and 'loving oneself'). As I will argue in the next chapter, there is still cultural discomfort, particularly within feminist theory, about the passive/object position.

The pairing of opposites that Freud establishes can also be found in the work of Silvan Tompkins, and is worth discussing in terms of the way Tompkins theorises the affect of shame. Tompkins's work has gained significance in the last few years as scholars consider the role emotion and affect within cultural theory (Ahmed 2004; Berlant 2004; Brennan 2004; Massumi 2002; Probyn 2005; Sedgwick 2003). Tompkins has been compared to Freud as a 'figure through whose work a lot of sharply different, competing, and often conflicting interpretive paths require to be cleared' (Sedgwick and Frank 1995, 24). In his work, Tompkins designates affects as a primary motivational system and considers shame, interest, surprise, joy, anger, fear, distress, and disgust as the basic set of affects (Sedgwick and Frank 1995, 5). However, he distinguishes shame and disgust from the others as affects that construct a 'boundary line or barrier' (Sedgwick and Frank 1995, 22).

In their introduction to reading Tompkins's work, Eve Sedgwick and Adam Frank argue that Tompkins's theory on affect works to resist teleological presumptions that are rooted in the disciplines of psychology. In other words, Tompkins resists a causal side to the affects as is evident in statements such as: 'It is enjoyable to enjoy. It is exciting to be excited' (Sedgwick and Frank 1995, 7). Unlike Freud's work, where to enjoy means one thing and to be excited means something else—and both have something to do with heterosexual sexuality and its repression—Tompkins's understanding of affect 'is indifferent to the means-end difference' (Sedgwick and Frank 1995, 7). This in itself offers an important counterposition to Freud and can be used to complement and deepen our understanding of Freud's work on scopophilia and its relation to shame.

For Tompkins, shame is activated by an incomplete reduction of interest or joy (Sedgwick and Frank 1995, 134). In other words, when we feel shame our feelings of joy or interest are reduced, but not completely lost. He offers the example of a child, who when meeting a stranger might peek at the person through his or her fingers. The child may feel shame but it is not completely uninterested in knowing or seeing who the stranger is. In this way, shame is also an ambivalent act, similar to the way Freud describes scopophilia. As Tompkins writes: 'In shame I wish to continue to look and to be looked at, but I also do not wish to do so' (Sedgwick and Frank 1995, 137). In this way, the distinction between subject and object is lost, and this is also similar to the way Freud describes scopophilia: 'In contrast to all other affects, shame is an experience of the self by the self' (Sedgwick and Frank 1995, 136). In considering the reasons why shame and pride are such central motives, Tompkins believes that the answer lies in the fact that the face is more prominent in shame than in other affects. Because the eyes both receive and send messages regarding shame, the face takes on an unusually significant role and therefore shame becomes a more potent affect than others, such as terror or anger. Here Tompkins privileges the role of the eyes in sexual experience which is contrary to Freud's interpretation. Freud argues instead that 'the object of the scopophilic instinct, however, though it too is in the first instance a part of the subject's own body, is not the eye itself' (2001 [1957], vol. 14, 132). As Tompkins argues: '[psychoanalysis] generated the concept of the eye as a symbol for the penis, as in the classical interpretation of the Oedipus myth' (Sedgwick and Frank 1995, 145).

In *Blush: Faces of Shame*, Elspeth Probyn draws on Tompkins's work (as well as others) to read for a positive and productive understanding of shame. She argues that 'In shame, the feeling and minding and thinking and social body comes alive. It's in this sense that shame is positive and productive, even or especially when it feels bad. The feeling of shame teaches us about our relations to others. Shame makes us feel proximity differently ...' (2005, 34–35). I want to take Probyn's idea of shame as productive, as something that teaches us about our relations to others and as something that causes us to feel proximity differently and apply this to the construction of shame in the melodramatic form. In melodrama, I will argue, shame is used to question the rightfulness of a couple's desire; it forces them to justify their desire, their interest, and even their *lack* of shame. The gaze functions both to keep the couple united in their desire for each other and also to heighten feelings of shame as others look disapprovingly upon their desire. Shame is intimately linked with interest in Tompkins work. If we take desire to mean intense interest then we can see how shame is connected to desire in the melodramatic narrative. Before moving on to discuss melodrama, I will continue to examine the way in which the gaze has been theorised within psychoanalysis, in order to explore its significance within cinema studies.

Lacan

Tompkins's theory of affect was first published in a collection edited by Jacques Lacan (Sedgwick and Frank 1995, 6). Indeed, Lacan's interest in affect and emotion had a profound influence on his theorisation of his 'mirror theory'. Bowie points out that the moment (down to the time and date) that Lacan first delivered his paper on 'The Looking-Glass Phase' is dutifully recorded in a bibliographic reference at the end of the first edition of *Écrits*.[1] Bowie suggests that this paper was not only important for Lacan in terms of his entrance into the psychoanalytic movement, but it also marked a time in which Freud's dominance seemed to shrink (1991, 17–18). Sean Homer suggests that the mythology that has developed around this moment helped to establish an image of Lacan as an 'outcast'—'a heroic figure battling for the truth against a conservative and reactionary establishment'[2] (2005, 17).

Like Freud, who looks to an earlier moment in scopophilia, one that involves a relationship solely with the self, Lacan looks to this moment in terms of setting up his understanding of how the subject enters into society—how we come to be an 'I.' Both Lacan and Freud stress the importance of identification, but the stress is in different places. For Freud, as discussed in Chapter 1, the Oedipal stage is the most important in terms of the lines of identification between children and their parents. A girl must identify with her mother and learn to be desirable, whereas a boy must identify with his father and learn how to desire. Lacan not only moves the stress to the castration complex but also shifts the focus to an earlier time, before the child realises that there is an Other to identify with. In this way, Lacan stresses a moment of alienation, in which the child realises that he/she is not complete and will never be again. As Bowie puts it: 'Lacan's account of the "specular" moment provides the ego with its creation myth and its Fall' (1991, 21).

Lacan's 'mirror stage' proposes that a child from the age of six to eighteen months experiences a moment of identification when looking at her image in a mirror:

> The *mirror stage* is a drama whose internal thrust is precipitated from insufficiency to anticipation—and which manufactures for the subject, caught up in the lure of spatial identification, the succession of phantasies that extends from a fragmented body-image to a form of its totality that I shall call orthopaedic—and, lastly, to the assumption of the armour of an alienating identity, which will mark with its rigid structure the subject's entire mental development.
>
> (1977, 4, author's italics)

The 'drama' that Lacan refers to stages a specular and spatial relationship between self and other; it is a drama that must be performed in order for a healthy relationship between self and other. Before seeing herself in the mirror, the child feels that she is fragmented, she does not have full control over her bodily movements, and yet, when she looks in the mirror, she recognises (with jubilance) that she is much bigger and more complete than she imagined herself to be. However, this jubilance is short-lived, for in the moment that the child accepts this image of herself she must also acknowledge that she is alone; she recognises that she is separate from her parent (who might also be in the mirrored image). In other words, the child loses a sense of completeness—hence Lacan's stress on alienation. What the child also recognises is that she cannot see a part of herself that she feels. The 'mirror stage' constructs the 'imaginary' and the 'real' and forces recognition that our sight is limited. It also sets up the child for the Oedipal stage: 'It is this moment that decisively tips the whole of human knowledge into mediatization through the desire of the other' (Lacan 1977, 5). Lacan moves the moment of identification to the 'mirror stage', thus creating an earlier entrance into the 'I' than Freud postulates and yet, at the same time, keeping the moment of the Oedipal complex important in terms of the self's relationship to the Other in desire.

Lacan stresses that the 'mirror stage' is a moment of identification: 'We have only to understand the mirror stage *as an identification*, in the full sense that analysis gives to the term: namely, the transformation that takes place in the subject when he assumes an image—whose pre-destination to this phase-effect is sufficiently indicated by the use, in analytic theory, of the ancient term *imago*' (1977, 2, author's italics). By this Lacan means that this stage, this recognition and assumption of the mirrored image, precedes a dialectical relationship with an Other, and a realisation of subjectivity in language (1977, 2). In other words, Lacan understands this moment as preceding social inscription, a phase the ego progresses through. The mirror stage establishes the relationship between the subject and his/her sense of reality (1977, 4). Lacan's theory outlines the movement from the 'specular *I*' to the 'social *I*' (1977, 5)—an *I* that must be mediated, and in a sense, contained, by an Other (or through the awareness that an Other exits).

In *Downcast Eyes* (1994) Martin Jay suggests that Lacan's 'mirror stage' is heavily influenced by his early case studies of paranoid women and violence. Jay understands the link between Lacan's early work on criminal madwomen and his theorisation of the 'mirror stage' to be a result of the way Lacan understood 'specular identification' (1994, 349). Although no conclusive connections can be drawn between Lacan's early work on Aimée and the Papin sisters and his theorisation of the 'mirror stage', bringing them side by side elicits parallels and intersections that are convincing.[3]

Lacan derives his understanding of the effects spatial awareness has on identity largely from Henri Wallon's work on 'transitivism'. Wallon studied the way in which children develop their emotional responses to other children. He noticed that children, at a young age, have trouble differentiating themselves from each other. That is, if a child hits another she often cries because she has not individuated herself from the other child. Wallon terms this phenomenon 'transitivism', and understands it to be a necessary and healthy progression into subjectivity. Lacan, on the other hand, notices the danger of spatial distance and argues that without knowing the self from the other, aggression develops. In her article on the differences between Wallon's work and Lacan's, Shuli Barzilai writes: 'Wallon's detailed experiments clearly established a conceptual paradigm for Lacan's understanding of the mirror stage. Yet Lacan decisively parts company with Wallon—and this departure is arguably the core of his theoretical innovation—on two points: the status of the mirror and the identity of the specular image' (1995, 372). In a departure from Wallon's findings, Lacan argues that the inability to individuate self from other leads the subject into aggression, not towards healthy subjectivity as Wallon suggests. As Lacan writes in the 1950s: 'We can observe it in these phenomena of transitivism in which one finds the infant taking as equivalent his own action and that of the other. He says—*François hit me*, whereas it was him who hit François. There's an unstable mirror between the child and his fellow being. How are we to explain these phenomena?' (1991 [1975], 169, author's italics).

Lacan continues to explain the importance and function of the gaze in his later work. In *The Four Fundamental Concepts of Psychoanalysis*, Lacan actually poses the question: 'what is the gaze?' (1994 [1973], 82) and sets about to explain the gaze from the point of annihilation in the subject. We must remember that the gaze is crucial in terms of the analytic session; it is necessary that the patient must not be able to 'see' the analyst. Diana Fuss and Joel Sanders draw attention to the physical layout of the analyst's office in their article titled 'Bergasse 19: Freud's office', in order to explain the connection between the architecture of Freud's room and the workings of the analytic mise en scéne. As Fuss and Sanders explain: 'The consulting room chair stands as a fundamentally uninhabitable space, a tribute to the imposing figure of the analyst who remains, even to the searching eye of the camera, totally and enigmatically other' (1996, 134). Lacan reiterates that

> This means that the level of reciprocity between the gaze and the gazed at is, for the subject, more open than any other to alibi. That is why we should try to avoid, but our inventions in the session, allowing the subject to establish himself on this level. On the contrary, we should cut him off from this point of ultimate gaze, which is illusory.
>
> (1994 [1973], 77)

Drawing on Sartre's conceptualisation of the gaze in *Being and Nothingness*,[4] Lacan argues that the 'gaze sees itself—to be precise, the gaze of which Sartre speaks, the gaze that surprises me and reduces me to shame, since this is the feeling he regards as the most dominant. The gaze I encounter [...] is, not a seen gaze, but a gaze imagined by me in the field of the Other' (1994 [1973], 84). Lacan makes a distinction between looking at a painting and watching a drama—whether between people or on screen. He argues that a painting invites the viewer to 'feed' on the work but also to 'lay down his gaze' (1994 [1973], 101). Lacan defines this as a 'pacifying' look and distinguishes it from the way one might look at an Other (in terms of desire). He relates a story of a time, as a young intellectual, he escaped to the coast and joined some fishermen in a small fishing boat. One of the men pointed to a sardine can in the water and said to Lacan: '*You see that can? Do you see it? Well, it doesn't see you!*' (1994 [1973], 95, author's italics). Lacan admits that he found it difficult at the time to see the humour in the man's joke, since he was the object of it. But in reflection, it is a parable that allows him to articulate the function of the screen.

Lacan's mirror theory stresses the importance of the articulation of an 'I' as the entrance into the symbolic order. As Patrick Fuery argues in his *Theories of Desire*: 'The subject, driven by desire, enters the mirror stage and subsequently the Symbolic in search of a satisfaction that can never be achieved. This is "desire" understood as an active process' (1995, 17). Fundamentally what Lacan does through the mirror theory is to suggest an earlier drama to the Oedipal complex and a relationship between desire and subjectivity.

Film

Jean-Louis Baudry's 'Ideological Effects of the Basic Cinematographic Apparatus', first published in *Cinethique* in 1970, was one of the earliest and most important essays to consider the importance of Lacan's work for film studies. Baudry considers the difference between paintings and the photographic image and film. Much like Lacan, Baudry points to the pacifying way paintings allow the eye to rest in their image; whereas film, with its continuous set of images, keeps the eye in motion/play. This movement, according to Baudry, creates 'a multiplicity of points of view' which effectively neutralises the fixed position of the eye (1974–75 [1970], 358). Another important distinction Baudry makes is that film, with its continuous set of images, 'lives on the denial of difference' (1974–75 [1970], 359). In other words, even though each frame is different, the film works to deny these differences in order to make the film appear seamless and continuous: 'if we look directly at a strip of processed film: adjacent images are almost exactly repeated, their divergence being verifiable only by comparison of images at a sufficient distance from each other' (1974–75 [1970], 359). What I want to draw attention to here is not only that the film denies difference but also the suggestion, within screen theory, that it is only via a position of distance that these differences are made visible.

Baudry engages directly with Lacan's 'mirror theory' in his attempts to explain the affects the cinematic apparatus has on the spectator: 'the arrangement of the different elements—projector, darkened hall, screen [...] reconstructs the situation necessary to the release of the "mirror stage" discovered by Jacques Lacan' (1974–75 [1970], 363). He claims that the cinema provides the spectator with the two conditions necessary to engage with the mirror stage—'sub-motor and super-perceptive state'.[5] The similarities between the cinematic experience, the cinematic apparatus and Lacan's theorisation of the 'mirror stage' are also taken up by Christian Metz in his work on the 'imaginary signifier'. Like Baudry, Metz sees connections between the primordial identification that Lacan establishes and the specular relationship between viewer and screen. However, as Metz points out, the identification that happens within the cinema presupposes that the spectator has already gone through the 'mirror stage' and this primary identification (1975, 49). Metz argues that the spectator is fundamentally identifying with the camera itself insofar as the images are projected from the back of his head and accepted (and then re-projected) within his mind. As he explains: 'during the performance the spectator is the searchlight I have described, duplicating the projector, which itself duplicates the camera, and he is also the sensitive surface duplicating the screen, which itself duplicates the film strip' (1975, 53). Metz considers the contribution psychoanalysis makes to the study of the cinematic signifier and unravels his answer through attention to history, linguistics, cinematic apparatus and to the act of theorisation itself. He concludes by suggesting that 'psychoanalysis does not illuminate only the film, but also the conditions of desire of whoever makes himself its theoretician' (1975, 75). His statement suggests that psychoanalytic theory is not only capable of making sense of film but also that it can expose the unconscious desires of the theorist herself. In each instance there is an assumption that unconscious desires are posited within a text and that psychoanalysis possess the tools to uncover them.

Screen theory derives its understanding of the gaze from Lacan's early work on the 'mirror theory'.[6] However, as discussed, Lacan went on to reconsider the significance of the gaze in his later work in *Four Fundamentals* and this is not reflected in the conception of the gaze in early film theory. In *Read My Desire*, Joan Copjec carefully examines the differences between the two interpretations and offers an important distinction: 'In film theory, the gaze is located "in front of" the image, as its signified, the point of maximal meaning or sum of all that appears in the image *and* the point that "gives" meaning. The subject is, then, thought to identify with and thus, in a sense, to *coincide with* the gaze. In Lacan, on the other hand, the gaze is located "behind" the image, as that which fails to appear in it and thus as that which makes all its meanings suspect. And the subject, instead of coinciding with or identifying with the gaze, is rather *cut off from it*' (1994, 36). This is a crucial dissimilarity and one that has often been overlooked in later understandings of the gaze and of the appropriation of Lacan's work within film theory. If we return to the description of the 'mirror theory', Lacan suggests that there is something that the jubilant subject cannot see but can sense—and this is the gaze that is located 'behind' the image, this is what the subject is *cut off from*. As Copjec goes on to explain: 'the gaze is not clear or penetrating, not filled with knowledge or recognition; it is clouded over and turned back on itself, absorbed in its own enjoyment' (1994, 36). Here we can return to Sartre's description of desire as 'troubled water', and see how the gaze constructs a subject who is desiring, seeking after an impossibility.

Feminism

'Seventies feminist film theory', 'gaze theory' and 'visual work' are phrases often used to encapsulate the contributions from feminists within film studies in the 1970s. However, these terms do not do justice to the rich terrain this work offers. The 1970s are often characterised by their debate, activity and movement. Ruby Rich's personalised account in *Chick Flicks* (1998) reflects some of the nostalgia that Rich and others such as Teresa de Lauretis and E Ann Kaplan share over the loss of these moments in intellectual history.

To begin it is useful to trace some of the fundamental ways in which feminism has met with film theory and psychoanalysis; one of the best places to look is at the contents pages of collections on feminism and film. For instance, in Sue Thornham's *Feminist Film Theory* (1999) she chooses the following sub-sections: 'Taking up the Struggle', 'The Language of Theory', 'The Female Spectator', 'Textual Negotiations', 'Fantasy, Horror and the Body' and 'Re-Thinking Differences'. Whereas E. Ann Kaplan's *Feminism and Film* (2000) offers the following: 'Pioneers and Classics: The Modernist Mode', 'Critiques of Phase I Theories: New Methods', 'Race, Sexuality, and Postmodernism in Feminist Film Theory', 'Spectatorship, Ethnicity, and Melodrama'. Each gives us a sense of the ways in which feminism has addressed film—primarily through struggle, representation, genre, language, sexuality, race and difference.

Following a feminist approach to language and difference, Laura Mulvey's influential article,[7] 'Visual Pleasure and Narrative Cinema' (1975), examines the gendered nature of the cinematic gaze identified by Baudry and Metz. She appropriates psychoanalytic theory as a 'political weapon' in order to demonstrate how the unconscious of patriarchal society structures film form (1989 [1975], 14). In her work she is attempting to 'conceive a new language of desire' (1989 [1975], 16), in part, by drawing on Freud's theorisation of scopophilia:

> Going far beyond highlighting a woman's to-be-looked-at-ness, cinema builds the way she is to be looked at into the spectacle itself. Playing on the tension between film as controlling the dimension of time (editing, narrative) and film as controlling the dimension of space (changes in distance, editing), cinematic codes create a gaze, a world and an object, thereby producing an illusion cut to the measure of desire. It is these cinematic codes and their relationship to formative external structures that must be broken down before mainstream film and the pleasure it provides can be challenged.
>
> (1989 [1975], 25)

Mulvey considers the way in which women become objects of the gaze, or spectacles ('to-be-looked-at-ness'). Psychoanalytic models of engagement such as Ien Ang's and Mulvey's pivot around lack, which is inherent to a psychoanalytic understanding of desire. For instance, Ang defines her 'tragic structure of feeling' as 'identification and distancing constantly alternating with one another' (1985, 61).[8] The lack maintained in these models is interpreted as necessary in that it allows the viewer a critical distance through which they can make a rational interpretation. However, it often negates an appreciation of the engagement—the close connection—viewers have with the text. This is primarily because there is still an assumption in film criticism, borne out of Brechtian and neo-Freudian film criticism, that this kind of emotional engagement does not enable viewers to be critical of the texts they watch. As Carl Plantinga argues: 'An emotional or pleasurable experience is often thought to be harmful or naïve of itself, while an alienated, distanced response becomes the mark of a knowing spectator' (1997, 373).

In her work on film and the masquerade, Mary Ann Doane argues that instead of thinking about female spectatorship in terms of an opposition between activity and passivity, as Mulvey does, we should consider the opposition between proximity and distance (1991, 21). Drawing on work by Burch and Metz, Doane argues that 'for the female spectator there is a certain overpresence of the image—she is the image' (1991, 22). Doane relies on Burch's mapping of the cinema to argue that part of the pleasure in watching films is derived from the spectator's spatial distance from the screen itself—you can neither be too close nor too far to appreciate your object of desire. She also draws on psychoanalysis, both Freudian and feminist interpretations (Kristeva and Montrelay), to suggest that the Oedipus complex necessarily creates a difference in distance and identification between the sexes. Drawing on Montrelay, Doane states that 'while the male has the possibility of displacing the first object of desire (the mother), the female must become that object of desire' (1991, 22). For Doane this means that the female is not given the distance Freud deems as necessary for knowledge. Returning to the Oedipal complex, she argues that the boy is afforded a chance to disown what is seen, and therefore, can make way for fetishism. In contrast, the female is unable to achieve this distance between seeing and understanding, which quickly leads Doane to link this over-identification to the 'women's weepie'. The connection Doane makes between the Oedipal stage and women's weepie is worth citing at length:

> The female, on the other hand, must find it difficult, if not impossible, to assume the position of fetishist. That body which is so close continually reminds her of the castration which cannot be 'fetishized away.' The lack of a distance between seeing and understanding, the mode of judging 'in a flash,' is conducive to what might be termed an 'over-identification' with the image. The association of tears and 'wet wasted afternoons' (in Molly Haskell's words) with genres specified as feminine (the soap opera, the 'woman's picture') points very precisely to this type of over-identification, this abolition of a distance, in short, this inability to fetishize. The woman is constructed differently in relation to processes of looking.
>
> (1991, 23–24).

This problem of closeness and distance and its relationship to spectatorship leads Doane to consider the viewing positions of the transvestite and of the masquerade as alternatives to this overidentification. Drawing on Rivere's concept, Doane argues that the masquerade 'confounds the masculine structure of the look' (1991, 26). Although Doane's work lays ground for important figurations of the femme fatale, I want to focus instead of the final part of her article: her analysis of Robert Doisneau's photograph 'Un Regard Oblique' and her analysis of female spectatorship. In the photograph a couple stare through a gallery window at a painting, invisible to the spectator. Although the woman is positioned in the centre of the photograph, her gaze is fixed at the painting we cannot see; her husband, who stands to the right side of her, in the margin of the picture, does not follow her gaze, but instead is looking at a painting of a woman who stands naked from behind in high black leather boots. This picture is visible to us and, as Doane argues, sets up a 'dirty joke' which only the woman in the photograph is oblivious to. Indeed, she argues that the 'the image is not readable by the female spectator— it can give her pleasure only in masochism. In order to "get" the joke, she must once again assume the position of transvestite' (1991, 32). This example leads Doane to conclude that the 'entire elaboration of femininity as a closeness, a nearness, as present-to-itself is not the definition of an essence but the delineation of a *place* culturally assigned to the woman' (1991, 31, author's italics).

There are many things to draw out here: the way Doane links closeness with a woman's position; the precarious link between the Oedipal complex, knowledge and 'women's weepies'—and finally the photograph by Doisneau, that becomes, for Doane, evidence of woman's inability to 'get' the joke. Before moving on to consider the issue of proximity and distance, I want to take another photograph by Doisneau, this one titled 'Le Regard Oblique II'. This photograph features the same scene discussed in the previous photograph. Except in this photo, a woman stands alone at the gallery window. Instead of fixing her gaze on the painting we cannot see, she is looking at the nude picture that served as the private joke. Her eyes are wide and her mouth shaped in such a way that you would imagine an 'oohh' coming out of it. In many ways this photograph carries elements of the camp or even the 'carry-on' film. Just behind her and slightly to the left a woman passes by. Her image is blurred but we can see that her gaze is fixed on the painting we cannot see. The series 'le regard oblique' ('the sideways glance') is of different people looking at paintings inside the Romi Art Gallery.[9] However, it is the photograph that Doane refers to that has become for her, and other critics, such as Griselda Pollock, evidence of the marginalisation of the female gaze.[10] What I would like to suggest is that the second image provides a different way of understanding the female spectator—one that cannot be reduced to the options Doane gives. Doane argues that 'above and beyond a simple adoption of the masculine position in relation to the cinematic sign, the female spectator is given two options: the masochism of over-identification or the narcissism entailed in becoming one's own object of desire, in assuming the image in the most radical way' (1991, 31–32). I cannot see either of these options embodied by the surprised and even somewhat excited onlooker in Doisneau's second photograph.

In her reconsideration of the 'masquerade' and female spectatorship,[11] and following criticism from Tania Modleski and Patrice Petro, Doane returns to some of the central issues she raises regarding proximity and distance and yet is still adamant that a closing down of distance and valuation of closeness is a sure way to return women to cultural denigration:

> Patrice Petro claims that the discourse of distance and differentiation is in itself a 'male epistemology.' I do not believe this is the case. What we are dealing with is an epistemology—that is, a theory of language and hence of knowledge—which is collapsed onto a theory of sexual difference that throws the epistemology into a phallocentric arena. But I would certainly hesitate to counter it with anything claiming to be a 'female epistemology,' with a theory which valourized closeness, nearness, or presence (and which therefore assumed that these qualities are essential female attributes). For the epistemology seems to me to have a certain force and explanatory power. Furthermore, it helps to delineate, with a great deal of persuasiveness, the positions, identities, and relations to power which accompany given cultural understandings of sexual difference. To embrace and affirm the definition of femininity as closeness, immediacy, or proximity-to-self is to accept one's own disempowerment in the cultural arena, to accept the idea that women are outside language.
>
> (1991, 37)

Doane's fundamental concern is that women spectators will overidentify with the image and therefore be barred from a critical appraisal of the text. As Petro argues: 'Doane surmises that when the female spectator fails to distance herself from the image of woman, she necessarily merges with that image, and, consequently, loses herself' (1989, 48). In this way, Petro argues that Doane ends up reinscribing woman in the model she initially intended to dismantle. Instead of affirming this model of spectatorship, Petro seeks to challenge psychoanalytic interpretations of perception. Drawing on work by Benjamin, Kracauer and Heidegger, Petro suggests that all three theorists demonstrate how sense perception is neither biological nor natural, instead it is the result of the process of differentiation (1989, 71).[12] What Petro's work, and more recent work,[13] suggests is that we need to reconsider the question of sexual difference within feminist film theory, and more specifically, how this difference is related to issues regarding identification and emotional engagement.

It is important to highlight that Doane's theorisation of closeness and distance is predicated on a psychoanalytic understanding of desire. As Geetha Ramanathan points out: 'Reviewing psychoanalytic work, Doane, in an analysis of the female spectator's lack of distance from the screen, or from the character in the diegesis, find that this inhibited the female's ability to desire as this specific identification mechanism does not posit lack, a necessary condition of desire' (2006, 141). Lack is a necessary condition for desire within a psychoanalytic understanding of desire, not an essential condition for other models of desire. Indeed, models of identification or recognition proposed within cognitive film theory do not posit lack as a necessary precursor to desire, nor do Deleuzian approaches, which will be discussed in more detail in Chapter 5. The assumption that distance is required to be a 'knowing spectator' needs to be critiqued, particularly in light of more recent theories on emotion and affect. It is interesting to note that the attachment to distance is held on to by some feminist film theorists who fear any reversal would only confirm woman's place as culturally inferior.

Indeed, there is very little feminist questioning of the distancing that is stressed in the process of identification within film studies. One of the only critiques of this distancing is offered within cognitive film approaches. As Carl Plantinga argues, there is an assumption that 'social criticism or critical judgment must come through distancing and alienation' (1997, 384). Cognitive film theorists such as Plantinga, Noel Carroll and Murray Smith rethink the concept of identification and use 'recognition' and 'emotional simulation' instead to describe the relationship between the spectator and screen. In his study of identification and audience, for instance, Smith contends that the word 'identification', that is often used to describe the relationship between spectator and character, is less important than the model of the experience itself. He argues that we could also refer to words such as 'absorption' and 'empathy' to refer to the relationship that exists between spectator and character (1995, 1–2). Smith also distinguishes between the 'levels of engagement' and 'structures of sympathy' that exists within this model of experience. He refers to 'emotional simulation' as a way of explaining the process of identification, defining it as: 'observing the behaviour of a person in a certain situation about which we have limited knowledge—as is often the case with a character in fiction—we imaginatively project ourselves into their situation, and hypothesize as to the emotion(s) they are experiencing' (1995, 97). The distinction that Smith makes allows us to concentrate on the emotions and affects the character's situation may have on the spectator. The emphasis on emotion and affect shifts the focus away from individual characters, and problematises any notion of 'overidentification'. In the cognitive model, spectators relate to the emotions the characters find themselves in, rather than the characters themselves. The point worth making here is that distance must no longer be considered a necessary component to the spectator's participation in desire, irrespective of gender. The elision made between 'distance' and 'intellect' and 'closeness' and 'sentiment' needs to be challenged within feminist film theory.

Melodrama and no sexual relationship

One of the most powerful filmic illustrations of melodrama's conventions and conceits is offered in Matthias Müeller's *Homes Stories* (1990).[14] The short film (6 mins) features a montage of images from the melodramatic form in which women are rising from beds, putting on silken peignoirs, listening intently at doors, turning on lights and turning off lights, all with a characteristic melodramatic expression. The short film, its repetitive images and its eerie accompanying music reminds us of some of the central themes and preoccupations within melodrama: the domestic, the home and female desire.

The history of melodrama, as a narrative form and a cinematic genre, is examined in great depth in Christine Gledhill's introduction to *Home is Where the Heart is* (1987). In her introductory chapter titled 'The Melodramatic Field: An Investigation' Gledhill discusses the critical, cultural, historical, ideological and cinematic background and the debates around melodrama and considers the ways in which the form has been dismissed as a 'women's weepie' and recuperated as a powerful critique of petit-bourgeois American ideology through its 'distanciation' (Willemen) devices (particularly with regards to Sirk). She also discusses the ways in which these competing arguments around melodrama's potential establish two different (and gendered) audiences: 'one which is implicated, identifies and weeps, and one which, seeing through such involvement, distances itself' (1987, 12). Part of what I want to argue is that these two different positions on melodrama are also at play within the theorisation of the gaze, as explored earlier. There is a contestation around whether the audience should maintain a distance to the text, or can be allowed to feel a sense of closeness, thereby participating with the emotion in the text. As also explored, these two different positions are gendered, and taken up accordingly within feminist theory—often, as discussed, there is an explicit cautioning against such closeness for fear of being positioned as the unintelligent weeping audience instead of the cool, distant audience. As theorists have noted, one of the weaknesses in both arguments is the fact that audiences take pleasure in these texts. What is also at stake is how we think about the theorisation of desire in terms of this constructed distance or unmediated closeness. And finally, as I will go on to argue, a debate between distance and closeness can be usefully linked to the concept of shame and its relation to interest.

In her guide to key concepts in cinema studies, Susan Hayward argues that 'Hollywood's great subject is heterosexuality, the plot resolution "requires" the heterosexual couple formation' (2000, 158). Although Hollywood might require heterosexual love, in the great romances, it also requires that this love is never truly realised. Anthony Easthope argues that Hollywood has developed three narrative strategies that make allusion to the sexual relationship while at the same time disguise its actual impossibility. One narrative involves the suggestion that the love will take place 'after the story ends' and there are countless examples such as *Pretty Woman* (1990) or *My Best Friend's Wedding* (1997). Another narrative implies that the love was really there before the story began, and *Casablanca* (1942) is a perfect instance of this kind of narrative. '"If only" is a very rich strategy, which includes: if only there hadn't been a Russian Revolution (*Dr Zhivago* 1965); if only he'd had normal fingers (*Edward Scissorhands* 1990); if only the ship hadn't hit an iceberg (*Titanic* 1997)' (1999, 69). The 'if only' that Easthope identifies is crucial to our interpretation of the gaze and of desire in film.

Distancing techniques, as have been discussed, and the 'if only' narrative strategy work together to keep us from the awareness that *there is no sexual relationship* but instead, a desire for self-love. What we truly desire, or so argue the psychoanalysts, is that unified relationship we had *before* our jubilant assumption of 'I' and concomitant awareness of an Other in the mirror. As Bowie argues: 'Lacan invites us to look back beyond the play of rivalries and aliases that the Oedipal phase initiates, and to behold an anterior world in which the individual has only one object of desire and only one alias—himself' (1991, 32). The emphasis Lacan places on the self within the play of desire establishes the self as the ultimate object of desire.

In order to consider these ideas further I want to explore how gaze and desire are figured in terms of the melodrama. The oft used phrase: 'their eyes first met' comes from Flaubert's *Sentimental Education* and is the focus of Mladen Dolar's insightful approach to the gaze and psychoanalytic theory. For Dolar, the phrase 'their eyes first met' 'epitomizes the gaze, the return of the gaze, as the crucial moment of that foundational myth of encounter. It is a moment of recognition: one recognizes what has "always already" been there, since the beginning of time, and the whole previous experience retroactively acquires the sense of leading just to this moment' (1996, 132–133). Here Dolar makes reference to the 'button tie' or 'quilting point' in Lacan's graph of desire, discussed in Chapter 1: this is the moment when meaning is fixed and all other meaning is affected. In simpler terms, the moment one meets this Other is also the same moment when meaning is established and reconsidered as the dominant meaning for all other encounters and narratives. When you 'fall in love' you believe that *this* person is and always has been the 'one' for you and so all others that came before have only helped in your journey to this moment (and person). As Easthope suggests, that leaves you wondering 'if only'. And yet it is the lack of a conventional 'happy ending' that ensures the melodramatic enjoyment of the film. As Mulvey points out, it is the contradiction not the reconciliation that allows the viewer a real escape in a melodramatic film (1989, 43).

In *Solaris* (2002),[15] for example, the moment that two strangers' eyes 'first meet' is privileged in the narrative and is often returned to in order to anchor the other storylines. The moment Chris (George Clooney) sees Rheya (Natascha McElhone) for the first time on the train is figured as the 'primal scene', the instant where both of their lives 'started' and a moment which is continually returned to as each tries to remember the story of their love. The 'truth' about this love, as Lacan would suggest, is that it is misdirected and misrecognised. What the two strangers should recognise is their own desire, not the desire of the Other. What they each truly desire is to have the Other return the gaze they solicit. As Lacan argues: 'when, in love, I solicit a look, what is profoundly unsatisfying and always missing is that—*You never look at me from which I see you.*' Conversely, *what I look at is never what I wish to see*' (1994 [1977], 103, author's italics). Lacan stresses that the eye can never see that which it wants to—that pure expression of desire, that something that would complete the person looking. As Žižek argues: 'there certainly is in the mirror image "more than meets the eye," yet this surplus that eludes the eye, the point in the image which eludes my eye's grasp is none other than *the gaze itself*' (2001 [1992], 127, author's italics). This surplus or excess can be found in melodrama and mirrors both the surplus that escapes the eye, and also the role fate and destiny play. As Mulvey writes: 'The aesthetics of the popular melodrama depend on grand gesture, tableaux, broad moral themes, with narratives of coincidence, reverses and sudden happy endings organised around a rigid opposition between good and evil. Characters represent forces rather than people, and fail to control or understand their circumstances so that fate, rather than heroic transcendence, offers a resolution to the drama' (1989, 73). Mulvey's description of the aesthetics of the melodrama fit perfectly with a film such as *Dr Zhivago*. The grand spectacle of the Russian Revolution is the backdrop for a very singular love story, and yet, it does not produce heroes but allows fate to control and inevitably dictate the events of their lives. Dolar goes further and argues that 'All melodramas also know very well that the moment one stops to reason about the viability of a certain choice, the moment one starts to calculate the advantages and disadvantages, one is heading for disaster. If one doesn't surrender unconditionally to fate, fate will inexorably revenge itself' (1996, 131). As Dolar emphasises, melodrama highlights the way in which desire is an incalculable force that makes even the impossible possible (and sometimes the possible impossible).

From *All That Heaven Allows* to *Fear Eats the Soul* to *Far from Heaven*

'Sirkian' has become a descriptor within film studies, much like terms such as 'Hitchcockian' or 'Chaplinesque', or so Thomas Doherty suggests in his article on Sirk (2002). However, as Doherty points out, the academic acceptance of Sirk's work has not always been as certain as the term might imply. Sirk's melodramas, *All I Desire* (1953), *Magnificent Obsession* (1954), *All That Heaven Allows* (1955), *Written on the Wind* (1956), *There's Always Tomorrow* (1957), *Time to Die* (1958) and *Imitation of Life* (1959), once categorised as 'women's weepies', were re-valued by feminist film scholars in the 1970s and given new importance by the New German director Rainer Werner Fassbinder. Sirk's melodramas are now understood not only to hold an important place within the study of melodrama but are also considered as offering some of the most damaging critiques of the American family (see Halliday 1971).

    All I Desire (originally titled *Stopover*),[16] starring Barbara Stanwyck, illustrates the powerful gaze of societal disapproval and the consequences of desire. Naomi, who leaves her husband and children to pursue a life as an actress, returns to the small town she lived in when her youngest daughter writes to her in hopes that she will attend her school play. The film is very advanced for its time in that it honestly and frankly addresses the dilemma some women face between a career and family. In the book, on which the film is based, Naomi leaves and returns to her life as an actress; however, the film version ends with Naomi's decision to stay and to resume her role as wife and mother. Although the ending is contrived it posits desire as the reason for Naomi's return to her family and for her triumph over societal disapproval.

The same trope of impossible love and societal intrusion is explored in Sirk's *All That Heaven Allows*. It is the first in a series of films that I will explore—all of which take on the notion of risk as a means of following one's true desire. Each film is also one of social commentary—each couple must face the shameful gaze of their local communities in order to prove their love to each other and themselves. The two later films, *Ali: Fear Eats the Soul* (1974) by Rainer Werner Fassbinder and *Far from Heaven* (2002) by Todd Haynes, draw heavily on Sirk's work but contemporise the issues, drawing in arguments regarding race and sexuality to Sirk's commentary on class.

All That Heaven Allows

Jon Halliday points out that *All That Heaven Allows* might be considered Sirk's most successful melodrama because it has a straightforward relationship between a confused character and a stable one. Sirk agrees that in 'melodrama it's of advantage to have one immovable character against which you can put your more split ones. Because your audience needs—or likes—to have a character in the movie they can identify themselves with' (1971, 98). Cary Scott (Jane Wyman) is unsure of her feelings for her young gardener Ron Kirby (Rock Hudson). Ron, on the other hand, is sure of his feelings for Cary and himself. Sirk makes reference to Ron's interest in Emerson's transcendental philosophy in order to establish him as someone with a more unconventional approach to life. In many ways the film can be read as a narrative of self-transformation: Cary, who begins as a bored, middle-class widow ends as a passionate and free-thinking woman in love with a man much younger than herself. Her transformation is marked by her desire for Ron. At first their love awakens feelings and ideas within her that she has not experienced before. However when the reality of their relationship comes up against the prejudices of her social circle and children's disapproval, she begins to doubt whether she is able to sustain the relationship. Believing she must leave him for her children's well-being, Cary ends up alone and without anyone. In the final scene, Cary and Ron are reunited, however as Laura Mulvey (1987) and Jackie Byars (1991) have suggested, the ending, with Ron incapacitated and Cary nursing him, suggests not the happy union of the couple but Cary returning to a more socially acceptable role as 'mother' to Ron.[17]

In his analysis of the film, Michael Stern draws on an interview with Sirk in which Sirk suggests that homes are like prisons or tombs, places people build to enclose themselves inside. Stern argues that Sirk's settings reinforce this idea, creating the sense that Cary is alive inside her own tomb (1979, 117). In one of the most powerful scenes, Cary is alone in her living room, neither of her children have returned home for the holidays. The TV she insisted she did not want has finally arrived, and she is left in the dark, her empty expression mirrored in the television screen. Stern suggests that 'her desire to escape a stultifying bourgeois life, her spiritual and sexual longings, all have been reduced to a pale reflection of the TV screen' (1979, 118). This low point however encourages the viewer to want Cary's reconciliation with Ron. Viewers who may have questioned her role as a 'good' mother in her initial decision to be with Ron will now feel Cary's desire is 'allowed', and a happy ending follows. Indeed we can read the film as a commentary on an 'older woman's' desire.[18]

It is interesting to note in her analysis of the film that Laura Mulvey refers to Cary's decision to reject Ron as a 'flight to illness' (1989, 42). The reference here to hysteria reiterates the way in which melodrama deals with inarticulable desires and is largely about trying to voice these repressed feelings, despite the damage their articulation might cause to the family structure. Mulvey points out that it is through Cary's doctor that she is convinced that she must pursue her feelings for Ron. He tells her that her headaches come from denying herself what she truly desires. The scene can be linked to the doctor figure in Haynes's *Safe* who is convinced that there is nothing physically wrong with Carol, instead he believes her problems are caused by her inability to articulate her desires (or perhaps to pursue her desires). In both cases, physical symptoms are diagnosed with emotional cures (Cary must give in to her desires and Carol must avoid 'stress'). The scientific establishment, as represented through the doctors, advises, as would Freud, that these inexplicable physical symptoms are the result of emotional repression—and, consequently, one only needs to express in order to be cured. Cary follows the doctor's orders and is 'rewarded' with a happy, albeit compromised, ending. Carol, on the other hand, resists the doctor's diagnosis and cure in pursuing her own solution. Read in this way, we can appreciate that the hysteric is not simply a 'repository for inexpressible desires' but a performative contradiction.

Distance, resistance and emotion

One of the preoccupations in criticism on Sirk regards his use of distancing techniques. Sirk himself has said that he believes 'art must establish distance', and achieves this, in part, through his use of mirrors'.[19] These distancing devices are apparent in *All That Heaven Allows* and as David Grosz argues, 'they are frequently employed to demonstrate the irreconcilable distances and separations of the characters from one another' (1971, 102). After her initial meeting with Ron, for instance, Cary sits in front of the mirror and yet does not look at herself directly. As viewers we can see her expression of confusion and excitement reflected in the personal mirror of her vanity table. In another scene, Cary's son tells her that he thinks she has been persuaded by Ron's muscles, and not true feelings for him. Sirk separates the mother and son through a screen which means viewers cannot see her expression: it is veiled. The screen represents the barrier the son places on Cary's sexual desires.

Although theorists seem to agree that Sirk uses distancing devices, there is debate about the purpose of these techniques: is it designed to separate viewers from the characters, to draw them in or to present a commentary on bourgeois ideology?[20] Or, as David Grosz has argued, do these devices signify the trapped nature of the characters themselves?[21] What is important to this analysis of Sirk and melodrama is the very fact that distance and proximity remain central concerns.

Indeed, in her article on Sirk's *Schlußakkord*,[22] Linda Schulte-Sasse is critical of the attention to 'distance' and 'resistance' so often found in relation to Sirk's work. She argues that 'although estrangement is central to Sirk's aesthetics, reliance on a Brechtian model may be misleading if it fails to accept the film's sentimentality and explains it away as hiding an intellectual message that needs to be decoded by a select few' (1998, 6). She suggests that instead of adopting a hierarchal model that would privilege intellect over sentiment, we should consider employing a horizontal model that would allow audiences to weep and get 'swept away' but still recognise a critical engagement (1998, 6). Schulte-Sasse's critique is not only important in terms of Sirk's work (and those that have followed him such as Fassbinder and Haynes), but is also significant in recognising the value of emotion within a text as an aesthetic quality. I have argued elsewhere that we can consider emotion as an aesthetic quality that not only *moves* audiences but allows for a critical engagement (Gorton, 2006).

Following her impressive reading of the musical and non-musical movements in *Schluβakkord*, Schulte-Sasse argues that 'what Sirk opens up is not a space of agency, in which I suspect he had little faith, but a space for understanding something that did not interest Brecht: desire, especially desire for what is impossible. Ultimately, however, one could scarcely find a phenomenon with greater political implications than the structure of desire, of desire's "impossibility"' (1998, 28). As Schulte-Sasse points out, the argument regarding distance and closeness is one predicated on an assumption that sentiment disallows or disables critical appreciation. This assumption does not take recent work on emotion and affect into account which re-values this closeness; more importantly, the preoccupation with distance overlooks one of the most important contributions within Sirk's work—that of desire and its impossibility.

Sirk's legacy: Fassbinder and Haynes

Mulvey suggests that there are two important ways in which Rainer Werner Fassbinder develops the American melodrama. Firstly, he takes hysteria as a central focus, and, secondly, he takes melodrama outside the confines of the bourgeoisie (1989, 45).[23] The movement of the melodrama from the privileged parameters of the upper middle class to the working class introduces new struggles and new boundaries to the happiness often anticipated in the narrative structure of the melodramatic form. Sirk's narrative in *All That Heaven Allows* is heavily referenced in Fassbinder's *Ali: Fear Eats the Soul* (1974) but is taken in new directions through the introduction of racial difference. In *Fear Eats the Soul*, the immovable character, Ali, a Moroccan immigrant, falls in love with Emmi, a German cleaner. The film opens with the statement 'Happiness is not always fun' and this underlines the film. What Fassbinder presents is not simply a 'love' story but a love story that involves struggle, disappointment and ultimately happiness, a happiness that is not always fun, but is nevertheless genuine.

The film begins with Emmi's entrance into a café that is a meeting place for Moroccans. Her 'otherness' is immediately established as all the occupants of the café stare at her. One of the women in the bar dares Ali to go have a 'dance with the old woman', which he agrees to. Having enjoyed their dance, Ali accompanies Emmi back to her modest apartment where she invites him up for coffee. The fact that they are very different in age becomes secondary to the fact that they come from different cultural backgrounds. Naïve to other people's reactions to her feelings of love for Ali, Emmi begins to suffer from the lack of social acceptance she finds in friends, work colleagues and her children. They all reject her when she announces her marriage to Ali. At first they are both determined to overcome the odds and work together to build savings for their own 'little piece of heaven'. However, the continual rejection starts to depress Emmi, and in a magnificent scene, Emmi shouts at the waiters and customers in a restaurant who have lined up to stare at the unlikely couple. She tells Ali that she did not think it would bother her, what other people think, but she begins to realise she does care: 'I pretend I don't care but I do, I do care! It's killing me.' 'Nobody looks me in the eye anymore. They all have such a horrible grin ... Stop staring, you stupid swine! This is my husband, my husband' (and she bursts into tears) (Fassbinder 1974). Following this public display they decide to go on a holiday together, some place where 'no one will stare'. The scene powerfully demonstrates their isolation from society and its penetrative gaze and, perhaps more importantly, the affect shame has on its objects. Emmi becomes aware that their interest in them, the reason they stare, has more to do with shame than happiness. They do not *see* the love she feels and shares with Ali—they only see the differences between them.

Upon their return, Emmi has a visibly new attitude towards her relationship with Ali. In one scene her work colleagues gaze on Ali like an object, remarking about how clean he is and at the size of his muscles. Emmi allows them to touch him, and inspect him as though he were her prized possession. She begins to be re-accepted by family, friends and colleagues, but as she is accepted back 'into the fold' Ali begins an affair with the bartender at the café where they first met. Fassbinder makes it clear that Ali is not in love with this woman but that she will make him the cous cous he so badly misses and which Emmi will not make for him. During this point the gaze between them is broken—they no longer look each other in the eye. When Ali does not come home, Emmi goes to the garage where he works. In this scene he will not look her in the eyes and when one of his colleagues asks whether she is her grandmother he joins in their laughter. Both Emmi and Ali internalise the shameful look they have received from others and begin to look upon each other in the same way. They no longer 'see' the love between them, but instead see the differences that separate them.

Eventually the two are reunited, but in the final scene, Emmi is by Ali's bedside in the hospital, determined to prevent him from suffering any longer. Like *All That Heaven Allows*, *Ali* ends with Emmi as caretaker/mother and Ali as patient/son. It is worth noting however that in *All that Heaven Allows* the film ends with Ron opening his eyes and seeing

Cary. He says 'you've come home' and the camera pans from the lovers to the open window where a deer stands majestically. In contrast, Ali never opens his eyes, and Emmi just sits by his side crying. The camera pans to the hospital window, which is covered by a white blind—no view is offered.

The most recent of the three films and the most loyal to Sirk's vision in *All that Heaven Allows*, *Far from Heaven*, tackles issues regarding race and sexuality as well as class and desire. The film begins with a similar montage offered in Sirk's *All that Heaven Allows*: the small town is highlighted as the backdrop and serves to emphasise the 'small town' values referred to throughout the film. Faithful to Sirk's plot, Haynes has the central female character, Cathy Whitaker (Julianne Moore) fall in love with her gardener Raymond Deagan (Dennis Haysbert); however, unlike Sirk's version, where age and social class construct barriers, in choosing an African-American gardener in 1950s America and having Cathy's husband leave her for another man, the emphasis is on race and sexual identity.

In an interview with Robert Fischer,[24] Todd Haynes argues for the political potential in the melodramatic form—a way of looking at powerless people trapped in houses and social society; trapped in moral, domestic culture. He also draws attention to compassion—he emphasises that many of the characters in melodrama are not heroic—they buckle under the pressure of societal demands. This inability to overcome the odds is highlighted in Haynes's film in particular. In both *All That Heaven Allows* and *Ali*, the couple are reunited over the sick bed, and although the scene makes clear that there is still work to do, they have resolved to do the work necessary to stay together. Haynes's *Far from Heaven* ends with Cathy on the train platform waving goodbye to Raymond as he leaves to start his new life. Unlike the first two films, the 'happy ending' has less to do with the couple and more to do with how their relationship has influenced each to pursue their own lives. The experience has transformed them and their relationship to the world.

Desire and (im)possibility

The point of bringing all three films together is to demonstrate a preoccupation with the 'impossible' love story and its resolution. These films draw attention to the focus in melodrama on the 'happy couple' and their relation to the world around them; they highlight how personal dramas are designed to speak of broader social dramas regarding class, sexuality and race. The melodrama moves its viewer from the personal to the social and back again, asking us, as viewers, to participate in the intimate development of a relationship that is unwelcome in the society it comes from. The function of the gaze is crucial here as it draws attention to the bond the couple establish and the way in which shame both draws them closer and tears them apart. The gaze also works to privilege the lovers' relationship over any other in the text. For example, in *All that Heaven Allows*, Ron's friends are presented as 'in love' with each other, but their relationship is constructed as 'simpler' than Ron and Cary's. They come from the same social class, they each made the decision to change their lifestyle, etc.: these similarities are established through the dialogue. However, the lack of any eye contact between them is what leads us to believe that their love is not as strong or as important as the one blossoming between Ron and Cary, who look deeply into each other's eyes at the party their friends host.

In her work on desire, Catherine Belsey argues that if there is a failure on the part of the happy, heterosexual couple it must be *our* failure—'the failure of the sexual relation, disappointment in love, the implicit argument goes, is our failure, the consequence of an afflicted personality or a repressive culture, or both, and the cure must be a return to nature' (1994, 5). However, as she goes on to argue, desire with its excess and contradiction is at the centre of the problem. In other words, desire and its restlessness keep us at work. Desire's insatiable nature requires the happy couple to focus on itself and its survival. As Belsey argues: 'Social stability thus depends in more ways than one on the profoundly anti-social couple, cultivating their relationship, tending it, agonising over its moments of crisis, anxiously watching it grow' (1994, 5–6). The melodrama performs this cultivation and struggle while also demonstrating the inherent value of overcoming the odds. In each film mentioned the ending is not a perfect resolution but recognition of the work that is to come: happiness, as Fassbinder emphasises, is not always fun. However, it seems to me that far from presenting desire as a threat to the happy couple, melodrama presents desire as the reason for the happy couple's continued struggle. Instead of a threat to their togetherness, desire is figured as the reason *for* their partnership. It is desire that allows them to overcome the differences that others around them perceive as a hindrance and obstacle. In this way, melodrama presents desire as something radical and life-changing, something that is capable of drawing together and keeping together even the most unlikely couple. Read in this way desire becomes capable of uniting people of disparate backgrounds, as a social leveller of class, gender, sexuality and race.

Geoffrey Nowell-Smith draws a parallel between the melodrama and 'conversion hysteria, arguing that 'it is not just that the characters are often prone to hysteria, but that the film itself somatises its own unaccommodated excess, which thus appears displaced or in the wrong place' (1977, 117). The 'if only' that conditions happiness in the melodrama also marks fantasy and melodrama's relation to desire. It also conditions the ending which either comes too late or almost too late which imbues the happy ending with a sense of loss. As Steve Neale suggests: 'The words "if only" mark both the *fact* of loss, that it is too late, yet simultaneously the possibility that things might have been different, that the fantasy *could* have been fulfilled, the object of desire indeed attained' (1986, 22, author's italics).

Neale also argues that if there is a desire central to melodrama 'characteristic form of desire in melodrama is adult, heterosexual desire, and that the aim of its fantasy is the union of an adult, heterosexual couple' (Neale 1986, 13). Embedded in Haynes's homage to Sirk's film is another story of desire: male homosexual desire. In *Far from Heaven*, Frank Whitaker (Dennis Quaid) begins to explore his feelings for men, which leads to his wife, Cathy, discovering him in his office in a compromising position with another man. At first his hysterical rejection of his own desire seems possible, but inevitably his feelings return, and in the end, he decides to leave Cathy for a man he has fallen in love with. The fact that Frank is able to attain his desired object is set in contrast with Cathy's loss—her fantasy of a happy marriage is shattered by Frank's acceptance of his homosexuality. '*If only* society was more tolerant' underlines the film and conditions the lives and desire of the characters within it.

Having a good cry

In her chapter on 'the invention of crying and the antitheatrics of the act' Joan Copjec playfully suggests that that melodrama was 'specifically designed to give people something to cry about' (2002, 108). Whether events happen too early or too late, the viewer of the melodrama is often filled with tears. Neale refers to melodrama's 'ability to *move* its spectators and make them cry' (1986, 6, author's italics). In the brilliantly titled *Having a Good Cry: Effeminate Feelings and Pop-Culture Forms* (2003), Robyn Warhol argues that sentimentalism is not cathartic, it does not drain or release emotions, rather it encourages its reader to 'rehearse and reinforce the feelings it evokes' (2003, 18). She goes on to argue that 'Feminist film theory—with its psychoanalytically inspired tendency to read women's crying over films as a masochistic pleasure and films' manipulation of women's sentiments as a form of textual/sexual violence—has not done much to ameliorate the negative associations of crying over stories' (2003, 30). There is still, as Warhol suggests and as I have discussed, a necessity to reconsider the negative connotations of 'having a good cry' within feminist film theory.

Indeed, if we return to the debate raised within feminist film theory over distance and closeness and use this to reconsider our reading of the melodrama, particularly work by or inspired by Sirk, it is striking that there remains a concern over female audiences weeping. And this seems partly related to shame/interest. Historically women have been cautioned against being interested in texts such as the melodrama, the soap or the chick flick—there continues to be a sense that these texts not only offer very little by way of intellectual challenge, but perhaps even more dangerously, can manipulate their viewers into thinking a whole host of bad things: like, women should believe in heterosexual marriage, they should avoid challenge, they should just want to love their man, etc.

In Linda Williams's 'Film Bodies: Gender, Genre, and Excess', she argues that what brackets genres such as the melodrama, the horror film and pornography from others is their 'apparent lack of proper aesthetic distance, a sense of over-involvement in sensation and emotion. We feel manipulated by these texts—an impression that the very colloquialisms of "tear jerker" and "fear jerker" express' (1991, 5). As Williams points out, these texts' ability to 'jerk' emotion from us lead to their cultural devaluation and to the perception that they are not 'good' for us, and, I would argue, a sense that we should feel ashamed or even angry if they have managed to make us cry or scream. And yet, many of us will admit not only to watching these texts, but enjoying them, and watching them again and again. At the centre of the enjoyment and pleasure viewers experience through these texts is an 'impossible' desire for the closeness they provide. Far from disabling critical judgement, an emotional engagement enables the viewer to appreciate the affects of shame and desire that circulate through texts such as the melodrama.

4
Shame and Desire

> Strung out between romance and pornography it is no
> longer clear what men and women want to use each
> other for
>
> (Adam Phillips 2005, 116)

As the last chapter explores, the 'happy' or 'triumphant' couple at the centre of the melodramatic narrative functions to draw viewers in, even to 'jerk' their emotions and provide a 'good cry' to what is ultimately a social dilemma of desire. The gaze functions to establish the relationship between the couple, and also to initiate the gaze of the viewer herself. She is drawn in to the scene of desire and its concomitant expectations and consequences. Also central to the melodramatic form is the notion of female desire, as this chapter will explore in more detail.

In a special edition of *Signs*, 'Beyond the Gaze: Recent Approaches to Film Feminisms', editors Kathleen McHugh and Vivian Sobchack argue that feminist film theory and media work is no longer dominated by psychoanalytic concepts such as 'the gaze' and 'desire', instead, they believe that feminist film theory is 'an increasingly heterogeneous and dynamic set of concepts and practices' (2004, 1205). In order to explore the efficacy of their claim, they invite some of the key feminist theorists of what is often referred to as 'seventies film theory', such as Annette Kuhn, Mary Ann Doane, E. Ann Kaplan and Linda Williams, to a round-table discussion of 'film feminisms' and then present the perspectives of a 'new' generation of film and media scholars. In many ways this edition adopts a 'then and now' framework: reflecting both on what affected women in the past and focusing on perceptions of women and film after the extensive development of feminist film studies. Its genera-tional approach reflects a difference that is often invoked between second-wave feminists and post-feminists or third-wave feminists and the concomitant knowledge and political positioning that characterise each interpretation of feminism. As Joanne Hollows and Rachel Moseley point out in their examination of feminism in popular culture: 'apart from women actively involved in the second-wave of feminism in the 1960s and 1970s, most people's initial knowledge and understanding of feminism has been formed within the popular and through representation' (2006, 2). The distinction that Hollows and Moseley make is crucial to understanding both the force of the work achieved by feminist film theorists in the 1970s and 1980s and the rejection and revision offered by theorists in the 1990s and today. Many academic women writing today about film theory have not only been informed by popular culture and representations of women, as Hollows and Moseley argue, but have also been influenced by the theoretical work offered by their 1970s 'foremothers'. They have been raised on a 'diet' of semiotics, psychoanalysis, feminism and sexual difference; they have been taught that woman is represented as 'lack', passive and an object of desire, and yet increasingly they find these interpretations to be unsatisfying given their social and personal experiences. This contradiction reflects the tension between 'politics and pleasure' that has been present within feminist film theory from the beginning (Smelik 1998, 7). Indeed, the gap between the imaginary 'female spectator' and her social counterpart is one of the fundamental contradictions within feminism film theory. As Anneke Smelik argues: 'Feminist theory is built on the very contradiction between the unrepresentability of woman as subject of desire and historical women who know themselves to be subjects' (1998, 17). The tension between 'politics and pleasure' and between the unrepresentability of woman as subject to her own desires and her historical experience continues to be articulated in recent work within feminist film theory. It can also be found within post-feminist and third-wave feminist work, which seeks to move away from the 'victim' mentality often associated with second-wave feminism. These tensions and their expressions within feminist work and film suggest that the question of woman and cinema is still relevant and necessary.

We might take the 1980s as the starting point for post-feminism, and indeed, theorists such as Faludi and Walters have cited Susan Bolotin's 1982 article, 'Voices from the Post-Feminist Generation', in the *New York Times Magazine* as the first time 'post-feminism' was used in public discourse (Projansky 2001, 77). Post-feminism is often associated with a media-induced version of feminism and this is the way Susan Faludi defines it in her influential *Backlash* (1991). However, it has also been understood as developing out of poststructuralism, in line with post-colonialism and postmodernism (Brooks 1997). In *Introducing Post-feminism*, Sophia Phoca and Rebecca Wright argue that in the 1990s, women 'began to feel alienated by what they saw as the policing of their sexuality'. For them, 'Feminism became reductively identified with political correctness and "victim politics"' (Phoca and Wright 1999, 170). Phoca and Wright's identification of sexuality and 'victim politics' as a key issue within post-feminism is important for this chapter and is resonant in much of the feminist work that is identified as post-feminist.

I want to isolate the historical context for this chapter between 1998 and 2004, for I feel it is a distinct moment in which issues regarding female sexuality, empowerment, desire and shame come to a head. This period saw the emergence of the genre 'chicklit', it witnessed the popularity, both in academic and mainstream audiences, of *Ally McBeal* and *Sex and the City*; it recognised new cinematic images of 'tough women', critically discussed in collections such as *Action Chicks* (2004) and *Action TV* (2001); and it also produced a multitude of popular feminist literature which questioned both the viability and relevance of feminism, texts such as *Bitch* (1998) by Elizabeth Wurtzel, *The New Feminism* (1998) by Natasha Walter and *Manifesta: Young Women, Feminism and the Future* (2000) by Jennifer Baumgardner and Amy Richards. This period can be characterised by its questioning of feminism for a new generation, its emphasis on sexual empowerment and independence, and its ambivalence over marriage and motherhood. It can also be seen as theorising what desire means to women in contemporary culture.

This period is also marked by the media's involvement in creating a generational gap between second-wave feminism and post-feminism. As Patrice Petro argues: 'The popular image of a moralistic and humourless feminism was reinforced by media-induced accounts of generational divisions among women, pitting younger, supposedly more sexually radical feminists against older, allegedly conservative ones' (2002, 11). This media-induced generational divide is best illustrated on the cover of *Time* magazine in June 1998. The cover featured four heads lined up against a black background. The first three heads, in black and white, were of Susan B. Anthony, Betty Friedan and Gloria Steinem: American icons of the second-wave feminist movement. The final face, in colour, is identified as 'Ally McBeal'. Underneath her head is the question: 'Is feminism dead?', thus implying that Ally not only symbolises a younger, sexier generation, but also one that does not need feminism (Gorton 2004). It is important to note that the cover establishes feminism as a white, middle-class and heterosexual politics. This choice not only offends those involved in feminist politics that do not fit this description but also erases the significant influences black, lesbian and working-class women have had and continue to have within feminist theory.

In her work on representations of rape in popular culture, Sarah Projansky argues that post-feminism should not be located historically, but rather post-feminism should be understood as a cultural discourse. According to Projansky, in thinking about post-feminism as a cultural discourse we can move beyond suggestions of progress that underlie the generational approaches to feminism. She also sees this understanding of post-feminism as offering a way of collapsing the tension between representation and subjective experience. As she argues: 'paying attention to post-feminism as a cultural discursive strategy, rather than as an "actual" historical event, also helps emphasize how easily the discourse moves between "real" women and fictional women (like the *Time* cover's move from Steinem to McBeal) without considering any difference between them' (Projansky 2001, 88–89). Although I find it very tempting to follow Projansky's model of post-feminism, in that it allows both an erasure of the notion of 'progress' and undoes the tension between the representation of woman and her social counterpart, I have deep anxieties about a discourse that moves between 'real' women and fictional women without a consideration of difference. In the case of the *Time* cover, the fact that the discourse moves between 'real' women and a fictional woman without any distinction glosses over the very real problem that Calista Flockhart (the actress who plays the fictional McBeal) loses her identity in favour of a fictional character written by a male television writer. Even if her character is written by a female writer (as she is in some episodes), this does not dismiss the suggestion that in contemporary popular culture there is confusion over 'real' women and fictional ones. The problem is that fiction often overlooks social realities such as equal pay, childcare and domestic violence. It might take these issues on board, but it will present them, as it does on *Ally McBeal* as humorous sidelines and sentimental moments. Nonetheless, what Projansky's work illustrates is a desire to move beyond these contradictions and false notions of progress; her work demonstrates that 1970s feminism is out of step with the experiences of young women today. 'As Angela McRobbie (1996) has argued in another context, the old vocabularies of 1970s feminism are not adequate to the experience of young women growing up today' (Brunsdon 1997, 101). And yet part of the reason for this inadequacy is that concepts such as 'desire' have yet to be fully theorised or explored within feminist theory. As Liz Constable argues in her insightful essay on women becoming sexual subjects, female sexuality is still addressed in terms of morality, disease and victimisation, and rarely in terms of desire or pleasure. Despite the best intentions of feminist theorists and researchers, there is still an absence of a discourse on desire and this absence has a profound affect on young women's self-construction as sexual subjects (Constable 2004).

The absence of a discourse of desire is cited as a reason for the problems women continue to experience in the process of becoming sexual subjects. And this is voiced by 'popular' feminism as often as it is in the academy. For instance, in raising the problems with social understandings of date rape, Elizabeth Wurtzel points out that 'many women—and to a greater extent, college girls—don't know how to say no because they don't know how to say yes. They cannot for the life of them register what their desire level is against what they think they should or shouldn't do [...] I wish I could get a grip on something as simple as desire, but it is so shrouded in other motives ...' (1998, 116). What Wurtzel points to is a lack of a discourse on desire that would allow women, particularly young women, to express the feelings they have and, at a basic level, as Wurtzel argues, to even know whether they should say 'yes' or 'no'. She also gestures towards the way in which female desire is mediated more by societal pressures and expectations than by bodily feelings. So although popular culture often represents women who know what they want, the reality seems to be that this knowledge is mediated by societal notions of what a woman *should* want. A gap emerges between what women desire and what they are *supposed* to desire. As Natasha Walter argues in *The New Feminism* (1998), young women 'may feel confident and believe that now, at the end of the twentieth century, the distinction between a slut and an independent woman has broken down. [...] But they live in a world which has not yet caught up with them and in which, crucially, they do not yet have the power to protect themselves from men who have not moved towards the same ideals' (1998, 123). Walter's point perfectly illustrates the results that Deborah Tolman's study of young women and desire produces. Tolman argues that although the girls she interviewed did experience intense sexual feelings, they were not able to articulate these feelings in the ways she expected (or hoped) they would be able to. As she explains: '(w)hat I heard instead was how the social dilemma that societal constructions of female and male sexuality set up for girls, a choice between their sexual feelings or their safety, was experienced as a personal dilemma by them. Given that this dilemma is framed *as if* it were an individual rather than a social problem—if a girl has a desire, she is vulnerable to personal, physical, social, material, or relational consequences—it is in a way not especially surprising that girls would experience their desire and these resulting difficulties as their own personal problem' (Tolman 2002, 44, author's italics). Tolman's findings not only give substance to Walter's suggestion that young women live in a world that has not yet caught up with them, but also points to the way this disparity (between social and individual experience) leads young women to experience profound feelings of isolation and alienation, and no doubt, shame.

In a collection on feminism and desire, titled *Jane Sexes It Up: True Confessions of Feminist Desire* (2002), editor Merri Lisa Johnson suggests that one of the central problems that remains an issue in terms of women's sexuality is the conflict between the notion of liberation and empowerment and women's personal experience of shame and confusion. Johnson uses the name 'Jane' (referring to Jane Gallop and a poem titled 'Jane Sexes It Up') as a way of describing the contradictions of female desire in contemporary society. *Jane* is the name Johnson uses to express the 'collisions of liberated ideas with real-life situations' (2002, 24), and to argue that many young women today are 'lodged between the idea of liberation and its incomplete execution' (2002, 25). Or as she puts it: '*Jane* is the conflict. And the glee' (2002, 11). We are returned here to the tension Smelik identifies between 'politics and pleasure'.

In her introduction, Johnson mentions a different roundtable discussion, but one that nonetheless featured some second-wave foremothers of sex-positive feminism: activists such as Betty Dodson, Susie Bright, Sallie Tisdale and Nancy Friday. Part of the discussion centred on the contradiction between feminism and sexual fantasies—someone asked how they reconciled their feminism with more traditional feminine roles, fantasies, positions, etc. Susie Bright responded by saying: 'What a weird question. I think you are trying to say, How can you be a feminist in the boardroom and a submissive in the bedroom? Is that it? I don't have to "reconcile feminism", how ridiculous—I challenged feminism and demanded that it get a grip and come to terms with human sexuality' (cited in Johnson 2002, 5–6). And yet pairing feminism with submission does need to be reconciled or at least re-understood. It continues to be a precarious and uncomfortable combination and perhaps part of the reason, as I will argue, for a post-feminist rejection of feminism as a label.

In citing Bright and others, Johnson links her collection with debates in the 1970s and 1980s around pornography and female sexuality. Sex-positive feminists such as Bright countered the reaction against pornography, and to some extent, against heterosexuality, as voiced by Catherine MacKinnon and Andrea Dworkin. The cover of Johnson's collection features a topless woman whose gaze is fixed directly at the viewer.

Her biographical information on the back cover reads: '[Johnson] earned her PhD in English and has worked as a stripper' (2002, back cover). The linking of an intellectual pursuit with a profession in the sex industry sets up the conflict Johnson wants to expose between sexual desire and feminist theory. As the tag line on the cover reads: 'Does feminism's legacy liberate or repress?' The central concern of Johnson's collection is how contemporary female desire is still mediated and understood through the lens of feminism and how this mediation continues to problematise female desire. Her work, and others in the collection, implies that shame now adheres to female desire when it does not conform to the ideological tenants of feminist theory. In other words, what Johnson argues is that if a woman shares a fantasy about being dominated by a man, she is immediately told that she is unable to critically deconstruct the messages she is given by society: that she is a victim. As cited earlier, Phoca and Wright believe that many post-feminists feel sexually censored by this line of thinking. What Johnson's work does is unsettle this assumption—she is an educated woman, a woman who is very aware of the theoretical arguments against her fantasies and yet she is trying to claim them regardless. Johnson argues that it is time to accept that these fantasies are not symptomatic of a victim mentality, but rather of an opening up of a discourse of desire.

Post-feminist romance

The bold and uncompromising stance that is reflected both on the cover of Johnson's collection and in her writing shares many similarities with French film director Catherine Breillat's work. Although Johnson, and others mentioned, is working from an Anglo-American perspective and Breillat from a French viewpoint, there are many similarities to be considered. Indeed, Breillat is known in particular for her unsettling material and for confronting desire, shame and women's sexuality in uncompromising ways. She is well educated in feminist film theory and yet also draws on pornographic cinema without apology. Breillat's work evokes the affect of shame in her viewer and she is dealing explicitly with feminist film theory (abject, gaze, identity, becoming). She brings these ideas forward in a way that is very uncomfortable to her viewer, particularly a viewer who is familiar with the feminist work that she self-consciously draws on. As Liz Constable argues in her article on 'unbecoming sexual becomings': 'it is crucial to understand how Breillat's combativeness and abrasiveness unsettle complacencies about the part humiliation and shame play in women's intimate relationality' (2004, 679).

I want to focus on *Romance* (1999) and *Anatomy of Hell* (2004) in particular because these two films mark out the time period that I have already discussed and suggest that Breillat is responding not only to feminist debates in the 1970s, but also to contemporary post-feminist issues, such as those discussed in Johnson's collection. Breillat started working on the ideas for *Romance* in the 1970s[1] so this film also illustrates the constitutive links between the debates in the 1970s and contemporary ones—thus reiterating the point that questions asked in the 1970s are still largely unresolved and being reconsidered today. I will argue that not only does Breillat offer a new theorisation of desire (in particular heterosexual desire) but her work also represents an inheritance and revision of 'seventies film theory'. The criticisms of her work also signify the way in which feminism becomes a contested site among feminists. In an article on Breillat's *Romance*, Emma Wilson asks whether it is liberating for women (as both authors and consumers) to recognise the victim position as pleasurable, and considers: 'Can such works open up the way we think about active and passive roles differently? Most simply, how do we judge films and texts that seem to perform female sexual fantasies?' (Wilson 2001, 145). I think these questions are crucial to an understanding of woman and cinema today and are at the forefront of how directors such as Breillat are able to describe what she refers to as 'female shame' (Sklar 2000). However, instead of questioning, as Wilson does, the victim position as pleasurable, I would instead like to point out how this question of passive/active roles in desire is still contested. In considering the unsettling nature of Breillat's work and the reactions against it, it is clear that there is still discomfort in accepting female desires that are perceived as submissive or passive.

In an interview, Catherine Breillat acknowledges that one of the reasons she makes films is because she wants to describe 'female shame' (Sklar 2000). She also suggests that cinema, as a mode of expression, allows you to film contradictions. This is important given that both feminist film theory and post-feminism, as discussed earlier, is often characterised by its contradictions and tensions. In order to understand or appreciate Breillat's work, it is necessary to contextualise it within a broader background of a feminist questioning of the victim position, of female desire and of shame. 'To Roberto Rossellini's question, "What would a woman's vision add to the vision of love in cinema?" Breillat responds: "A woman would add the point of view of shame [...] something that people have never talked about' (cited in Constable 2004, 676). Because of Breillat's cultural cachet, the British Board of Film Classification passed *Romance* uncut, claiming that the explicit sex scenes were allowable given the film's status as a 'serious' and 'philosophical' text (Mazdon 2001, 7). And yet, as Lucy Mazdon points out, 'although the film itself may make high cultural demands upon its spectators, it does this through a negotiation of non-high cultural forms which led to a widespread media response which in turn may have created a new audience for the film' (2001, 7).

The title of Breillat's *Romance* is ironic. Indeed, Breillat's version of romance can be termed 'post-feminist' in its revaluation of previous understandings of romance. The film's beginning has attracted attention from critics such as Liz Constable and Emma Wilson who notice the way in which the male protagonist, Paul (Sagamore Stévenin), is privileged visually over Marie (Caroline Ducey), who is only visible from the back for the first few shots. When the camera does focus on Marie, she appears in stark contrast to her boyfriend Paul. As Constable points out: 'Paul's emphatic and rigidly proud body language for his photo-shot contrasts with Marie's crumpled body language of crushing dejection and humiliation despite the elegance of her immaculately tailored clothes' (2004, 689). Marie is there to watch Paul; she is situated as submissive to the dominance of his 'look'. The director, whose voice we can hear but who we cannot see, tells the female model to: 'look down, be a bit submissive' (Breillat 1999). In response to his request, she dramatically tilts her head down to Paul's shoulder. 'Not too submissive' the director responds, 'A bit submissive to the man [...] It's all in the look'. This scene sets up the central theme of the film perfectly. A man poses as a matador, the woman with him is directed on how to look submissive, and reminded that it is 'in the look'. Meanwhile, Marie looks on as observer in a pose of humiliation and shame.

In the next scene, Marie and Paul sit in a café together. He tells her that he no longer desires her physically but does not want to end the relationship. Apparently she is lucky, as he usually feels this way about a woman sooner. The next few scenes feature the couple walking along the beach, going to restaurants—typical romantic scenes—and yet the dialogue undermines any notion we might have of romance. After feeling rejected by Paul, Marie drives to a bar where she picks up Paulo (Rocco Siffredi). Marie narrates her encounter with Paulo, the first moments of touching, as 'pure desire'. She says she is 'giving in to a childish longing—a stranger making love to you'. They begin an affair, but one solely to do with physical sex. Marie leaves Paulo when she feels there is too much intimacy. The opening scenes with Paul and Paulo, who are held in contrast with each other and yet whose names imply that they are two sides of the same coin, serve as the beginning of

Marie's search for sexual intimacy. She is lacking this in her relationship with Paul but afraid to find it with Paulo.

After a shameful encounter with the school's principal, Robert (François Berléand), who has observed Marie badly misspelling words on the chalkboard in front of her young students, Marie goes over to his house. Robert presents himself as a kind of modern-day Don Juan. He has slept with over 10,000 women and believes this is because he listens to women and because his ugliness appeals to their narcissism. In the scenes between them we see the first visual expression of desire on Marie's face. Following Emmanuel Ghent's work on 'Masochism, Submission and Surrender: Masochism as a Perversion of Surrender' (1990), Liz Constable argues that: 'For Ghent, surrender, quite distinct from masochistic sub-mission, defines experiences of being "responded to" or "acted on" in adult life, experiences when subjects feel "met", or "known" without having given expression themselves to the needs that the other articulates for them and helps them construct' (2004, 692). Constable's point is crucial insofar as it makes a distinction between 'submission' and by extension 'victim' and 'surrender' which, as she argues, can lead to subjectivity. Breillat engages with the difference between these two positions in the S/M scenes between Marie and Robert. In these scenes, Marie 'surrenders' herself, and in so doing, is able to release herself from the sadness and rejection she has experienced with Paul. She is 'met' by Robert, who is interested in her pleasure as much as his own.

In keeping with her uncompromising view of desire, Breillat does not allow Marie's transformation to stop at the point she is 'met' by Robert—at the point in which we, as viewers, begin to witness a change in Marie. This transformation is represented both in terms of the emotional changes Marie goes through—we witness her sobbing in Robert's arms and confronting Paul's refusal to have sex with her—and in terms of her physicality. In the opening scenes, Marie is always dressed in white with her hair pulled back. Her posture is often hunched and submissive to Paul's confident, sexually secure body language. After her meetings with Robert, Marie begins to wear red and leave her hair down. She walks with a seductive, sexual energy. And yet it is at this moment in the film, the moment where we can visually see a positive change, that she is subjected to rape by a stranger. However Breillat leaves it somewhat unclear whether the rape is 'real' or is a fantasy. A man meets her on the stairway; he offers her a 'tenner' if she will let him lick her. She agrees and after he has done this (Marie as subject), he rapes her (Marie as object). As he runs away she shouts 'I'm not ashamed asshole'. On the one hand, her comment refuses the position of victim, but the brutality of the rape evokes both pity and discomfort on the part of the spectator.

In her article on submission and domination in *Jane Sexes It Up*, Johnson points out that it is difficult to discuss rape because there are very few ways available to women to talk about it. She argues that there are 'no words for how thin the line is between desire and domination [...] There is a cultural logic, unspoken but implacable, that if I want some (oral sex), I better want it all (a dick in me)' (Johnson 2002, 37). This logic is taken on board in Breillat's depiction of Marie's rape. The logic of 'if you want some, then you better want it all' is played out and illustrated as one of the problems women encounter in their journey towards sexual intimacy. However, Breillat chooses to deal with the consequences of Marie's rape in unexpected ways. Marie waits on the steps until it is 'time' to return home (even though she knows that Paul has returned). She does not tell him about the rape, and it is not mentioned again. Instead she is seen enjoying a decadent meal with Robert. In this way, Breillat does not allow the possibility of the viewer perceiving Marie as victim. Indeed, it is only at this point that Marie is able to articulate what she enjoys about her relationship with Robert. She reveals that she takes pleasure in his ability to 'Tie me up without tying me down'. This admission is crucial to the point Constable develops in the distinction between 'submission' and 'surrender'. Robert allows Marie the sexual pleasure of being dominated without feeling like an object of his fantasy. She feels in control of the way he controls her sexually which is contrasted with the way she is rejected by Paul. She cannot control the fact that Paul does not desire her sexually.

In the final scene we witness Marie as triumphant and alone with her child. Motherhood becomes the ultimate transformation. Although Robert is present at the birth of her child, Breillat ends the film with Marie alone, with child, barefoot, and burying Paul. His refusal to wake up and help her as she goes into labour prompts Marie to leave him in the apartment with the gas on, knowingly leaving him to die: their son's first scream as he enters the world is in sync with the apartment exploding. Marie has undergone a complete transformation, and again this is represented as much through emotional cues as through costume. In the final scene Marie is wearing a dress with red, black and white colours—embracing the full palette Breillat uses throughout the film. In this way, Breillat suggests that Marie has become a woman in control of her emotions, desire and intimacy. As Wilson suggests: 'Breillat's film shows us the way in which a woman learns to desire, and indeed perceives her affective and sexual life, in the terms of a set of classic fantasy scenarios. Reality and fantasy are utterly fused. The course of the film allows Marie through these fantasy scenarios in a line which leads ultimately to the production of a new identity, the explosion of the past and a new autonomous future' (2001, 149).

But what does this new autonomous figure offer us in terms of representations of women in contemporary European cinema? In her influential work on intimacy, Lauren Berlant reminds us that the 'inwardness of the intimate is met by a corresponding publicness' (2000, 1). No matter how private or individual the love story it must always be contained in what Berlant calls 'the institutions of intimacy'. As she argues: 'Romance and friendship inevitably meet the instabilities of sexuality, money, expectation, and exhaustion, producing, at the extreme, moral dramas of estrangement and betrayal, along with terrible spectacles of neglect and violence even where desire, perhaps, endures' (Berlant 2000, 1). Berlant's point addresses the gap between the desired image and the reality of that experience. In Breillat's handling of Marie's sexual becoming we witness Marie as object of desire and her transformation into desiring subject. We can see what Berlant refers to as the 'institutions of intimacy' in the scenes when Marie is pregnant and beholden to Paul. The realities of life intrude on any notion of 'romance' and she makes a decision (prompted by the birth of her child) to literally explode him and his version of romance. Although Marie's decision to blow up the apartment can be read as liberating, it can also be seen, along with the apocalyptic ending, as Breillat needing to resort to fantasy because reality will not allow for such a permanent and violent transformation.

Woman, man, desire

Whereas *Romance* considers the shame that accompanies fantasies of surrender/submission, *Anatomy of Hell* takes shame a step further in considering how the female body itself is positioned as shameful, particularly in terms of the male gaze. The film begins in a gay nightclub. A woman walks towards the toilets and on her way brushes past a man. He turns around, affected by her touch, and goes into the bathroom to find her cutting her wrist. In the next scene, the woman has been treated by a doctor, as she goes towards the man, he imagines her cutting her throat open. Both scenes are very graphic and unsettling—again, as in *Romance*, Breillat is uncompromising in her choice of images. She upsets the viewer and unsettles any possibility of watching her film for entertainment only. As the couple walk away from the clinic they argue about the positions men and women take in desire. The woman kneels down and gives the man fellatio, then offers him money to come to her house and 'observe' her as she is observed by other men. Again, within the scene we are given an example of a woman being both submissive, but also taking responsibility for her own desires, being in control of the situation.

The rest of the film takes place in an abandoned house on the coast. The man arrives, ready to be paid to observe the woman. What follows are confusing, dream-like 'nights' (four in total) where the two learn about each other and their sexuality. For the most part, the woman is perceived as 'in control' of the situation (particularly since we know she is the one paying and the one who owns or is renting the house). And yet in most scenes she submits her body for the man's gaze: she willingly surrenders herself to his touch, desires and interest. The fact that he is gay adds a different dimension to the encounter and does not allow us to think about the engagement between them as simply 'heterosexual': instead we are forced to consider them solely as 'man' and 'woman' and any relation between them as one of intimacy and curiosity. In this way, Breillat creates new terms for intimacy between men and women, and in the end, the man has been permanently altered in his thinking. He tells a stranger at a bar: 'I experienced total intimacy with her and I don't even know her name' (Breillat 2004). He can no longer conceptualise 'woman' in the same way (and perhaps Breillat's hope is that neither can her viewer). In other words, he now understands that women are not as different from men as he imagined; they are not as 'other' to him as he once expected, or even desired, them to be.

The characters in *Anatomy of Hell* are known solely as 'the man' (Rocco Siffredi) and 'the woman' (Amira Casar). The fact that Breillat casts Siffredi as 'the man' again evokes the pornographic as Siffredi is a well-known Italian porn star, director and writer; his recent films include *Dirty Dreams* (2005), *Nasty Trails* (2005) and *Rocco Ravishes Ibiza* (2005).

As in *Romance* Breillat is not only evoking the pornographic but is also making reference to Lacan's infamous edict that 'there's no such thing as a sexual relationship' (1998 [1975], 12). However, with this phrase, Lacan is not referring to sexual relations, instead he suggests that 'the impossibility of founding the sexual relationship is strictly coextensive with the conundrum of sexual difference' (Fink 2002, 6). In this instance we are presented with the impossibility of the sexual relationship in terms of linguistic structures versus the impossibility as experienced through social experience. Breillat manages to convey this contradiction through the juxtaposition of this 'man' and 'woman' and through her narration. It is worth noting that at the end of *Romance* Marie states unequivocally that 'love between man and woman is impossible', which again reiterates both Lacan's point and Breillat's interpretation of his theorisation of sexual difference.

Sexual difference and anatomy are taken on directly in *Anatomy of Hell*. In one scene, the woman asks the man she has paid to observe her to pull out her tampon. She then dunks it into a glass of water again and again until the glass is filled with red liquid. She reminds him that people used to 'drink the blood of their enemies' and then hands him the glass. They both drink the blood-soaked water which becomes a suggestion of a mutual pact—or a unity between this man and woman over the shame that she might have felt from her menstruation. The woman asks why men are afraid of menstrual blood. She tells him that he probably feels that if his penis is covered in blood that he is injured. Does he become a victim, tainted by the same blood as woman? Knowing this man is gay, she asks why he is not troubled by faeces and yet is uncomfortable with blood. She answers for him and guesses that what is inert is not as threatening as that which is life-giving. He does not respond but continues to observe her with a mixture of curiosity and disgust.

Iris Marion Young discusses the potential shame in menstruation that faces women: 'No matter how hard she works to conceal this fact of her womanliness, however, others, especially men, always have it as a switch to beat her with, a stigma with which to mark her as deviant, a threat of exposure which to harass and humiliate her' [...] 'The harm here is that of producing shame and stigma by others revealing what the dominant norms say should be hidden' (2005, 116–117). Young's comment reveals several important aspects of shame: its public nature—there is always an 'other' involved with shame (even if this is an imagined self); there is a interplay between concealing and revealing that is inherent to shame; and finally, women must act according to the dominant norms or risk being exposed (and therefore shamed) by others. Using film as a medium of expression, Breillat is able to illustrate the public nature of female shame. In viewing a scene such as described above, viewers are literally caught in the moment of shame, witness to the exposure, involved in the interplay of concealing and revealing. As Jennifer Biddle reminds us: 'shame is even more contagious. [...] Witnessing someone else being shamed and/or the converse, witnessing when someone ought to be ashamed and they aren't, is likely to induce shame in response' (1997, 230). As viewers, we are shamed both in terms of watching this woman and also in terms of what this woman exposes us to. This is one of the strengths of Breillat's work— to expose us to the 'point of view of shame' and to allow us to see how intimately it is linked to female desire and sexuality.

In the final scene of *Anatomy of Hell* the 'man' pushes the 'woman' over a cliff and into the sea. Similar to scenes discussed in *Romance*, the ending is artistic and dream-like, and we are left unsure whether it is a fantasy or reality. The blurring once again suggests an unfinished nature to the questions and issues Breillat raises. It also suggests that although the man has learned something about female sexuality and intimacy, he cannot live with this knowledge—and so must kill her in order to survive. We are returned here to Berlant's notion of intimacy and the limitations in which new constructions of intimacy are allowable. The knowledge that the man and woman have achieved through their excessive experience of intimacy cannot be contained, instead this intimacy is violently rejected.

Post-feminism and shame

In her work on shame in cultural theory, Elspeth Probyn begins her chapter on feminism and shame with the following statement: 'I've been shamed by feminism—what feminist hasn't?' (2005, 75). She goes on to recount an experience of being shamed when asking a question at a feminist conference. The keynote speaker publicly ridiculed her by asking 'What is it about these frigid women?'(Probyn 2005, 76). This is a telling kind of shame: to reduce a woman to shame by referring to her sexuality. Despite all the work that has been done in feminism, it is still the case that even feminists themselves will often shame other women because of their sexual practices. Sexuality and desire continue to be areas which draw shame and morality from their feminist readers more so than pleasure and enjoyment, and this paradox is explored within Breillat's work.

However, shaming can also be found in criticism of Breillat's work and underlines the discomfort viewers have with Breillat's presentation of shame and desire. Emma Wilson points out that the film's 'too excessive material' often invites 'knee-jerk and macho derision' (2001, 156); it is hard not to hear in this analysis a resonance of 'she asked for it' and reiteration of Johnson's point that there is an unspoken cultural logic that if a woman expresses her desire then she better be ready to receive a full and even violent response. One might expect to hear this kind of 'knee-jerk' derision from male journalists who are uncomfortable with the 'unbecoming' nature of the desire Breillat describes. However, there is also criticism from feminist theorists who understand Breillat to be re-inscribing objectification of women through her references to the pornographic. I would argue, however, that this criticism is as 'knee-jerk' as the macho derision from male journalists. It does not take on board what the allusions to the pornographic allow—that they re-consider and re-appropriate these images in terms of female desire. In other words, Breillat offers up these fantasies not to objectify the women in her films but to suggest that not all women's fantasies are the same and that some women fantasise about being submissive. This does not make them victims or objects, particularly because Breillat contextualises these fantasies in the minds (and also in the control) of her female characters. Dismissing these moments and claiming the women are not 'in control' of their own desires or shaming them for having these desires perpetuates both repression and anger on the part of women who feel censored and morally judged. Probyn argues that 'any politics not interested in those who are placed beyond its ken will continue to be a politics of shaming: a bastion of moral reproach' (2005, 106). Her comment suggests that feminism must take seriously and analyse critically the 'choices' and sexual practices of women within contemporary society if it is to progress and adapt its politics.

In her work on Deleuze and nomadics, Rosi Braidotti argues that 'becoming nomadic means you learn to reinvent yourself and you desire the self as a process of transformation. It's about the desire *for* change, for flows and shifts of multiple desires. Deleuze is no Romantic. Deleuze's nomadology stresses the need for a change of conceptual schemes altogether' (2003, 53, author's italics). What comes through post-feminist work and recent work within feminist film criticism is a desire to change the conceptual frameworks that have held 'woman' in place over the last thirty years. However, as Constable's article illustrates so well, there is a resistance within critical theory to accept these 'unbecoming' sexual becomings. Instead of seeing shame and humiliation as degrading, for instance, Constable reads these affects as constitutive of transformation and as playing a role in women's intimate relationality. Breillat's films are capable of opening up new ways of understanding female desire, but only if these representations are considered within a new framework, not if they are going to be consigned to old debates and tensions. I am not suggesting abandoning the work that has been done, but rather recognising the limitations and parameters that new representations are set in and arguing that these need to be carefully reviewed. Indeed, feminist work has confronted these issues before now. In her work on feminism, Sheila Rowbotham remembers experiencing the contradictions between feminist ideology and her own desires. In 1966, at a meeting discussing Juliet Mitchell's 'The Longest Revolution', 'a woman got up and said, "Women should control their own bodies". The thought flashed through my head, "What about the times I want to be out of control?" Twenty years later the thought still hovers' (Rowbotham 1989, 61). The point that Rowbotham makes is that she wants to be in control of when she is out of control—that she might fantasise moments of surrendering and does not want these to be figured as 'unallowed'. Another twenty years on and feminists such as Johnson and Breillat are still questioning why women must censor their fantasies, their sexual desires and their sexual becomings. It is perhaps important then to think about the productive potential in shame, as Probyn does in *Blush*, to consider how shame allows women to imagine and invent new relationships to desire.

Although I am indebted to Constable's work, I think that her use of surrender over submission effectively dodges the problems feminists have with submission and with the idea of woman in a passive posture. It is a clever and important way of re-thinking this relationship, but it does not address the issues from the 1970s regarding submission head on. In work such as in Johnson and Breillat, they are not renaming the experience of submission, they are claiming it for everything it represents, and there is a power in this acceptance. On the other hand, there is clearly a danger that is felt by feminist theorists around the acceptance and approval of submission, which suggests that there has not been any real development in the way we consider the relationship between submission and power.

To return to the problem posed at the beginning of this chapter, in order for feminist film criticism to truly become 'an increasingly heterogeneous and dynamic set of concepts and practices', it need not get rid of concepts such as 'desire' and 'gaze', but instead to challenge and reconsider the frameworks that have been used to understand these concepts. We need to review the way they have been theorised and consider new ways of doing so, particularly through the work of contemporary film makers. We also need to challenge the framework, used so often by the media that holds the 1970s film criticism on one side, and new, recent film theory on another. As I argue, there are not enough developments or differences to pit one as 'old and frumpy' and announce the next as 'new and sexy'. Understanding the arguments, tensions and contradictions that took place in the 1970s enables us to avoid falling into the same traps and encourages us to reconsider our fears and discomforts with 'unbecoming' becomings. This knowledge allows us to review work such as Catherine Breillat's in terms of how it constructs a new discourse on female desire instead of dismissing it with knee-jerk reactions and feminist shame.

Breillat's work is unknown to many and so it seems necessary to pose a question regarding how these representations, these unbecoming becomings, are handled within the sphere of popular culture? Probyn argues that 'popular culture is a rich ground for the propagation of shame'; 'Television', she suggests, 'in particular exploits the individual viewer's response to what resembles an intimate shameful moment, which is aired for all to see' (2005, 85–86). Her observation raises questions such as how are issues concerning submission, surrender and shame dealt with in mainstream work? And how might we theorise desire on television? In order to address these questions and raise others, I will turn to the popular, mainstream television programme *Sex and the City*.

Sex, shame and the city

Popular television programmes such as HBO's *Sex and the City* have been appropriated by a diverse range of feminist and non-feminist readings. Many have celebrated their empowering effect on audiences—encouraging girls and women alike to feel more comfortable to talk about sex and desire. Articles such as Astrid Henry's 'Orgasms and Empowerment: *Sex and the City* and the Third Wave Feminism' not only suggest that the programme allows for female empowerment through a renewed discourse of desire but also that it engages directly with third-wave feminism. Others such as Joke Hermes's '*Ally McBeal, Sex and the City* and the Tragic Success of Feminism' take a different tack, firstly in identifying the programme as post-feminist, but also in taking on board the viewers' perspectives through her engagement with 'jumptheshark.com', an online web forum. Her conclusion: 'There is a lot of feminism in popular culture, but there is also a lot of old rot, that, it needs to be said, apparently continues to offer a great many viewers much pleasure' (2006, 93). Hermes's diagnosis is an important one, for, however much we may deconstruct, analyse, or apply our feminist theoretical toolbox, there is always the reality that viewers want, enjoy and take pleasure in these kinds of representations. My point here is not to write another 'ur' article, as Brunsdon so aptly puts it, in which I would apply my feminist critique to the programme and assess the ways in which it succeeds and fails; I have done this before (Gorton 2004), along with many others. Instead, the reason I refer to these programmes in my examination of female desire in contemporary culture is because they are so accessible, so enjoyed and for the most, so celebrated. The other way to look at this is through more popular images of surrender/submission.

Sex and the City has received a wide range of feminist responses: from empowering to consumeristic. 'Great Sexpectations' begins with Carrie's new romance with Berger (at a burger joint). They are going through the 'firsts' of their relationship ('it's a very intimate thing, shopping for a shower curtain') before leading up to their first time having sex. Despite passionate kisses in stores and restaurants, when they reach the bedroom there is silence and apathy. The couple are shown having mechanical, passionless sex. Carrie tells the girls later that it was so quiet that she could hear the 'M11 Bus'. She tells Miranda in confidence that the sex was 'not good' that there was 'no throw down, more like a slow down'. Later in the narration of the programme Carrie describes Charlotte's boyfriend Harry as 'definitely having throw down'. This phrase 'throw down' refers to the act of surrender, however it is couched in the anodyne rhetoric of the programme. When Carrie asks Samantha for advice she tells her: "Fuck me badly once, shame on you; Fuck me badly twice, shame on me.' Again the notion of shame accompanies desire—this time the lack of it.

Samantha's character is perceived as sexually liberated—in control of her desires. We, as viewers, have every confidence that Samantha is not submissive. She surrenders herself to her desires, not someone else's. In the final series, Samantha meets Jerry Jerrod (who she re-names 'Smith Jerrod'). On their 'first date' we see them in every imaginable position with each other throughout the night and far into the next day. In 'Pick-a-little, Talk-a-little' they begin a series of fantasy scenarios—she is tied up and he is physically dominating her, they are both detectives, etc. The episode opens with a domination fantasy in which Samantha is the housewife (complete with rollers in her hair and slippers on her feet) and Jerrod is the intruder. She tells her friends: 'And then he pretended to tie my hands behind my back and the whole time he kept screaming "Shut the fuck up." I tell you, it's so refreshing to be with someone who likes to fuck outside the box.' Charlotte replies: 'That is incredibly offensive. Violence against women is a very serious issue' to which Samantha replies: 'All fantasies are healthy and harmless.' When asked what he thinks about all this, Berger responds: 'As a guy I've always been under the impression that rape or anything in the rape family is not a good idea. Can I go home now?' His mock innocent question is met by laughter from the women, and the scene shifts from a discussion of Samantha's fantasies to Carrie's friends 'accepting' her new boyfriend.

Initially the fantasy is destroyed when Smith Jerrod admits that he does not drink—and so Samantha's order of two martinis is re-phrased as 'a martini and seltzer' which destroys the aesthetics of her fantasy. She meets him again and he offers her a new game. 'Hotter than secret service sluts?' she asks. He replies: 'I'm me, you're you.' 'It spoils the fantasy' Samantha tells him. She is very reluctant, but surrenders, giving in to his desires to 'know her'. In another episode, Samantha runs into her old love, Richard Wright, and goes with him to a hotel room. They have sex over the bathroom sink which allows us to see Samantha's expression. For once it is clear that she is not enjoying herself and it appears as though she is crying. The camera then closes up on her as she takes a very slow ride down the elevator. The doors open and Jerrod is there waiting for her. 'I don't know what is wrong with me. I hate myself for doing this to you', after which she breaks down and is helped out of the hotel by Jerrod. The voice-over tells us: 'Even in the dark, Smith could still see Samantha, and for the first time, she could see him', thus explaining the episode's title: 'Let there be light'. The scene is very uncharacteristic of Samantha's character and leads to an intimate and monogamous relationship with Smith, also uncharacteristic for Samantha.

This popular example allows us to think through the more complex and arguably more problematic examples offered by Breillat. It also raises the way in which these examples offer us a 'becoming' reading of becoming—the transformation, desire, shame and surrender is watered down, dressed up and made palatable for more mainstream audiences. This is as much a consequence of television as it is a consequence of what we are willing to take in.

In her work on melodrama, Mulvey argues that

> It is as though the fact of having a female point of view dominating the narrative produces an excess which precludes satisfaction. If the melodrama offers a fantasy escape for the identifying women in the audience, the illusion is so strongly marked by recognisable, real and familiar traps that escape is closer to a day-dream than to a fairy story. Hollywood films made with a female audience in mind tell a story of contradiction, not of reconciliation. Even if a heroine resists society's overt pressures, its unconscious laws catch up with her in the end.
>
> (1989, 43)

Here we have a possibility of engagement with the contradiction and ambivalence that is noted in feminist criticisms of television programmes such as *Sex and the City* and *Ally McBeal*. We also have the notion of a woman's point of view—and perhaps not only one of excess, as Mulvey suggests, but also one of shame (as Breillat's work suggests). Mulvey's final point—that the unconscious laws of society catch up with women in the end is perfectly illustrated in the final episode of *Sex and the City*. Carrie finally gets 'Mr. Big', Miranda settles down with Steve and her son in the suburbs, Charlotte and Harry adopt and Samantha finally settles down with Jerrod. Each woman is monogamously coupled and returned to the certainty of heterosexuality, and, one could say, an unspoken script of Western society (that a woman in her thirties or early forties should marry and 'settle down'). It would be impossible to suggest that this is in any way a challenging or unconventional end to what is a contradictory and dynamic text.

What Breillat's work and popular television programmes such as *Sex and the City* suggest is that discomfort and shame around female desire persists. As Tolman's study illustrates, there is still a need to discover a discourse on desire. There is also the need to have various representations of desire presented on screen, as it remains the most accessible way for women to engage and think about their own relation to desire, particularly sexual desire. Indeed, Probyn suggests that 'popular representations of sexuality can provide fertile ground for the airing of shame' (2004, 86), which allows new discourses to emerge and new relationships to desire to be formed. From something as simple as *Sex and the City* which presents Carrie's desire for true love, Samantha's desire for consistently good sex, Miranda's desire for self-fulfilment and Charlotte's desire to love and be loved, to Breillat's critique of surrender and submission in heterosexual romance, these various representations of desire allow viewers a chance to consider their own desires and their relationship to them, however fragile and tenuous.

Televisual desire

A reading of desire in *Sex and the City* invites a consideration of how to theorise desire on television. John Ellis has argued that 'TV is more about the look, and the glance and sound' than the cinematic gaze (cited in Moore 1989, 50). However, with the increase in DVD box sets and digital recording devices (such as Tivo) we might question whether viewers are watching more intensely than a look or a glance. Indeed, the popularity of television programmes such as *Sex and the City* suggest that their audiences are watching with an intense gaze and that they might often re-watch episodes (or seasons) on DVD.[2] Instead of addressing the question of how to theorise desire on television with a conclusive answer, I want to pose various possibilities. To begin it seems useful to think about the space between the viewer and the screen itself and to consider some ways of theorising both this space and our relationship, as viewers, to it (Elsaesser 1992). Sara Ahmed's *Queer Phenomenology* (2006) considers the ways in which we orientate ourselves towards objects— she is thinking in particular how this orientation or direction affects sexuality, but I think her argument can be extended to think about how we orientate ourselves towards the television. The object, television, directs our gaze, our attention and our emotions. Or do our emotions direct our bodies? Can we consider desire on screen part of how we think people respond to that desire, what it means to them, how they relate to it and to what extent it is desirable for them.

One of the most successful ways television represents desire is through tension—and we can think of numerous examples in which characters are held in tension with each other in order to elicit this desirous response, and yet the parameters of the episodic structure often mean that this desire inevitably needs to be 'solved'—the viewer wants the couple to get together. In terms of the narrative, this poses a fundamental difference from film—film can leave desire elusive and abstract, 'ineffable' as Pence suggests, whereas television must remedy the tension and expose the desire.

We could take a Deleuzian approach and think about the materiality of television and perhaps we are talking here of the white space, the empty time—which some have called television's 'raw materiality'.[3] This empty time can be theorised as a place for viewers to enter in their own desires—to imaginatively project their emotions and to explore these through the emotional situation the characters are in. Ien Ang has gone some way to consider this, in particular with her theorisation of 'melodramatic identification' (1985, 1996), however her theorisation is couched within psychoanalytic understandings of fantasy. Instead, we could consider Deleuze's theorisation of 'affective-images', which will be explored in more detail in the next chapter, to consider how, for instance, close-up shots are used to elicit affective responses. One of the obvious problems with this approach, however, is the increasing lack of white space on television.

Or we could think about desire in terms of how people watch television. In his lecture on 'broadcast television and the social contract', Thomas Elsaesser argues that 'desire when watching TV becomes manageable and meaningful by making not morons, but specialists of us all' (1992, 14). He refers to the ways in which we watch for the smallest details in order to confirm our knowledge of a programme or character. He goes on to suggests that 'we watch in the endlessly renewable hope that politicians and celebrities will give us the "psychopathology of public

life," when a momentary hesitation, a sideways look, an unguarded gesture, an awkward stride will unmask them as impersonators and impos-
tors, catch them out as players and performers' (1992, 14). Elsaesser's
suggestion that desire comes through in the ways in which viewers
want to know the intimate details of television's content can be linked
with Lauren Berlant's work on the intimate public sphere. We can theorise desire in terms of the ways in which viewers gain knowledge about
the intimate lives of their favourite soap characters, reality show partic-
ipants or talk show guests. The desire for the details of these characters
functions in a similar way to the process of getting to know a beloved
(and we can extend this theorisation to think about why people enjoy
celebrity magazines). It reiterates the suggestion made by contemporary
theorists that we are living in an increasingly isolated and alienated
society—where people look for intimacy on screen (whether on television,
the internet, film) instead of finding it in other people.

Following recent work by Ahmed on 'orientation', I want to think
about the possibility of moving beyond psychoanalytic models or
Deleuzian approaches (lack vs production) in order to think through a
phenomenological approach. Ahmed's work on sexual orientation and
phenomenology encourages us to think about how we are orientated
or directed physically—and I think there is room here to consider the
space between the screen and the viewer as an object of study, as discussed previously. Ahmed argues that certain objects act as 'anchoring
points' (2006, 1)—and what better one in the home than the television
itself, which often provides its occupants with a sense of home and, as
Ahmed suggests, of orientation. Theorising desire from this perspective
allows us to think more concretely about how viewers orientate themselves towards what they watch and allows us to consider what they
want to get out of that experience. It also allows us to consider how the
'lived body'—the one snuggled up on the couch with a glass of wine,
responds to something as abstract and enigmatic as desire. Television,
perhaps more than film, allows us to consider how desire is theorised
through the everyday.

And finally, I think we could usefully consider Sartre's concept of
desire as 'trouble' and think of the moments in television where 'trouble' is used to create the tension and struggle that I referred to earlier—
a moment when the programme attempts to work through desire and
does so by troubling the situations the characters find themselves in;
though, as previously discussed, this is usually resolved—whether that
means bringing two people together or allowing a character to achieve
something he or she desires.

What this brief consideration of theorising desire on television demonstrates is that a combination of approaches, psychoanalytical, philosophical, phenomenological, work better to begin answering the question of desire than following one theoretical model. It also reminds us that desire, as a concept, is elusive and therefore requires a multi-layered approach to considering how it affects its audiences. Furthermore, juxtaposing a reading of shame and submission in French film with a mainstream American television programme illustrates the limitations and possibilities of each medium to tell us something about desire, and more specifically to transmit the 'point of view' of shame that accompanies female desire.

5
Melancholia and Desire

> Desire presses to be written, to be narrated: people find
> it exhilarating to tell their stories
>
> (Catherine Belsey 1994, ix)

The preceding chapters have theorised desire in terms of risk, hysteria, melodrama and shame—the final chapter will consider the relationship between desire and melancholia. Melancholia, like shame, has a profound affect on the viewer, drawing the spectator in and making her feel the sadness and loss that the characters experience. I will argue that this affect lends a new dimension to a theorisation of desire.

This chapter will also address how films tell stories about desire and yet do so in a way that resists any final interpretations. In creating ambiguous terms, ones that resist meaning and formulation, films suggest that language is incapable of speaking the 'beyond' of desire; to insist on a singular meaning of desire denies its elusive nature. The directors discussed in this chapter, Alain Resnais and Wong Kar-wai, achieve this partly through their use of repetition, and this formal characteristic will be examined in particular. This chapter will consider psychoanalytic concepts such as melancholia and lack, but will do so in conjunction with affect theory and Deleuze's work on cinema. One of the aims of this chapter is to argue that affect theory dislodges the centrality of desire within psychoanalytic theory and moves it along a register of affect. This movement is important because it suggests a way of theorising desire that moves beyond the restrictive boundaries of psychoanalytic theory and away from any simple opposition between psychoanalysis and Deleuzian conceptualisations of desire.

Duras and desire

I have chosen to focus on Marguerite Duras's work, in particular *Hiroshima Mon Amour* (1959) (for which she wrote the screenplay), because Duras's work has been deployed in psychoanalytic, feminist and Deleuzian interpretations of desire. Lacan wrote a 'Hommage' to Duras in which he claimed that 'Duras proves to know without me what I teach';[1] Feminist scholars have long been interested in Duras, and as Karen Ruddy's article on the 'ambivalence of colonial desire' in Duras's *The Lover*, suggests: 'there has been a veritable explosion of scholarship on Duras's work, particularly amongst feminists' (2006, 78), and Deleuze draws on both Duras's work and Resnais', who directed *Hiroshima Mon Amour*, in *Cinema 2*. Because Duras has been claimed by psychoanalytic, feminist and Deleuzian models of desire, her work provides an opportunity to think through these various models and to the problems that surround each competing interpretation. Her work also gestures towards her own understanding of the concept of desire, as this chapter will explore.

What Duras's films present is a troubling understanding of the concept of desire and of desire as a process that does not have any finite beginnings or endings. The women in her films are represented as inhabiting desire in a melancholic state. Desire is embodied in the characters and expressed in various ways: as something that can release the past, as something that is contained in the past, as something that produces connections and forges new bonds and as something that is destructive and annihilating. Desire is about the potential to cause all these things and is foremost an unsettling affect—it is characterised by its movement, its intensity and its ability to cause change.

In *India Song* (1975), for instance, Duras disrupts the continuity between the images on screen and the soundtrack which creates an unsettling affect for the viewer. Although the viewer might see two characters on screen talking to each other, they may hear the sound of crickets or of a woman's painful mourns or the background hum of a cocktail party. The lack of continuity between image and sound forces the viewer to take in the images and their noises, rather than following the narrative itself. As Duras explains:

> The 'voice-off' is completely justified to my mind. I find it totally satisfying. I had the actors record the voices first. Delphine Seyrig heard her own voice and so she didn't have to worry about her lines. She no longer had to use her memory to act. She was freed from the script. All she had to do was listen. So, then we got a sort of simultaneous

absence/presence of the actors. The image loses its supremacy and the spoken word becomes more important. So then the dialogue is no longer between a particular man and woman but rather between their essences.

(Duras, *South Bank Show*, 17.11.85)

The 'voice-off' creates a disruption between dialogue and image that encourages the viewer to enter into the affect of desire created on screen. In this way, desire is theorised as something both inside and outside the text—something that can be captured by the senses and something that eludes them.

Duras's *India Song* develops from a moment, which I have referred to elsewhere as a 'critical scene of desire' (Gorton 2003; 2007). By 'scenes of desire' I mean a textual location where an author or critic attempts to define or interpret desire. I use the word 'scene' for several reasons. The first refers to the descriptive quality in an author's or a critic's attempt to construct an event of desire. She or he paints a 'scene' of desire in language or constructs one within a theoretical framework. For example, in *The Ravishing of Lol V Stein* the 'critical scene of desire' is a moment during the South Tahla Ball when Michael Richardson, fiancée to Lol V Stein, is seduced by Anne-Marie Stretter, a woman who literally haunts Duras's texts, and whom she has described as a muse for her work.[2] Both the novel and the film end with Anne-Marie's suicide and with a sense of loss: the melancholia that pervades the film is still present at the end. Despite an author's or critic's attempt to pin down desire in language, it often remains a mystery. For this reason, I suggest that 'scene' reflects a performative quality in desire. Desire can be thought of in terms of movement—it moves within literary and theoretical texts. Any attempt made by a critic or reader to formulate an answer or construct a framework to contain the question of desire usually results in failure.

In Duras's film *Moderato Cantabile* (1960), again based on the novel of the same name, similar themes of melancholia and loss are explored, this time through the narrative of Anne Desbaresdes (Jeanne Moreau), the wife of a wealthy factory owner. *Moderato Cantabile* begins with a *crime passionel*, a man has murdered a woman in a crowded café. The woman's dying screams are heard through the small town, and Anne is mesmerised by the noise. She is in the middle of listening to her son's piano lesson and his teacher's demands that he play 'moderato cantabile'. She leaves her child's lessons and goes to look through the café window, along with the other townspeople who have now gathered around the crime scene. She is transfixed by the man's expression as he gently caresses the face of the woman he has just murdered. The police pull the man away as his gaze meets Anne's. The following day Anne returns to the café, curious to know more about the crime. She begins to talk to a man, Chauvin (Jean-Paul Belmondo), who works at her husband's factory and spends his days in the café. The two begin a relationship that is based solely on their curiosity about the crime passionel. They meet to discuss the possible reasons why the man killed his lover in such a public place; they consider the events that led to this passionate moment. As they discuss their ideas in intimate conversations, the townspeople begin to suspect them of having an affair. As a result, Anne is no longer able to carry out her daily routines and can no longer keep up the appearance expected of her. For instance, at a formal dinner party at her house, she is seen drinking too much and leaving the table to find refuge in her son's bedroom. Her husband comes upstairs and expresses his disappointment, and yet it is clear that she is too far removed from the situation to feel any sense of embarrassment or shame. Indeed, when she takes her son to his piano lessons and the teacher tells her she should be ashamed, she responds in a desultory tone: 'So they say'. At the end of the film, Anne returns to the café in the middle of the night to meet Chauvin. He is leaving the town and her, and she is devastated by this loss. She tells him that she will never be able to talk to anyone again, to which he replies: 'Yes, one day you'll talk to a child, or just anybody. It will be a fine day and you will want to tell someone. It will begin again, for us' (Duras 1997 [1958]). The final line, the promise of a refrain gives the viewer some hope, and yet the harsh lights that fill the café, coming from her husband's car, offer a bleak future for Anne. The film closes with her getting into the car: returning to the closed and passionless confines of her suburban existence.

The central female figures in Duras's fiction are often housewives, mothers or schoolgirls, people who would be considered ordinary and yet, as the texts reveal, they are enigmas to other characters as well as to their readers and critics. Duras's choice of an 'ordinary' woman can be interpreted as a way of undermining assumed and enculturated images of desirable women or as offering her male voyeur a clichéd fantasy: a nameless, faceless woman who is solely interested in his own desires. Although similarities can be drawn between Duras's female characters and Lacan's theorisation of lack and 'woman', the 'lack' in Duras's fiction is not filled or constituted by male desire. The sense of absence that begins the text is still in place at the end of the narrative. Duras does not try to 'cure' the 'lack' in either character. Instead, Duras's texts demonstrate how desire creates connections and builds foundations. In other words,

Duras's texts allow us, as readers, to think about the productive possibilities in the movement of desire. Duras's work gestures towards a way
of thinking about desire outside of 'lack' and acquisition (Gorton 2007).

Hiroshima Mon Amour

Hiroshima Mon Amour, directed by Alain Resnais and written by Duras,
is the story of a man and a woman who meet in Hiroshima and have a
brief affair. The woman is in Hiroshima starring in a film about peace;
the man, an architect, is from Hiroshima. They are both happily married with children, but nonetheless find passion and comfort with each
other. Neither character is given a name, and we never find out how
they met.

The film begins with the couple in bed together, their bodies indistinguishable and covered in a sparkling mist, which Duras writes can
represent 'ashes, rain, dew, or sweat, whichever is preferred' (1961, 15).
Emma Wilson argues that the 'shots of the lovers exist as a metonym ...
which functions both as part of the film, and as a sequence of images
which sums up the film's themes' (2000, 35). According to Duras, the
image of the embrace should 'produce a violent, conflicting feeling of
freshness and desire' (1961, 15). The first line of the film: 'You saw nothing in Hiroshima. Nothing' evokes the notion of remembering, forgetting and loss which dominates the text. However, the historical event of
Hiroshima becomes secondary to the love affair between the man and
woman, a problematic aspect of the film that I will return to later.

The couple meet again during a peace march, and return to the man's
home. There the woman begins to remember the traumatic loss of her
first love, a German soldier who is killed just as the war comes to an
end. The process of her remembering and 'letting go' dominate the narrative and is the primary focus of their conversations. When they move
from his house to a local café, she continues to tell the man the story of
how she met this German soldier, how she was physically and verbally
abused by the townspeople from Nevers when they discovered her
transgression, how her parents kept her hidden in the cellar, and eventually how she left Nevers and the tragedy behind her and went to Paris.
As she tells the man her story she begins to become hysterical, and as
she shouts, 'He was my first love ...' (1961, 65), the Japanese man slaps
her (1961, 66).

One of the reasons I have chosen this scene is that it responds well to
Marks's concept of the 'skin of the film', discussed in Chapter 1. There
is a materiality to the scene that draws the viewer in and involves her,

so much so, that the slap is almost experienced by the viewer. The snap return of the sounds of the café slaps the viewer back into the social reality of the present in the film—it returns the spectator from the past to the present and to the forgetting that is taking place. Deleuze suggests that 'whether it is visual or of sound, the image already has harmonics which accompany the perceived dominant image, and enter in their own ways into suprasensory relations' (2000, 158). There is a tension produced here with the quick cut from the flashback to the scene in the café. The pace of cutting speeds up and we are presented with close-up shots of the present landscape having been in the world of both the past and of Nevers. The contrast between these two worlds: both of Hiroshima and Nevers, and the past and present is ruptured through the physicality of the slap. It draws us out of the past, out of remembering/forgetting and into the process of 'letting go' that is presented to us. We can also understand this moment to function to what Deleuze refers to as an 'interval' 'which divides immediate action and reaction (what Deleuze refers to as a 'degree zero' of perception) from affects (where I feel but do not act) and acts (where I respond *for* this sense I have of what life ought to be)' (Colebrook 2006, 75). In other words, it divides the image from actions: 'I feel but do not act, or I recall another image that alters how I might respond' (Colebrook 2006, 75–76). Resnais constructs this interval—dividing us from the action of the slap and the reaction of the woman by splicing images from the reactions of people in the café into the pause. This alters how we, as viewers, might have responded initially and delays our reaction until we are returned to the close-up shot of the woman and her perplexing smile. In the screenplay the stage directions read: 'The Japanese slaps her. [Or, if you prefer, crushes her hands in his]. She acts as though she didn't know where it had come from. But she snaps out of it, and acts as though she realised it had been necessary' (Duras 1961, 66).

The woman's ambiguous smile is troubling and is difficult to know how we, as viewers, are supposed to respond to the fact that she has been slapped. She seems to appreciate the way it draws her back, keeps her from entering into a hysterical fit. And yet we as viewers might resent this action, particularly on the part of the woman. It creates a tension and unease—and constructs a limit to how far the Japanese man is willing to participate/collaborate in the forgetting. Following Butler's work on melancholia and power, we could read the scene as a kind of 'acting out', 'an aggression that break[s] out of that circuit only to heap itself, through displacement, on objects which signify ... the remains of the lost other' (1997, 162).

In the flashbacks to the woman's past, we are invited into the way the trauma of losing her beloved not only made her experience grief and loss, but also shame at the hands of the women in the town. They cut her hair, a symbol of her beauty, in order to punish her for her transgression. Desire functions in many ways here: as a mode of self-definition—the young girl falls in love with a German soldier, goes against everything she has known in her town, and risks losing everything—and eventually does. It functions as a rite of passage, a becoming and as a mode of destruction. Desire also functions in the present as something that can retrieve the trauma of the past and let it go and this is signified both in her recollection of the past (the moment when she starts to see things again and 'winter is over' and in the moment with the Japanese man ('I tremble at the thought of having forgotten so much love' (Duras 1961, 63–64).

This is where problems begin to emerge, however, and we see the limitations of psychoanalysis and the intervention of work on affect. Freud argues that '[i]n melancholia the relation to the object is no simple one; it is complicated by the conflict due to ambivalence' and this 'ambivalence' is either something that resides in the person or 'else it proceeds precisely from those experiences that involved the threat of losing the object' (2001 [1957], vol. 14, 256). In other words, it is a relation that is always there, in the person, or is present in the situation that proceeded 'falling in love'. The ambivalence structures both the feeling of loss, and I would argue the expression/affect of desire.

Desire and melancholia

Joanne Brown argues that Freud's 'Mourning and melancholia' (1917) 'challenges [Freud's] Cartesian frame of reference, i.e. the sharp division between the body and the mind ... and between the split subject/object' (2000, 41) in her work on the 'psychoanalytic sociology of emotion'. This confusion is visually represented in the scene between the Japanese man and French woman: she confuses the Japanese man with her beloved German soldier. She talks to the Japanese man as though he were the German soldier. In so doing, she transfers her desire from the lost object (German soldier) to the Japanese man.

Freud suggests that 'each single struggle of ambivalence loosen the fixation of the libido to the object by disparaging it, denigrating it and even as it were killing it' (2001 [1957], vol. 14, 257) and this is clear in *Hiroshima*—the woman is aware of the way she is 'forgetting' and how this forgetting will lead to a second death of her beloved (this time in her mind). One death is physical (she could not tell which body was her) and one is mental (she begins to own her own desires again).

In her work on 'unbecoming' sexual becomings in Catherine Breillat's films, discussed in the last chapter, Liz Constable argues that through shame, Breillat's female characters are able to 'let go' of past trauma. Following Emmanuel Ghent's work on 'Masochism, Submission and Surrender: Masochism as a Perversion of Surrender' (1990), she argues that: 'For Ghent, surrender, quite distinct from masochistic submission, defines experiences of being "responded to" or "acted on" in adult life, experiences when subjects feel "met", or "known" without having given expression themselves to the needs that the other articulates for them and helps them construct' (2004, 692). I see a similar model operating in Duras's work, where the woman and man feel 'met' for whatever reason, and that this connection, forged through desire, allows them each to unfreeze past psychic trauma—to 'let go'. And yet, I am cautious here because I do not think that this 'letting go' should be given such a precedent, nor do I think Duras's work insists upon this kind of reading. Duras's women are melancholic and this is something that irritates Kristeva in *Black Sun*. Kristeva argues that Duras's women have a 'sickly core': 'It is a non-dramatic, wilted, unnameable sadness. A mere nothing that produces discreet tears and elliptical words' (1989, 239) and yet, it is this 'unnameable sadness' that moves the narrative along. In *India Song* and *Moderato Cantabile*, the women are left with this 'sickly core' they are not as redeemed or liberated as the woman in *Hiroshima* appears to be. I think we, as feminists, often want to read for this kind of ending. And this call to a positive or joyful conceptualisation of desire has recently been expressed by Rosi Braidotti. She tells us that 'I actively yearn for a more joyful and empowering concept of desire and for a political economy that foregrounds positivity, not gloom' (2002, 57, see also Braidotti 2006, 230). However, as Sara Ahmed has suggested, 'the very assumption that good feelings are open and bad feelings are closed ... allows historical forms of injustice to disappear. Or if they do appear, they would be read as symptoms of stubbornness rather than present and ongoing aspects of the world we have inherited. We need to think about how histories of injury stay alive and how the demand for happiness can make those histories disappear or project them onto others, as a kind of bad inheritance: as melancholic ...' (2006, 16). In an excellent collection by David L. Eng and David Kazanjian titled *Loss: The Politics of Mourning* Judith Butler argues that 'Loss becomes condition and necessity for a certain sense of community, where community does not overcome the loss, where community *cannot* overcome the loss without losing the very sense of itself as community' (2003, 468). I would argue that Duras's texts keep melancholia in place and I think this is linked to her theorisation of desire, which I will go on to explain further.

In their introduction to *Loss*, Eng and Kazanjian suggest that 'melancholia results from the inability to resolve the grief and ambivalence precipitated by the loss of the loved object, place or ideal' (2003, 3) (hence why they divide their collection into 'bodily remains', 'spatial remains' and 'ideal remains'). And there is clearly a reference to the remains of loss in *Hiroshima*. The two characters are named by the places they have endured loss: Hiroshima and Nevers; they are haunted by the loss and by the discovery of a loved object. Desire attaches them to this object and to the grief that accompanies losing this object.

Butler suggests that loss has its own 'dynamism, if not its own dance' (2003, 469) and this is a persistent theme in Duras's work, particularly in *The Ravishing of Lol V Stein* and in *India Song*. The entire narrative of *Ravishing* revolves around the night of the South Tahla Ball when Michael Richardson leaves his fiancée, Lol V Stein, in order to dance with Anne Marie Stretter—a figure that haunts most of Duras's texts. In *India Song*, the central female figure is constantly dancing with different men in slow, tired waltzes, which evokes both the heat and humidity of India and the languorous movement of desire Duras captures. Butler argues that 'If suffering, if damage, if annihilation produces its own pleasure and persistence, it is one that takes place against the backdrop of a history that is over, that emerges now as a setting, a scene, a spatial configuration of bodies that move in pleasure or fail to move, that move and fail to move at the same time' (2003, 472). Hiroshima emerges in the film as a setting, a scene and as a backdrop to the very personal, individual and intimate relationship between this man and woman. What is the effect of using Hiroshima as this kind of landscape? Emma Wilson suggests that '*Hiroshima Mon Amour* seems to testify to the failure of memory and the artifice of representation' and goes on to suggest that 'For the female protagonist, forgetting seems to bring little solace but only horror at the loss of memory traces which have allowed her to remain present in her own past history' (Wilson 2000, 33). Deleuze argues that '*Hiroshima Mon Amour* complicates matters still more. There are two characters, but each has his or her own memory which is foreign to the other. There is no longer anything at all in common. It is like two incommensurable regions of past, Hiroshima and Nevers. And while the Japanese refuses the woman entry into his own region ('I've seen everything ... everything ... You've seen nothing in Hiroshima, nothing ...), the woman draws the Japanese into hers, willingly and with his consent, up to a certain point. Is this not a way for each of them to forget his or her own memory, and make a memory for two, as if memory was now becoming world, detaching itself from their persons?' (Deleuze 2000, 117–118)

In citing these interpretations I want to draw attention to two things: firstly the suggestion that Wilson makes that 'forgetting' brings little solace to the woman, and secondly, Deleuze's notion of memory becoming 'world'—of memory becoming detached from the individual and entering the social. What is illustrated here is a long standing contrast between a feminist reading which perceives lack as something negative—Wilson is concerned, as Kristeva has been before her, about how Duras leaves her female characters with melancholia—how her narratives keep this in place. In contrast, Deleuze offers a productive reading of the loss that remains (and therefore we can understand why many feminist film scholars, such as Kennedy and Marks, have turned to Deleuze to re-theorise feminist understandings of materiality and desire). However, what I want to draw from this is Duras's use of melancholia as a fundamental part of desire and as something that has its own movement, its own intensity. As Butler suggests, melancholia is often perceived as static and stagnating, however, if we think counter-intuitively we might begin to appreciate the way in which the loss which remains becomes part of the desire which emerges.

Colonialising desire

Work by Homi Bhabha, Gayatri Chakravorty Spivak and Edward Said constitute what Robert J.C. Young refers to as the 'Holy trinity of colonial-discourse analysis' (1995, 163) and have inspired analyses that consider the implications of colonialism on desire and desire on colonialism. In this section, I want to return to Deleuze's suggestion that the two memories become 'world' and make a link here with Ranjana Khanna's work on 'worlding' in *Dark Continents*. I am conscious that I have not addressed the colonising aspect of Duras's film, and although I do not have room to adequately explore these ideas, I want to consider ideas that are inherent to the rethinking of psychoanalysis offered in Khanna's work and to refer to the potentially problematic way in which Duras uses Hiroshima as a landscape.

First, drawing on work by Heidegger and Spivak, Khanna offers an understanding of 'worlding' that positions psychoanalysis as a 'colonial discipline' (2004, 6). Second, she argues that the 'individualisation of memory and the individual's responsibility to *remember* historical events for the sake of the group enables "successive generations to mediate their cultural myths by inculcating them with their desires" ... the group or nation is to *remember to forget* in order that the future can be willed into existence' (2004, 12, author's italics). Part of what *Hiroshima* explores is the way in which memory, desire and melancholia are fused together and linked to the process of remembering and forgetting. However, the woman's narrative of loss dominates the text and begins to take precedence over the landscape of Hiroshima. As Duras writes: 'Their personal story, however brief it may be, always dominates Hiroshima. If this premise were not adhered to, this would be just one more made-to-order picture ... If it is adhered to, we'll end up with a sort of false documentary that will probe the lesson of Hiroshima more deeply than any made-to-order documentary' (1961, 10). Duras imagines the love story and its dominance to give greater depth to the history of Hiroshima, however, it can be argued that the precedence of the love story moves Hiroshima to the background and privileges a white, Western woman's loss and grief over the loss and suffering of those who experienced and continue to experience the devastation of Hiroshima.

Indeed, it can be argued that Duras's female character maintains her position as 'other' and as 'stranger' to the landscape—she is able to leave her mourning behind. At the end of the film the Japanese man calls her 'Nevers' as if to name her distance from Hiroshima. And yet she calls him 'Hiroshima' which suggests the closeness between them. In her work on 'strange encounters', Sara Ahmed argues that colonial encounters necessarily involve a complex relationship between distance and proximity: 'Colonial encounters disrupt the identity of the "two" cultures who meet through the very process of hybridisation—the meeting of the "two" that transforms each "one."' This intermingling and closeness is demonstrated through the intimate relationship the couple form and the way in which their melancholia affects each other. And yet, as Ahmed goes on to argue: 'just as the conditions of meeting are not equal, so too hybridisation involves differentiation (the two do not co-mingle to produce one). How others are constituted and transformed through such encounters is dependent upon relationships of force' (2000, 12). Although the two are affected by each other, the woman is able to leave— she does not need to take responsibility for the distance and difference between them.[3]

In her article on the ambivalence of colonial desire in Duras's *The Lover*, Karen Ruddy argues that the 'city of Saigon provides not only the backdrop for the narrator's reconstruction of her desire ... Saigon itself is produced in the text as a territory inscribed with the flows of colonial desire' (2006, 82). Following Ruddy's analysis, it is possible to suggest that Hiroshima, as backdrop to the love affair between the man and woman, becomes a space for remembering and forgetting. At the end of the film, it is clear that the woman will leave both her lover and her past behind, thus constructing Hiroshima as a repository of loss. This argument throws the notion of the woman's liberation from her past through her involvement with the Japanese man into racialised borders. As Ruddy goes on to suggest in terms of *The Lover*: 'Duras elaborates a fantasy of the Orient that simultaneously ruptures and recuperates Orientalist discourse by presenting the white woman as the subject of colonial desire' (2006, 83). Reading the girl in *The Lover* as melancholically attached to her whiteness, Ruddy argues that this attachment highlights the 'ambivalence of both white identity and colonial desire' (2006, 93).[4]

However, in leaving her female characters with an 'unnameable sadness', Duras keeps the melancholy in place; she does not seek to clarify this ambivalence rather to maintain the messiness. What this does is suggest a kind of agency within melancholia regarding those feelings, emotions and desires that cannot be resolved. As Khanna suggests, there is a critical agency in melancholia, 'melancholia represents the ghostly workings of unresolvable conflict within the colonial subject' (2004, 30). Far from simplifying or overlooking the affects of colonialism, Duras's work illustrates the unresolvable consequences they have on desiring subjects.

Instead of thinking through desire and colonialism through the lens of psychoanalysis, it may be useful to think through the ambivalence with regards to work by Deleuze and Guattari, which Robert J.C. Young does in *Colonial Desire* (1995). Noting that Deleuze and Guattari's work has been relatively absent from discussions regarding postcolonial theory, Young argues that their work produces a social theory of desire that 'cuts through the problematic psychic-social opposition of orthodox psychoanalysis' (1995, 168). For Young, Deleuze and Guattari's representation of capitalism as a desiring machine in *Anti-Oedipus* not only reflects the development of industrialisation but also the violent process of colonialisation. Deleuze and Guattari's figuration of the desiring machine and their concept of territorialisation allow Young to map out an 'ethnography of colonial desire' which is marked by a 'dialectic of attraction and repulsion' (1995, 174–175). Although Khanna and Young approach the notion of colonial desire through different theoretical registers (psychoanalysis and Deleuze and Guattari), they each stress the ambivalence that marks the movement of desire.

Desire and affect

I want to gesture towards the ways in which work on affect dislodges the centrality of desire in psychoanalytic interpretations and moves it along a register of emotions from desire to loss, desire to anxiety and desire to melancholia.[5] What Duras's films evoke is the importance desire has on one's emotional state and the way these affects (melancholia, loss) act together to produce transformation or change within the subject. Once the subject has lost her co-ordinates of desire she must re-map them, and this is what Duras's films present: a way in which desire is re-mapped, re-coordinated through loss, forgetting and melancholia. In this way, desire is both an individual and a social experience. Unlike a psychoanalytic model of desire which poses the question of desire in terms of the Other, and in terms of the individual, desire is figured in terms of what it does and how it moves people.

I would also argue that Duras's presentation of desire's affect on the subject affects her viewers. Viewers are moved by the desire, loss and melancholia within the film and in a sense can begin to appreciate the importance desire has on identity, self and culture. Duras's work captures the affect of desire and translates this 'feeling' to her viewers. In so doing, her work presents a unique opportunity to reconsider what desire does and how it is theorised.

In the second half of this chapter, I want to introduce Wong Kar-Wai's work in *In the Mood for Love* for it explores similar issues regarding desire and melancholia, but uses repetition in particular to draw out a different understanding of desire's relationship to melancholia. Like Duras's work, Wong Kar-wai's films also manage to capture a 'feeling' of desire through his use of melancholia and repetition; he creates situations in which his characters must return to events in order to make sense of them. However, in the case of *In the Mood for Love*, the couple is not remembering past events, instead they are trying to repeat events in order to understand them. In so doing, they begin to fall 'in the mood for love', which leads to further complication. Whereas *Hiroshima Mon Amour* deals with the memory and its relation to desire, *In the Mood for Love* focuses on loss and the performance of desire.

Desire and repetition

In order to consider how repetition functions within *In the Mood for Love*, I will first outline the way repetition has been understood within psychoanalytic theory and in work by Deleuze. Freud reflects on the developments within psychoanalysis in *Beyond the Pleasure Principle* and explains that psychoanalysis was 'first and foremost an art of interpreting' (2001 [1955], vol. 18, 18). In other words, the analyst's job was to uncover unconscious material, construct a history from the patient's memory and explain it to her. As Freud points out, however, this method did not prove successful. And so, another aim, to compel the patient to confirm the analyst's construction from her own memory, also came into play (2001 [1955], vol. 18, 18). This aim involved trying to overcome the patient's resistances and was achieved through transference. However, as Freud points out, transference requires the patient to '*repeat* the repressed material as a contemporary experience instead of [...] *remembering* it as something belonging to the past' (2001 [1955], vol. 18, 18, author's italics). This process sets up a difference between what is remembered and what is reproduced, the former being more desirable than the latter.

What Freud argues is that the compulsion to repeat overrides the pleasure principle—that is, patients will repeat repressed and often painful material even though it is not pleasurable to do so. So, for example, Freud refers to people whose love affairs constantly go through the same phases and reach the same ends and yet they do nothing to avoid this kind of repetition. And here we might think of the cliché that women like 'bad boys'—although women often know certain kinds of men are not 'good' for them, they will get involved with them all the same. For Freud this is understandable because the subject is actively making this choice. On the other hand, what Freud finds more unbelievable are the examples of people who keep getting themselves into situations over which they have no control. Whether passive or active, these instances prove to Freud that there is a compulsion to repetition that is more powerful than the pleasure principle and which demonstrates the ability of the mind to work through and remember trauma.

Lacan claims repetition as one of the four fundamental concepts of psychoanalysis. Following Freud's work in *Beyond the Pleasure Principle* (1920–22), Lacan understands repetition not as a return of the same thing, but as an entirely different thing: the two events are separate.[6] Lacan argues that Freud's theory on repetition compulsion was based on the insistence of speech, the compulsion on the part of the subject to have the final word (1993 [1981], 242). For Lacan, nothing is more enigmatic than the process of repetition (1994 [1973], 50–51). The word repetition itself is close to the verb, 'to haul', as Lacan points out, 'very close to a *hauling* of the subject, who always drags his thing into a certain path that he cannot get out of' (1994 [1973], 51).

In his seminal work on difference and repetition, Deleuze argues that the turning point in Freudian psychoanalysis appears in *Beyond the Pleasure Principle* where Freud discovers that the death instinct is in connection with the repetition phenomena (1994 [1968], 16). He points out that Freud noted that in order to 'stop repeating it was not enough to remember in the abstract (without affect), nor to form a concept in general, nor even to represent the repressed event in all its particularity: it was necessary to seek out the memory there where it was, to install oneself directly in the past in order to accomplish a living connection between the knowledge and the resistance, the representation and the blockage' (1994 [1968], 18). The dramatic process that this involves is transference, which for Deleuze is repetition: 'If repetition makes us ill, it also heals us; if it enchains and destroys us, it also frees us' (1994 [1968], 19). For Deleuze, repetition is a powerful way of freeing the subject from its own repression.

Happy Together

Wong Kar-wai's films *In the Mood for Love* and *Happy Together*, both evocatively titled, gesture towards a way in which desire is theorised through repetition and melancholia, through the repeated instances of love offered in the texts. My primary focus will be on *In the Mood for Love*, but I want to begin with reference to *Happy Together* because most of this book has centred on heterosexual desire. *Happy Together* (*Cheun gwong tsa sit*, 1997), set in Argentina, is the love story of two Chinese men who have left Hong Kong for a holiday. The film begins with their 'starting over' and with their attempt to go see the Iguazu Falls. Lai Yiu-Fai (Tony Lueng Chiu Wai) narrates their story and tells us from the beginning that Ho Po-Wing's (Leslie Cheung) favourite phrase is 'Let's start over' which, as he suggests, has many meanings. Indeed the phrase 'let's start over' becomes a dominant trope in the film— initially referring to their relationship, but eventually used by Yiu-Fai as he tries to reconcile his relationship with his father. The film uses the phrase 'let's start over' to mark out the different attempts the couple take at a 'new' beginning. At first they 'start over' by deciding to drive to the waterfalls, but along the way they get lost and instead return to Buenos Aires. When Po-Wing is badly beaten after prostituting himself, they 'start over' by living together in Yiu-Fai's flat. This period is the happiest for Yiu-Fai, or so he reflects once Po-Wing has left him again. While Po-Wing is recovering he cannot leave Yiu-Fai or go back to prostitution, so for once, they are 'happy together'. Frustrated with his life in Argentina,

Yiu-Fai returns to Hong Kong to 'start over', primarily in terms of his relationship with his father, although the film does not explore this in any detail.

On the one hand, the film considers the futility of 'starting over' when one partner is unable to change. We can return here to Belsey's construction of the 'profoundly anti-social couple', discussed in Chapter 3, and to the way in which this couple obsesses over every argument or happy moment. Indeed, the film revolves entirely around the couple itself and their inability to be 'happy' together. On the other hand, the film introduces this repetition, this 'starting over', as part of what it means to be 'happy together'. In order for both characters to move forward they must first move backwards with each other. Their inability to be 'happy together' is not so much a failure of their love for each other, but rather, an indication of their individual need to be happy on their own. In the end, Yiu-Fai achieves this happiness, but it is at the expense of his relationship with Po-Wing.

In the Mood for Love (Fa Yeung Nin Wa, 2000)

The intensity of the relationship created between Yiu-Fai and Po-Wing is similar to the attention paid to the two central characters in Kar-wai's acclaimed *In the Mood for Love*. Set in 1962 Hong Kong, the film centres on two neighbours, Chow Mo-wan (Mr Chow) and Su Li-zhen (Mrs Chan), who discover that their partners are having an affair with each other. Mrs Chan's husband is often away travelling, and Mr Chow's wife is often away visiting her parents. It is not until Mrs Chow is seen with the same handbag Mr Chan has given his wife that the truth of their continual absence is revealed. When Mrs Chan discovers her husband's infidelity she decides to tell Mr Chow and the two become involved in an attempt to figure out how the affair began.

The act of repeating and performing the imagined affair results in an erasure of the original moment—the path is repeated endlessly which slowly erases the reason for their mimicry. The affair that is at once so central to the text slowly becomes secondary, if not invisible, to the process of repetition—to the performance of the affair itself. In this way, the film emphasises the movement of desire as more important than an arrival or ending. In the act of repeating the affair the couple begin to recognise a desire for each other that they had not previously felt. In the case of *In the Mood for Love* we might also refer to the repetition the couple perform as a kind of mimicry. And therefore we might think of considering work by Luce Irigaray, who understands mimicry as a kind of 'playful repetition' constituted as a challenge to masculinised discourse (1985 [1977], 76). Indeed, there is an inherent playfulness to the text regarding the way the couple perform at being their partners and play at what they might say if confronted by the affair.

Kar-wai uses music to underscore the melancholic atmosphere of the film. He uses shots of Mrs Chan walking down steep concrete stairs to get noodles from the 'congee' again and again, which underlines her loneliness and isolation. The music which accompanies these scenes, in conjunction with the slow panning of the camera, emphasises the sadness Mrs Chan feels even before she is aware of the affair between her neighbour and husband. The majority of camera shots in the film position the viewer as someone who is peeking in on the events happening on screen, which emphasises both the enclosed atmosphere in the film and builds the sense that the couple are being watched or feel watched. In one scene, for instance, the corner of the building is held in frame and the couple are off to the right, as though, we, the viewers, are watching them unnoticed. This camera angle positions the viewer, in some respects, as a voyeur and invites us to fetishise their relationship in the same way they are fetishising the affair between their partners.

Kar-wai also uses shots of the characters' legs, or feet, or the backs of their heads—fragments of the body. As spectators we never actually see Mr Chow and Mrs Chan's partners. We see Mr Chow's wife from the back as she talks to him on the phone, again from the position of someone watching from afar. In many scenes the camera shoots down the narrow hallways in the apartments where Mr Chow and Mrs Chan live. These tight shots emphasise the way in which each couple is watched by the other members of the house. When Mrs Chan starts coming home late, she receives a lecture from her landlady, Mrs Cheun, who advises her to tell her husband that he should not travel as much as he does. The fragmented shots also function to keep our attention on Mr Chow and Mrs Chan; indeed, we never see the faces of the other couple. In choosing to keep them anonymous from us, as viewers, Kar-wai places emphasis on the repetition, rather than the 'original'—there is no chance for us to privilege the other couple's desire over the one between Mr Chow and Mrs Chan. As viewers, we are not allowed to see what is happening between the other couple—like Mr Chow and Mrs Chan we are kept from knowing what their desire really looks like, and so the repetition becomes more important than what is being repeated.

In the process of comforting each other, the couple begin to fall in love with each other, as if by mistake. 'I thought we wouldn't be like them. But I was wrong', Mr Chow tells Mrs Chan. 'I didn't think you'd fall in love with me', she replies. 'I was curious to know how it started. Now I know. Feelings can creep up just like that' (Kar Wai Wong 2000). The notion that feelings 'creep up' and can take hold without notice suggest the power of desire's movement, as I will go on to discuss in terms of affect. It also suggests that repetition does not only produce the same thing, but also constructs new formations. Following Deleuze's notion of repetition, Colebrook writes: 'Any repetition, because it is a repetition *of* something that is not itself, is also the production of a difference: one can either play down this difference or push it to its limit' (2006, 15–16). *In the Mood for Love* plays with the consequences of repetition pushed to its limits and thus offers a productive interpretation of desire.

In the final scene, set in Cambodia in 1966, Mr Chow has taken his secret, the secret of his desire for Mrs Chan, to a sacred site and whispered it into the hole of a tree, thus rendering any possibility of their desire impossible. The final refrain goes as follows: 'He remembers those vanished years as though looking through a dusty window pane; the past is something he could see, but not touch. And everything he sees is blurred and indistinct.' As mentioned previously, the camera shots make us, as viewers, feel as though we are watching the events from behind a window pane—from the position of a curious onlooker. This establishes the way in which the couple themselves look on, in their imagination, at what they imagine their partners to be doing. There are no scenes of confrontation between the couples, only a rehearsed one in which Mrs Chan practices asking her husband about his affair with Mr Chow. She cries in his arms, taken by surprise by how much it hurts. In the end of the film we know that Mrs Chan has left her husband and lives alone with their son, but the two are never reunited.

However, in the film often referred to as a sequel to *In the Mood for Love* titled *2046*, Kar-wai revisits the narrative and suggests new possibilities for the desire between the two lovers. Although the film captures a similar sense of melancholia and repetition to *In the Mood for Love*, it lacks narrative continuity and loses the viewer in its attempts to theorise desire in terms of time and space. The movements from 2046 to 1966 suggest a linearity and continuation of desire; however, the development of this cinematically is difficult to follow.

In both *Hiroshima Mon Amour* and *In the Mood for Love*, the labour of memory work is presented and, in both cases, it is performed by a couple that is relatively unfamiliar with each other. The intimacy that develops between the couple is a direct result of the memory work they perform. In each case this memory work involves narratives of desire—whether of the past, in the case of *Hiroshima*, or, of the present, in the case of *In the Mood for Love*.

In her work on 'resisting left melancholia', Wendy Brown reminds us that 'the irony of melancholia, of course, is that attachment to the object of one's sorrowful loss supersedes any desire to recover from this loss, to live free of it in the present, to be unburdened by it. This is what renders melancholia a persistent condition, a state, indeed, a structure of desire, rather than a transient response to death or loss' (Brown 2003, 458). Both films deal with this structuring of desire through melancholia. Not only do the stories tell us about their desire and melancholia but the camera angles, the music and the lack of narrative closure allude to the potency of this mixture.

Affective-images

In the final part of this chapter I want to think about the structuring of desire through melancholia by focusing in particular on each director's use of partial/fragmented shots. Drawing on work by Deleuze in *Cinema 1* I want to suggest that each film creates what Deleuze refers to as 'affective-images' through the use of close-up shots. Part of Deleuze's project in his turn to cinema is to consider how it creates new ways of seeing things and even new ways of understanding philosophy. As discussed in Chapter 1, unlike a psychoanalytic approach to cinema, where meaning or interpretations are drawn from the text, Deleuze is interested in seeing what the text *does* instead of what it *means*. Instead of applying philosophy to cinema, Deleuze is interested in mapping out how cinema can teach us something about philosophy.[7] As Colebrook writes: 'Our everyday seeing of the world is always a *seeing from* our interested and *embodied* perspective ... Cinema, however, can present images or perception liberated from this organising structure of everyday life and it does this by maximising its own internal power' (2002, 31, author's italics). Deleuze is interested in how the cinematic apparatus opens up new connections and therefore encourages us to think differently about the world.

In *Cinema 1*, Deleuze distinguishes between two points of view used in the close-up: the face as an outline which includes all the features of the face (the mouth, the nose, even a hat) he refers to as 'faceification' [visagéification] and the fragmented parts of the face (the lips, a certain look' he refers to as 'faceicity' [*visagéité*] (2005 [1983], 90). Although Deleuze puts desire under the categorisation of 'faceicity' he reminds his reader that a distinction should not be made between the full face as reserved for 'tender emotions' and the fragmented face for 'dark passions' (1986 [1983], 91). Deleuze draws on work by Balázs (1952) in order to consider how the close-up removes the image from its spatio-temporal co-ordinates. However, unlike Balázs, Deleuze argues that this affect is not just reserved for the close-up of the face, but can also be extended to consider fragmented parts of the body such as the hand, or the back of the head. In other words, Deleuze argues that any close-up on the body is able to tear the image away from its spatio-temporal co-ordinates 'in order to call forth the pure affect as the expressed' (1986 [1983], 99). He goes further to add that 'even the place, which is still present in the background, loses its co-ordinates and becomes "any space whatever"' (1986 [1983], 99).[8]

In *What is Philosophy?* Deleuze and Guattari argue that 'affects are no longer feelings or affections; they go beyond the strength of those who undergo them. Sensations, percepts, and affects are *beings* whose validity lies in themselves and exceeds any lived' (1994, 164). Affect therefore is something more than simply *feeling*; affects produce sensations that *move* those who experience them. Deleuze and Guattari's notion of affect lead them to consider artists as creator of affects, capable of drawing us, the audience, into their understanding of the world. As they write: 'It should be said of all art that, in relation to the percepts or visions they give us, artists are presenters of affects, the inventors and creators of affects. They not only create them in their work, they draw us into the compound' (1994, 175). 'Drawing us into the compound', artists possess the ability to invent new worlds, create new ways of seeing things and therefore, to *move* their audiences through affect. In her work on Deleuze, Claire Colebrook writes: 'Affects are not actions (or powers exerted) but *powers to*. Is not cinema the power to *feel* fear, desire, tragedy or melancholy without oneself being afraid, desirous, afflicted or depressed?' (2006, 63, author's italics). Colebrook's question regarding the cinema's power to present affect is addressed at the beginning of Brian Massumi's work on movement, affect and sensation in *Parables for the Virtual* (2002). At the start of his chapter on the 'autonomy of affect', Massumi refers to an audience research project involving nine-year-old children. They were asked to watch three version of a short and simple film (of a snowman melting): one wordless, one with a factual narration and one with an 'emotional' narration and to rate the scenes both on a '"happy-sad" scale and a "pleasant-unpleasant" scale' (2002, 23). The results illustrated that the children preferred the 'sad' scenes, as Massumi puts it: 'the sadder the better' (2002, 23). However, this data only revealed one half of the story. The children were wired to monitor their physiological reactions, and these findings suggested that the version that made them happiest was the one with a factual narration, even though this one was rated as the most 'unpleasant'. For Massumi and the other researchers, this study illustrates the *'primacy of the affective* in image reception' and the gap between *'content* and *effect'* (2002, 24, author's italics). The study illustrates Deleuze and Guattari's assertion than affects 'go beyond the strength of those who undergo them' and highlights the inter-relationship between body and mind in terms of affect and desire.

In thinking about the opening montage in *Hiroshima Mon Amour*, described earlier, we can connect the movement of bodies with Deleuze's assertion that 'the close-up does not divide one individual, any more than it reunites two: it suspends individuation' (1986 [1983], 102). There is a difference in thinking about the bodies as united or reunited and indistinguishable from each other. The lack of individuation draws the spectator's attention to the affect the bodies produce—the sense of 'desire and freshness' that Duras is alluding to. In considering the way in which affects are registered, Deleuze argues that 'Affects are not individuated like people and things, but nevertheless they do not blend into the indifference of the world [...] It is like points of melting, of boiling [...] This is why faces which express various affects, or the various points of the same affect, do not merge into a single fear which would obliterate them' (1986 [1983], 106). This idea is important in terms of a theorisation of desire—because desire can be understood as containing a variety of affects (joy, shame, disgust) which produce an affect of desire. In other words we do not need to think about desire as just one affect but the presence or the melting of many affects.

If, as Deleuze suggests, that the close-up is able to tear a part of the body away from its spatio-temporal co-ordinates, then there is a link to be drawn here between the way in which desire draws the subjects out of their spatio-temporal co-ordinates and the way the camera sustains this through close-up shots. In other words, the camera heightens the narrative displacement and emphasises the way in which desire causes the subject to lose his or her sense of self and belonging in the world. If we return to Michael Winterbottom's *Code 46*, it can be argued that in meeting Maria, William loses the co-ordinates of his desire—he is no longer sure of himself or of his actions, instead he finds himself drawn to her almost hypnotically.

Once the subject has lost her co-ordinates of desire she must re-map them,[9] and this is a way in which desire is re-mapped, re-coordinated through loss, forgetting and melancholia. In this way, desire is both an individual and a social experience. Unlike a psychoanalytic model of desire which poses the question of desire in terms of the Other, and in terms of the individual, desire is figured in terms of what it does and how it moves people, in other words, it is figured in terms of movement.

In *In the Mood for Love* desire is re-mapped through repetition and performance. One couple follows the others' movements and in so doing, begins to feel the affect of those movements: they begin to fall in love in spite of themselves (or in spite of their partners). The film implies a deep connection between affect and desire. It suggests that the affects of desire are powerful enough to change the feelings of those who perform their movements.

Examining issues of melancholia and repetition lead us to a fundamental critique of desire—that of movement, and it is present in all the models of desire discussed so far—in the risk-taking individual, the repressive hysteric, the excessive melodramatic, the shameful submissive and the melancholic lover. It also underlies a psychoanalytical, Deleuzian, feminist, cinematic and an affective theorisation of desire. Therefore, if we take movement, we can theorise the way it affects the audience, particularly, with regards to this chapter, how this functions in terms of melancholia and repetition. In her reading of Deleuze and cinema, Colebrook argues that 'Cinema frees affect or the power of images from a world of coherent bodies differing only in degree, and opens up divergent lines of movement to differences in kind ... For Deleuze this has political ramifications, for it helps to explain how we *as bodies*— respond and desire forms (such as Fascism) even when they would not be in our interest' (2002, 39–40, author's italics). Colebrook offers the example of political rallies, where the music, speeches and colours draw demonstrators in both in terms of what we can see and hear, but also what we feel; as Colebrook suggests: 'our bodies respond positively to these pre-personal "investments"' (2002, 40). Part of what we respond to are the affective memories we may have about these kinds of events and this propels our desire to participate and to respond to the affects these events produce. In her work on trauma, sexuality and lesbian public cultures, Ann Cvetkovich talks about the all-girl mosh pits at the Michigan Womyn's Festival and relates her own positive experiences participating in these seemingly dangerous spaces. She argues that 'The "violence" of Tribe 8's performance, and the physical release that the mosh pit enabled, can be understood as a ritualised repetition that transforms earlier scenes of violence [...] Indeed, the power of the notion of safe space resides in its double status as the name for both a space free of conflict *and* a space in which conflict and anger can emerge as a necessary component of psychic resolution' (Cvetkovich 2003, 87, author's italics). Cvetkovich's discussion of 'safe space' and mosh pits provides us with an opportunity to draw out some of the central ideas this chapter has raised. Her argument takes on both a psychoanalytical and an affective account of space, desire and embodiment which is related, in part, to the examples we have explored in *Hiroshima Mon Amour* and *In the Mood for Love*. In each film, the couples' desire for each other creates a 'safe space' through which they can re-visit past traumas and which enables them to release the pain and anger that accompanies trauma. However, the emphasis of this movement is not on psychic resolution, rather on the affective-images these couples produce. In other words, the emphasis within the cinematic examples is on producing the affect of desire on the psyche rather than on resolution. What this offers the viewer is the sensation of desire—of desire as affect and of desire as *movement*. It also provides a model of desire-as-process which enables us to focus more specifically on what desire *does* rather than what it *is*.

Conclusion:
Desire and Embodiment

Throughout the book I have made reference to ways in which the body is affected by desire. By means of conclusion, I want to focus on this issue, in particular, in order to attend to the ways in which the body and desire work together to figure desire as movement. In her work on 'embodiment and moving image culture', Vivian Sobchack reminds us not only of the vast amount of work done in contemporary theory on 'the body', but also that 'we matter and we mean through processes and logics of sense-making that owe as much to our carnal existence as they do to our conscious thought' (2004, 4). The distinction Sobchack draws between 'carnal existence' and 'conscious thought' seems apt in a theorisation of desire and this book has admittedly focused more on the thought than the carnality, but, as Sobchack points out, we owe both for our ability to make sense and to make meaning. We also need to avoid falling into an opposition between mind and body and instead move towards thinking about how the two function together, particularly in terms of what desire does.

In addressing notions of embodiment, sexual difference and the materiality of the subject in *Metamorphoses* (2002), Rosi Braidotti argues that the 'construction of a thinking subject cannot be separated from that of a desiring subject' which reminds us that 'desire is the first and foremost step in the process of constitution of a self' (2002, 71). Following the concept of 'becoming' that is fundamental to both Irigaray's and Deleuze's theoretical work, Braidotti argues that 'nomadic embodied subjects' demonstrate that their power of thinking is not a reflection of interiority but an expression of the 'outward-bound nature of the subject' (2002, 70). In other words, the nomadic subjects' mobile nature illustrates their ability to think differently and establish connections. Although my reading of Michael Winterbottom's *Code 46* in Chapter 1 drew more from a psychoanalytical tradition than a Deleuzian one, it is possible to return to the issues the film raises and consider how Braidotti's figuration of the 'nomadic subject' becomes useful in thinking about Maria's character, how embodiment and desire are figured in terms of William's rehabilitation and how the two present ideas about theorising desire.

At the end of the film, Maria is exiled to 'al fuera' (the outside); she has been sent there as punishment for her transgression of 'code 46'—for her affair with William. As discussed, it is from this position, from the outside, that Maria questions the role of destiny and fate; she considers: 'If we had enough information we could predict the consequences of our actions [...] If we knew what would happen in the end would we ever be able to take the first step to make the first move?' (Winterbottom 2003). Maria's questions echo Braidotti's assertion that desire is the first and foremost step—it is our desire to know that draws us into action, whether or not we know what consequences will accompany our decisions. It is William and Maria's desire to know more about each other that leads to their self-knowledge. Maria's return to 'al fuera' repositions her as a nomad—as someone without a home, someone who is looking to belong somewhere. This status as 'nomad' is emphasised by Maria's appearance and the desert-like landscape that is used to represent 'al fuera'. She is alone, moving and yet we are sure that she has no real destination. In her figuration of the 'nomadic subject', Braidotti argues that the nomad 'does not stand for homelessness, or compulsive displacement; it is rather a figuration for the kind of subject who has relinquished all idea, desire, or nostalgia for fixity' (1994, 22). If we imagine Maria as a 'nomadic subject', as someone who has given up any hope or desire for permanence, then she stands in direct contrast with William, who is figured in the final scenes as someone who possess an entirely fixed sense of self: reflected in his home, wife, child and career. And yet it is Maria who possesses and retains the desire shared between her and William. His desire for Maria has been removed through a surgical operation.

One of the implications in the different fates for William and Maria is surely a difference around gender, but also there is a difference here around desire. William has had his desire 'cured' and has been returned to the safety and security of the 'family', represented through a traditional constellation of wife and son. We can read this 'curing' of desire and reinsertion into the family as one of the goals of psychoanalysis. As discussed, Freud used the 'talking cure' to rehabilitate his patients in order that they could better participate in the family. Desire here is figured as something that is dangerous to the stability and security of the traditional family and as something that needs a direct focus. It cannot be figured as something fluid and multiple, as something that supports and builds connections, especially if that desire involves a woman other than a man's wife.

In contrast, Maria's desire for William can be figured in terms of Deleuzian production. Although Maria is left in the less desirable 'al fuera' and in a position of otherness to the rest of the world, she is seen as 'happy'. She is contented with her memories of William and the love they shared; even though William is no longer with her physically, her desire for him has not been taken away. She is the archive for the love they experienced. Here desire is figured as something fluid and multiple. It allows Maria a becoming that is not propped up by material belongings or familial constellations—it is the one thing she is left with and that cannot be taken from her. These contrasting images of desire and its resolution reflect the two fundamental ways desire is theorised (psychoanalytic vs Deleuzian) and the vast difference between them. However, to merely state this opposition is as unsatisfying to a scholar learning to theorise desire, as this ending is to the viewer of *Code 46*. What is most enjoyed is when the two come together and when their differences produce meaningful possibilities.

It is important to note that William's feelings for Maria are physically removed from his body. In the scene that follows his departure from the hospital William and his wife make love—she has his body back and his desire. Desire is, after all, an affect of the body. And yet, what the film reminds us is that this desire resides in the brain—in thoughts, in feelings. So desire is posited here as part of the body, but even more specifically as part of thoughts and feelings.

Hysterics imagine things wrong with their bodies: legs don't work even though there is nothing physically wrong with them. Freud and those following him believe this to be caused by a problem in thinking, in the way the patient relates to her body, and even more specifically regarding a sexual problem. However, it is not just Freud for whom the ideas matter more than the body—as Elizabeth Wilson points out: 'following Breuer and Freud, feminists have tended to retreat from the biology of hysteria and theorize hysteria as primarily ideational' (2004, 5). As she goes on to argue: 'Hysterics do indeed suffer from reminiscences; they also suffer from bodily symptoms: they are paralyzed, blinded, in physical pain, they cough incessantly, they have difficulty breathing'; for Wilson, this preference of ideas over the body illustrates the fact that the question of the body has not been explored as fully as it could be (2004, 5). Wilson's point reiterates the way in which theoretical work on hysteria privileges the ideational over the body/biological.

Todd Haynes's *Safe* offers an important contemporary discourse on hysteria partly because it places the viewer in a position of being unsure whether to believe that Carol's illness is a result of her mind or her body. Viewers are left confused whether she has allowed herself to become physically sick or to believe that external toxins are penetrating her body and making her sick. Perhaps one of the consequences of the preferences in theoretical work Wilson notes is that we, as viewers, are more likely to think that Carol imagines this fear of contamination rather than actually experiencing it. Carol's fear of contamination can also be read as a metaphor for the growing sense of concern within society around contagion. Teresa Brennan suggests, for instance, that the rise in depression in the US and the concern with boundaries have led to 'the Western individual especially more concerned with securing a private fortress, personal boundaries, against the unsolicited emotional intrusions of the other' (2004, 15). Her work suggests that the 'fear of being "taken over" is certainly in the air' (2004, 15) which has led to a desire to protect ourselves from others, even at the expense of cutting ourselves off from the world. *Safe* illustrates an extreme reaction to the fear of being 'taken over' and of the desire to protect oneself from the emotional intrusion of the other. It also demonstrates the alienation that accompanies such a move inwards.

Brennan begins *The Transmission of Affect* (2004) with the following question: 'Is there anyone who has not, at least once, walked into a room and "felt the atmosphere"?' (2004, 1). This question, which sets up Brennan's brilliant examination of the way in which affect is contagious and permeable, also typifies the moment in melodrama when the central character enters the room for the first time after her desire has been exposed. In Sirk's *All I Desire*, for instance, when Naomi returns to town after leaving her husband and children to pursue her stage career, she walks into the auditorium to watch her daughter's play and the 'atmosphere' is palpable. She enters wearing an elaborate gown, and everyone, despite their moral disapproval, is drawn to the atmosphere of success and glamour she exudes. Everyone is drawn into the emotions that mark her return. These moments demonstrate Brennan's point that affect is contagious, however, as Sara Ahmed points out, not everyone will have the same relationship to these feelings. Ahmed argues that it is important to make a distinction between thinking about catchy emotions as property, something one has and then passes on, and thinking about how the objects of emotion circulate. As Ahmed suggests: 'even when we feel we have the same feeling, we don't necessarily have the same relationship to the feeling' (2004, 10). This distinction is illustrated in the example offered earlier. Naomi's entrance makes her daughter, who longs to be just like her, fill with pride and excitement; whereas her other daughter, who was left to fill her role as caretaker, resents her glamorous presence and sees it as nothing more than an attempt to draw attention to herself. In other words, the same affective moment produces very different feelings in the individuals involved. Although, as Brennan points out, bodies are capable of affecting each other, they affect in incalculable ways.

Brennan's model of affective contagion can be used to think about the ways in which melodrama marks bodies with desire. In melodrama the physical space of the couple's desire becomes a threat within the small communities and towns it flourishes, drawing the critical gaze of the other to bear down and make judgement. It forces the couple to prove the worthiness of their desire. In Fassbinder's *Ali*, for instance, the couple sit together in the middle of an empty outside café while the customers and waiters stand in a line and stare at the unlikely couple. Emi shouts at them: 'Nobody look me in the eye anymore. Stop staring! This is my husband, my husband' to defy their physical stare. In another scene the women Emi works with sit a flight of stairs away from her, just as they do to the foreigners, to register their need for physical distance from her—from the desire she has confessed to possessing. The physical distance is used as a way of disapproving of desire and as to suggest that this person's body is contagious. In these examples the body is physically othered by the social gaze—it is excluded from a sense of belonging. Here desire rubs off and infects the person making them undesirable to those around who disapprove (if even because they feel they must). Desire works as an affect which can attract interest and shame to the body. As discussed in Chapter 3, Silvan Tompkins pairs shame with interest; shame 'only operates after interest and enjoyment has been activated, and inhibits one or the other or both. The innate activator of shame is the incomplete reduction of interest or joy' (Sedgwick and Frank 1995, 134). Tompkins points out the way in which shame and interest function together and are intimately connected to the way in which we relate to others. As Elspeth Probyn argues: 'Shame illuminates our intense attachment to the world, our desire to be connected with others, and the knowledge that, as merely human, we will sometimes fail in our attempts to maintain those connections' (2005, 14). Melodrama reveals the intense attachments and desires people share—the desire to belong and yet the desire to be part of something greater than us. It illustrates how shame and interest work together to challenge and often to strengthen desire.

Shame, as discussed in Chapter 4, is an affect felt by many women in terms of desire, particularly if their desire is deemed unacceptable.

Postfeminism has, in part, attempted to reconfigure the parameters of desire, believing that second-wave feminists have policed women's sexuality. This question of whether feminism regulates desire is one which regards the body and the way in which desire affects the body. There is an implicit concern within second-wave feminist discourse that women's bodies need to be protected from the threat posed by male bodies—that the physical differences between the sexes means that women are more 'at risk' than men. The logic inherent to this thinking is part of what post-feminists take objection to—they see this as contributing to a victim mentality in which women are robbed of their agency via the fear and concern of their feminist foremothers. One of the responses therefore from post-feminist writers such as Merri Lisa Johnson, Elizabeth Wurtzel and Sarah Projansky is to re-write desire, to re-map the boundaries of female desire to be more inclusive and less proscriptive. This project of re-mapping can also be found in French filmmaker Catherine Breillat's work, as discussed, but also in more mainstream work, such as the HBO series *Sex and the City*. In *Sex and the City* the phrase 'throw down' is used to suggest that some women desire surrender or even submission. Reminiscent of 'swept off your feet' or 'weak at the knees', these phrases emphasise the pleasure in being physically affected by desire. At the centre of feminist concern over the notion of submission and surrender is a fear that women might allow themselves to become out of control of their desires and therefore not in full possession of their bodies. The post-feminist and even third-wave feminist response to this fear has been a suggestion that women *are* in control of their bodies even when they take pleasure in surrendering themselves to other bodies.

In chapter 5, I discussed the physical and mental affect of melancholia, embodied in characters such as Duras's 'sickly women'. Psychoanalytic theory conceptualises melancholia as a malaise—an infection that takes hold of the body. And yet, as the last chapter explored, it is this embodiment of melancholia that allows us to see how movement underlines desire, how it propels characters, moves them to do things. This movement is linked to a notion of becoming (discussed in Chapter 1 through Grosz and Probyn) and to the use of the body to demonstrate this affect on screen (Deleuze's affective-images). Cinema produces an affect of desire that resonates with its viewers.

Beyond the body?

So where does this lead us? The embodiment of desire necessarily means the risk of inviting in trouble—whether contagious, imagined or social. This risk has arguably led to figurations of desire that transcend the body.

You've Got Mail (1999), a relatively simple and even trivial film starring Tom Hanks and Meg Ryan is one of the first films to use the Internet as a place where 'lovers' eyes first meet'. Instead of the figuration explained in Chapter 3 where the gaze functions in constructing a deep and potentially meaningful desirous relationship—this film foregrounds the virtual as a place for meeting and falling in love (we could say their 'I's meet rather than their 'eyes'). Adapted from a play by Miklós László titled 'The Shop Around the Corner', the film begins with the sounds of the computer: clicking noises, dialling up sounds and with an image of New York city as inter-connected, drawing our attention to the 'Internet-age'. In the opening scene, Frank (Greg Kinnear), Kathleen's (Meg Ryan) partner, comes into the bedroom with the paper telling her that solitaire has been taken off computers in West Virginia because of the impact it has had on work production. He moans that this is a symptom of the 'end of Western civilisation' and tells her, as he looks towards the computer, 'you think this thing is your friend but it's not'. As soon as he leaves, Kathleen goes to the computer, logs on with the screen name 'shopgirl' and smiles when 'you've got mail' is announced. As she begins to read her mail out loud her voice is replaced with that of Joe Fox (Tom Hanks) and we cut to the morning rituals at his house. Both Kathleen and Joe are involved in relationships but each is more interested in their online companions than their live-in ones. Kathleen's email to Joe reads as follows: 'I turn on my computer. I wait impatiently as it boots up. I go on line, and my breath catches in my chest until I hear three little words: You've got mail. I hear nothing, not even a sound on the streets of New York, just the beat of my own heart. I have mail. From you' (Ephron 1998). Words and their power to construct impossible love stories are foregrounded, both 'on line' through email exchanges and with regards to the places where each works: bookstores. The notion that 'someone you pass on the street may already be the love of your life' fuses new technology with the 'if only' trope—re-figuring destiny and desire.

You've Got Mail provides an easy segway into contemporary society's use of the Internet to facilitate desire—whether in chat rooms or online dating agencies. These sites flourish and offer people a chance to 'meet'. This proliferation of desire on the internet can be thought of in terms of the internalisation of desire (McGowan 2004; Verhaeghe 1999b)—and other psychoanalytic work which suggests that we have become increasingly alienated from others and even ourselves—and therefore some find the anonymity of the Internet the perfect place to communicate and experience desire.

It could also be argued that the increased use of the Internet and other new media technologies to express and fulfil desire is a by-product of 'confessional culture' or further evidence of what Berlant calls an 'intimate public sphere'. In *The New Individualism*, Elliott and Lemert argue that 'in terms of transformations of intimacy, we can see that aspects of the contemporary media age can protect people from the anxiety of feeling overwhelmingly alone' (2006, 123). Mobile phones, the Internet and other new media allow people to interact virtually and to avoid the perceived messiness of physical contact. As Luciana Parisi tells us: 'in the age of cybernetics, sex is no longer a private act practised between the walls of the bedroom' (2004, 1), which has led to what she refers to as 'abstract sex'. Parisi's work illustrates a shift in terms of thinking about desire—a move towards thinking about the ways in which advances in contemporary science and in media/information technologies change our conceptions of sex and our relation to it.

Finally, I want to suggest that we can understand the proliferation of desire in new media technologies in terms of Deleuzian assemblages to consider machinic productions of desire. In *Volatile Bodies* (1994), Elizabeth Grosz points out that 'while psychoanalysis relies on a notion of desire as lack, an absence that strives to be filled through the attainment of an impossible object, desire can instead be seen as what produces, what connects, what makes machinic alliances. Instead of aligning desire with fantasy and opposing it to the real, instead of seeing it as a yearning, desire in an actualization, a series of practices, bringing things together or separating them, making machines, making reality' (1994a, 165). Here Grosz draws out the distinction between psychoanalytic conceptualisations of desire which posit lack and Deleuzian interpretations of desire which foreground production and connection. Instead of seeing new technologies as opposite to the real, it is possible to understand them as opening up new possibilities and alternatives to expressing desire. In her work on the body and new technology Braidotti suggests that 'whether we take bio-technologies, or the new information and communication technologies, the evidence is over-whelming. Capital flow, unfettered by topological or territorial constraints, has achieved a double-goal. It has simultaneously "dematerialised" social reality and hardened it' (2002, 17)—which as she argues, opens room for a renewed interest in the emotional and affective ties that bind us and to the role they play in both private and public life.

In conclusion, I want to refer briefly to Ann Cvetkovich's beautiful phrase, 'an archive of feeling', which she uses to explore cultural texts as repositories of feelings and emotions which are bound not only by their content but by their production (2003, 7). I want to suggest that one of the affects of desire is the construction of an 'archive of feeling' which in turn constructs a notion of selfhood and a relation to the world. In *Code 46* we end with Maria's archives—she will remember her desire even though it has been removed from William. Desire resides in the body and mind and enables a sense of movement. This notion of movement and transformation returns us to the images with which this book opened—moments when desire moves the characters to become something different, moments when the 'archive' of their feelings opens and invites in new possibilities.

I will end with a final image from *Safe*. As Carol stands in her 'safe hut' in front of the mirror, she is finally able to tell herself 'I love you, I really love you', which is meant to signal a development in her personal transformation. The first time I saw this scene I experienced it as something eerie and alienated—detached from the 'real' world. However, in reflection I think this moment exemplifies an instance of uncomplicated desire and one that, Lacan would argue, is at the centre of our sexual relationships: that of the desire for self. As Carol faces the mirror/camera, her gaze fixes on the viewer as if to invite a reciprocal moment—as if to challenge us to become free from everything else around us and to accept ourselves completely. Perhaps this is the most powerful theorisation of desire: desire as awakening and acceptance of the self.

Notes

1 Theorising Desire

1. This approach, of theorising what desire *does* rather than what it *is*, can also be linked to work by Elizabeth Grosz and Elspeth Probyn, as will be discussed later in the chapter in terms of work on feminism and Deleuze.
2. For further reading, see: 'Spinoza: Desire and Power', *The Warwick Journal of Philosophy*, vol. 14 (2003); 'Spinoza on the Politics of the Passions', Wiep van Bunge, *Cultural and Social History*, 2005; 2: 99–111.
3. In *Cahiers pour une morale* (published posthumously in 1983), 'Sartre describes at length what he calls "the universe of desire" (p. 364 et seq.); this is the "primitive" universe in which the interpenetration of human freedom and matter is not "lived" as the technical and productive phantasm of subordinating matter to human freedom but as fascination with the inherent powers of this interpenetration, that is, as a feeling of the sacred and the magical. Lack, which Sartre here calls "desire," aims at fulfilment not through changing the world but through incantatory passivity; the work required for the satisfaction of desire is considered to be nonessential and the objective and static world to be essential' (Simont 1992, 186–187).
4. Of course these texts are not the only ones, and criticism of Freud is far from new—as will be explored later, Deleuze and Guattari mounted an attack against Freud in the 1970s as did Freud's contemporaries. See Elizabeth Wilson's (1998) '*Post-Dated*: A Review of *Freud 2000*, ed. by Anthony Elliott'.
5. Silverman goes on to clarify that she believes that the Oedipal complex allows for 'permutations' and 'hybrids' and adds that the main point of her contribution was to demonstrate that the terms 'mother' and 'father' are 'themselves meaningless' (2000, 169).
6. 'Freud recollected a screen-memory (a trivial childhood memory that covers an important one) of his mother at the time of her confinement with his sister Anne (Freud was two and a half years old at this time) which he was to use later in *The Psychopathology of Everyday Life*' (Mitchell 2000 [1974], 61).
7. The concluding lines read: 'It is dangerous to answer riddles, but some men are born to answer them. It is the gods' doing. They hide themselves in riddles. We must not try to understand too much' (Sophocles 1972, 80).
8. Freud writes in a footnote added in 1920: 'Every new arrival on this planet is faced by the task of mastering the Oedipus complex; anyone who fails to do so falls a victim to neurosis. With the progress of psycho-analytic studies the importance of the Oedipus complex has became more and more clearly evident; its recognition has become the shibboleth that distinguishes the adherents of psycho-analysis from its opponents' (2001 [1953], vol. 7, 226, footnote 1).
9. See also Diana Fuss, *Essentially Speaking: Feminism, Nature and Difference* (New York: Routledge, 1989), p. 66.

10. For an extensive analysis of Irigaray's theory on 'two lips', see Margaret Whitford, *Luce Irigaray: Philosophy in the Feminine* (London: Routledge, 1991), pp. 170–175; Diana Fuss (1989), *Essentially Speaking*, pp. 62–66.
11. Lacan uses the metaphor of Orpheus and Eurydice to explain Freud's understanding of the function of the unconscious. As soon as something is found, there is the possibility of losing it: 'Eurydice twice lost, the most potent image we can find of the relation between Orpheus the analyst and the unconscious' (1994 [1977], 25).
12. See Shattuc's (1998, 212–225) discussion of the shift from the social to the personal in the talk show genre; A discussion could also be extended to consider Michel Foucault's work in *The History of Sexuality, vol. 1* (1978).
13. For further reading, see Jean-Michel Rabaté's discussion of Lacan and *Hamlet* in *Jacques Lacan: Psychoanalysis and the Subject of Literature* (London: Palgrave Macmillan, 2001), pp. 54–68.
14. Elizabeth Wright suggests in *Speaking Desires Can Be Dangerous* that the emphasis Lacan places on Gertrude marks a different reading of the Oedipal drama from Freud's. Instead of focusing on Hamlet's repressed desires and his inability to let them go, Lacan places the 'blame' on Gertrude. As Wright suggests: 'The (m)Other is showing no lack, and this is the essential cause of Hamlet's inability to act. He cannot conclude the Oedipal journey' (1999, 84). Wright's analysis argues that Gertrude's failure to expose herself as lacking undermines Hamlet's success. Hamlet's desires are privileged over his (m)Other's desires.
15. Mari Jo Buhle, *Feminism and Its Discontents: A Century of Struggle with Psychoanalysis* (Cambridge, MA: Harvard University Press, 1998). Buhle's work provides her readers with an exhaustive and well-researched analysis of the relationship between psychoanalysis and feminism.
16. Juliet Mitchell, 'Introduction, 1999', in *Psychoanalysis and Feminism: A Radical Reassessment of Freudian Psychoanalysis* (London: Penguin Books, 2000; first published 1974), p. xxxii.
17. In *Écrits: A Selection*, Alan Sheridan translates *point de caption* as 'anchoring point' (1977, 303); whereas in *Écrits: The First Complete Edition in English*, Bruce Fink translates *point de caption* as 'button tie' (2006, 681). Žižek refers to the *point de caption* as a 'rigid designator' (1989, 101).
18. In her article entitled 'Feminist Assessment of Emancipatory Potential and Madonna's Contradictory Gender Practices', Lynn O'Brien Hallstein argues that Deleuze and Guattari introduce Georges Bataille's theorisation of excess into their understanding of desire: 'Thus, Deleuze and Guattari argue that desire, the investment of human energy for satisfaction, is fuelled by excess energy and lacks nothing, which means desire is excessive, has no permanent object, structure, or pre-ordained form; it is characterised by continual flows of connections. Desire, then, is the radically free investment of energy without any boundaries, with the capacity to create a radically free unconscious' (1996, 126).
19. Grosz's *In the Nick of Time: Politics, Evolution, and the Untimely* and Braidotti's *Metamorphoses: Towards a Materialist Theory of Becoming* draw on Deleuze and Guattari's work as theoretical allies in their discussions on 'becomings' and 'evolutions'. Although Grosz does not engage explicitly with Deleuze in her reading of time through Darwin, Nietzsche and Bergson, she attempts to

'run Deleuze's and Irigaray's concepts underneath [her] reading of the others, as a kind of (ghostly) guide to the untimely, the crack, the unexpected resonance, that each prefigures' (2004, 14). Braidotti's engagement with Deleuze and Irigaray is more explicit, but similarly to Grosz, she believes the two philosophers can be read together to elucidate notions such as embodiment, nomadism and sexual difference (2002, 65).

20. I am thinking here of Michael Moore's work, in particular *Bowling for Columbine* (2002). Also, Morgan Spurlock's *Supersize Me* (2004).

21. See Brian McNair's *Striptease Culture: Sex, Media and the Democratisation of Desire* (London: Routledge, 2002).

22. In the introduction to *The Brain is the Screen* (2000), Gregory Flaxman makes a convincing argument that although Bordwell and Carroll denounce 'grand theories' they 'continue to proceed on the basis of their own schematic, and universal, assumptions'—because of this, Flaxman argues that Deleuze is much more the 'avatar' of grand theories' (2000, 9).

23. The idea of mapping out the co-ordinates of one's desire comes from Slavoj Žižek's work in *The Pervert's Guide to Cinema* (*Film Four Cinema*, 2006a), which will be explored in more detail in Chapter 5.

24. As Sean Homer points out, Freud had two notions of the father: one is the father of the Oedipus complex and one is the 'primal father of *Totem and Taboo*' who, as Homer points out, 'is perceived as outside the law'. As Homer argues, 'identification with the primal father involves an ambiguous process whereby the subject simultaneously identifies with authority, the law *and*, at the same time, the illicit desires that would transgress and undermine the law' (2005, 59). This relationship to the father(s) places the subject in a paradoxical relationship in terms of desire and enjoyment.

25. Mary Kay was sentenced to seven and a half years, which was mostly suspended until she was caught having sex with Mr Fualaau, at which time she had to serve the full sentence. She eventually married Vili in 2005. The couple have two daughters together, both conceived while Mary Kay was serving her prison sentence (http://news.bbc.co.uk/2/hi/americas/4569259.stm, accessed 9 February 2007).

2 Hysterical Desire

1. We could turn here to Foucault's theorisation of 'discipline and punishment'; indeed as Joseph Rouse argues: 'These practices of surveillance, elicitation, and documentation constrain behaviour precisely by making it more thoroughly knowable or known. But these new forms of knowledge also presuppose new kinds of constraint, which make people's actions visible and constrain them to speak' (1994, 96).

2. For instance, the 1984 edition of *The International Journal of Psychoanalysis* suggests that: 'today we face the question of the existence or non-existence of hysteria' (Verhaeghe 1999a, 92).

3. See 'Is Hysteria Real? Brain Images Say Yes' by Erika Kinetz, *New York Times*, 26 Sept 2006, pp. D1, 4.

4. See *Does the Woman Exist? From Freud's Hysteric to Lacan's Feminine* (1999), Paul Verhaeghe.

5. See Todd McGowan, (2003) *The End of dissatisfaction? Jacques Lacan and the Emerging Society of Enjoyment*, Albany: SUNY and McGowan (2000) *The Feminine "No!" Psychoanalysis and the New Canon*, Albany: SUNY.

6. For a more detailed, albeit 'short' history of hysteria, see Micale's excellent 'Short history of hysteria' (1995, 19–29).

7. For an excellent exploration of Charcôt's work on hysteria at the Salpêtrière, including many images from Charcôt's *Iconographie photographique de la Salpêtrière*, see Georges Didi-Huberman's (2003) *Invention of Hysteria: Charcôt and the Photographic Iconography of the Salpêtrière*.

8. 'Freud, who studied at the Salpêtrière from October 1885 to February 1886, gave Charcôt the credit for establishing the legitimacy of hysteria as a disorder' (Showalter 1985, 147–148).

9. See Gorton, *Psychoanalysis and the Portrayal of Desire in Twentieth-Century Fiction: A Feminist Critique* (2007).

10. Freud titled his first case study of Dora 'Dreams and Hysteria' in 1901. However, the analysis does not actually appear until 1905, along with the publication of *Three Essays on Sexuality*. For an analysis of whether his case history is a 'fragment or a whole', see Toril Moi's 'Representation of Patriarchy: Sexuality and Epistemology' (1990 [1985]), 184–187.

11. Because of the short length of the session and the manner in which he interprets the case, Freud concludes that he can 'present only a fragment of an analysis' (2001 [1953], vol. 7, 12).

12. As Freud points out: 'In the first place the treatment did not last for more than three months; and in the second place the material which elucidated the case was grouped around two dreams' (2001 [1953], vol. 7, 10).

13. See Erik H. Erikson's 'Reality and Actuality: An Address', in *In Dora's Case*, 44–55.

14. Freud remarks that 'such women (and this applied to the patient's mother) are entirely without insight into their illness, so that one essential characteristic of an "obsessional neurosis" is lacking' (2001 [1953], vol. 7, 20).

15. Freud writes: 'From the very beginning I took the greatest pains with this patient not to introduce her to any fresh facts in the region of sexual knowledge; and I did this, not from any conscientious motives, but because I was anxious to subject my assumptions to a rigorous test in this case (2001 [1953], vol. 7, 31).

16. An extended justification is offered by Freud which directly precedes his explanation of the working of the unconscious (2001 [1953], vol. 7, 48–52).

17. Freud writes: 'Taking into consideration, finally, the indications which seemed to point to there having been a transference on to me—since I am a smoker too—I came to the conclusion that the idea had probably occurred to her one day during a session that she would like to have a kiss from me' (2001 [1953], vol. 7, 74).

18. Lacan's search for an 'original sin' is, in part, motivated by his own desire to establish his own school of psychoanalysis which is the impetus behind his work in *The Four Fundamental Concepts of Psychoanalysis*.

19. See Gorton (2007).

20. For a more exhaustive survey of the feminist literature on hysteria, see Micale's *Approaching Hysteria* (1995, 66–107).

21. It is important to note that hysteria is not understood solely as a 'female malady'. In Showalter's work on women, madness and English culture she devotes

a chapter to male hysteria and 'shell shock'. She explains that men coming out of World War One displayed symptoms of hysteria which meant that this could not be simply a 'female malady' but a problem of enduring trauma. Indeed Charcôt admitted that men displayed hysterical symptoms and devoted a special wing in the Salpêtrière to male hysterics. Charcôt's acknowledgement of male hysterics meant that hysteria could not simply be linked to the female reproductive system. Yet, as Showalter points out, hysteria remained symbolically for Charcôt a 'female malady' (1985, 148). Lacan writes: 'This is what the hysteric's discourse means, industrious as she is. In saying "she," we are making the hysteric a woman, but this is not her privilege alone. Many men get themselves analysed who, by this fact alone, are obliged to pass through the hysteric's discourse, since this is the law, the rule of the game. It is a matter of knowing what one deduces from this concerning the relations between men and women' (2007 [1991], 33).

22. Indeed, as Felix Deutsch's essay on Dora reminds us, she did not overcome her symptoms and died in relative unhappiness. Deutsch, a consulting physician, was called to see Dora who was complaining of various illnesses, but promptly forgot about them in favour of telling Deutsch that she was the famous Dora Freud worked with. Dora died of colon cancer which seemed, in Deutsch's opinion, a blessing to those around her. He writes that 'she had been, as my informant phrased it, "one of the most repulsive hysterics" he had ever met' (Deutsch 1990, 43).

23. In *Madness and Cinema* (2004), Patrick Fuery discusses what he terms 'hysterical flesh', 'the negotiation of meaning through the body that challenges the epistemes through the conversions of flesh' which draws both issues regarding the body and those concerning the psyche together his analysis of hysteria and cinema (1995, 120).

24. See Imelda Whelehan's *The Feminist Bestseller* (2005) for her commentary on both *Fear of Flying* and *Kinflicks*, as well as Rosalind Coward's *Female Desire: Women's Sexuality Today* (1984).

25. For a reading of *Safe* as an AIDS allegory, see John David Rhodes 'Allegory, mise-en-scène, AIDS: Interpreting *Safe*,' in *The Cinema of Todd Haynes* (2007), ed James Morrison, pp. 68–78.

26. See also *The Hysteric's Guide to the Future Female Subject* (2000).

27. The term *jouissance* has many meanings, even in Lacan's work. In *Love in a Time of Loneliness*, Paul Verhaeghe writes: 'It is striking that the period of pregnancy is described by the majority of women, once it has come to an end, as a condition of unparalleled well-being. To describe this situation, Lacan used the term *jouissance*, which has all sorts of layers of meaning. In the first place, it means pleasure. In the French language, the word also has a legal meaning, in the sense of the profit arising from the use of something that belongs to someone else' (1999, 38). As Verhaeghe suggests, jouisannce can stand for pleasure (or as some define it, ecstasy) or in a more material sense, as excess or profit. Verhaeghe's reference to both a sense of enjoyment and the law reflect Lacan's opening chapter in *Encore* titled 'On Jouissance'.

28. Thanks to Patricia O'Neill for pointing this out.

29. Thanks to Sarah Franklin for her thoughts on Bridget Jones and rebellion.

30. See Joke Hermes's (2006) 'The Tragic Success of Feminism', in (eds) Joanne Hollows and Rachel Moseley, *Feminism in Popular Culture*, Oxford: Berg, 79–96.

3   Gaze and Melodrama

1. As Bowie writes: 'At three forty on the afternoon of 3 August 1936, Lacan began to deliver his paper on "The Looking-Glass Phase" to the fourteenth International Psychoanalytical Congress, which was being held in Marienbad. The bibliographical guide placed at the end of the first edition of *Ecrits* piously records the details of time and date and in so doing suggests that the paper was an event of unusual historical significance' (1991, 17).
2. Incidentally, the paper that is referred to here was given by Lacan at the 14th International Congress of Psychoanalysis in Marienbad, 1936. As Homer points out, there is no known version of this paper, and the 'Mirror Stage' most of us are familiar with is the one dated from 1949, a paper Lacan delivered 13 years later at the 16th International Congress of Psychoanalysis in Zurich (17th July, 1949), as reprinted in *Ecrits: A Selection*. As Homer explains, Lacan was actually prevented from offering his full paper in 1936 by Ernest Jones, Freud's biographer, who stopped Lacan ten minutes into his paper (see Homer, 2005, 17–18).
3. See Gorton (2007), *Psychoanalysis and the Portrayal of Desire in Twentieth-Century Fiction: A Feminist Critique*. For an interesting article on the problematic 'origins' and chronological ordering of Lacan's 'Mirror Stage', see also, Jane Gallop, 'Lacan's "Mirror Stage:" Where to Begin', *SubStance*, No.37/38 (1983), 118–128.
4. Sartre writes: 'It is shame or pride that which reveals to me the Other's look and myself at the end of that look. It is the shame or pride which makes me *live*, not *know* the situation of being looked at (1956, 261).
5. See Christian Metz, 1975, 'The Imaginary Signifier', 51.
6. The use of psychoanalysis within cinema studies led to a debate, both on the pages of *Screen* and within their editorial board. Film theorists contested the use of psychoanalysis and its dominance. For an excellent reflection on this period within cinema studies, see Andrew Tudor's *Decoding Culture* (1999).
7. Although published in 1975, Mulvey's article still remains influential in discussions of female spectatorship and the gaze and has inspired numerous articles/books to consider the function of the gaze in cinema studies—notably Loraine Gamman's and Margaret Marshment's edited collection *The Female Gaze: Women as Viewers of Popular Culture* (1989), Jackie Stacey's 'Desperately Seeking Difference' (originally titled 'An Investigation of Desire Between Woman in Narrative Cinema') and E. Ann Kaplan's *Looking for the Other: Feminism, Film and the Imperial Gaze* (1997). Mulvey's work has also perpetuated an interest in psychoanalytic engagements in film studies, such as *The Couch and the Silver Screen: Psychoanalytic Reflections on European Cinema* (2003), ed. Andrea Sabbadini, for which she wrote the foreword.
8. See also Ang's (1996) 'Melodramatic Identifications: Television Fiction and Women's Fantasy', in *Living Room Wars*, pp. 85–97.
9. http://www.michaelhoppengallery.com/artist,show,1,40,0,0,0,0,0,0,robert_doisneau.html
10. See Griselda Pollock (1988) *Vision and Difference*, pp. 121–123. Pollock uses the picture to argue that 'texts made by women can produce different positions within looking' (1988, 122).
11. Doane returns to her analysis of the photograph in 'Masquerade Reconsidered: Further Thoughts on the Female Spectator' and argues that 'Doisneau's

photograph *is* a joke which is funny only at the expense of the woman, but it is not the only way of visualizing female spectatorship' (1991, 42–43). She also draws attention to Tania Modleski's critique of her use of the phrase 'get the joke'; see Modleski (1988), *The Women Who Knew Too Much: Hitchcock and Feminist Theory*, New York: Methuen.

12. For Petro, 'male or female spectatorship [...] cannot be theorized apart from questions of gender and experience, for perceptual response is constructed as much in history as it is by positioning and address within individual films' (1989, 77).

13. Alternative approaches to the question of sexual difference, posed by feminist film theorists such as Doane and Petro, are being re-evaluated. In her work on film and spectatorship, for instance, Jan Campbell returns to work on sexual difference within feminist film theory, particularly to Doane's and Petro's analysis, in order to re-read these debates in terms of a phenomenological approach. By drawing on a phenomenological imaginary, Campbell suggests that 'All spectatorship is over-identified narcissistically with the cinematic image, but this is an active as well as a passive position' (2005, 47). Arguing that Petro's contemplative gaze can be re-read in terms of a phenomenological imaginary, Campbell also suggests that 'Such a phenomenological reading of the melodrama situates the spectator not with fixed textual identifications of sexual difference but within a more experiential space—a place where melancholic, distracted and hysterical identifications can potentially become mobilised within a more embodied, contemplative looking' (2005, 62 63).

14. Thanks to Zoe Beloff for drawing my attention to this film.

15. Remake of Andrei Tarkovsky's *Solyaris* (1972).

16. In Halliday's *Sirk on Sirk*, Sirk explains that he did not like the title change; 'I was attracted to the title, *Stopover*. Stanwyck doesn't get into her love again— there is something blocking her. A woman comes back with all her dreams, with her love—and she finds nothing but this rotten, decrepit middle-class American family'; '... I wanted to keep *Stopover* as the title for the picture. It was a much darker title. It would have deepened the picture and the character— and at the same time the irony' (1971, 89).

17. As Mulvey argues: 'How can a mother of grown children overcome the taboo against her continued sexual activity in "civilised society", when the object of her desire is reduced to child-like dependency on her ministrations?' (1989, 79).

18. See Gorton (2008b), 'Domestic Desire: Framing Representations of Older Women's Sexuality in *Six Feet Under* (HBO) and Hanif Kureishi's *The Mother* (2003),' in *Homes Fires: Representations of Domesticity in Popular Culture* (eds) S. Gillis and J. Hollows, London: Routledge.

19. Sirk: 'I believe that art must establish distances, and I've been astonished in seeing my films again at the number of times I've used mirrors for they are the symbols of that distance', from Fred Camper's 'The Films of Douglas Sirk' (1971), *Screen*, 12: 2, 44.

20. Camper argues that Sirk's use of mirrors and screens give us, as viewers, a sense that we are separated from the characters, and thus enhance our feeling of powerlessness (1971, 50). Whereas Willemen argues that Sirk does not distanciate his audience, instead Sirk involves the spectators in the action (1971, 65). Indeed, what Willemen argues is that, through Sirk's use of cliché, his films distance themselves from bourgeois ideology (1971, 67).

21. David Grosz argues that Sirk frames are 'flat, surfaces of glass' which trap the characters and prevent them from any attempt at escape (1971, 100).
22. *Schlußakkord* (Final Chord, 1936) 'was one of Sirk's three major German melodramas' (Schulte-Sasse 1998, 3).
23. For a fascinating account of Fassbinder's television adaptation of Alfred Döblins's novel *Berlin Alexanderplatz*, 'the longest (sixteen hours), most expensive ($6 million), and most widely seen television project in German media history' (1995, 1), see Jane Shattuc's *Television, Tabloids and Tears: Fassbinder and Popular Culture*.
24. See *far from Heaven* (2003) DVD Extras.

4   Shame and Desire

1. As Liz Constable points out: 'Breillat's idea for the film *Romance* dates from the late seventies' (2004, 675).
2. I expand and develop this idea in *Media Audiences: Television, Meaning and Emotion* (2008a).
3. Thomas Elsaesser, 'Broadcast Television and the Social Contract', http://home.hum.uva.nl/oz/elsaesser/essay-television.pdf.

5   Melancholia and Desire

1. Jacques Lacan, 'Hommage Fait a Marguerite Duras, Du Ravissement de Lol V. Stein', *Ca(s)hiers de la Compagnie Madeleine*, Paris: Renard-Jean Louis, vol. 52 (1965), pp. 7–15, (p. 9). 'C'est précisément ce que je reconnais dans le ravissement de Lol V. Stein, où Marguerite Duras s'avère savoir sans moi ce que j'enseigne.' The translation is my own. See Jean-Michel Rabaté's interesting account of this in *Jacques Lacan: Psychoanalysis and the Subject of Literature* (2001).
2. In 'Marguerite Duras' *The South Bank Show*, ITV, 17.11.85, Duras talks about the real woman who inspired the figure in *India Song* (Anne-Marie Stretter) and her work in general; 'It's she that made me become a writer'.
3. In her reading of women and globality, Ahmed argues that 'Cultural relativism assumes distance and difference in order precisely not to take *responsibility* for that distance and difference' (2000, 167).
4. In her work on 'women, natives and other', Marie-Paule Ha also finds a contradiction in Duras's work, particularly in her representation of women characters, who, she argues, 'both challenge and reaffirm the colonial hegemonic discourse' (2000, 95). Exploring the roles of women in her Asian novels, Ha argues that 'in her representation of white and native women Duras both reproduces and subverts the gender code that regulates the colonial society' (2000, 106–107).
5. Thanks to Jackie Stacey for her help in formulating these ideas.
6. See 'The Real Cause of Repetition' (1995) by Bruce Fink for further explanation of Lacan's understanding of repetition, in *Reading Seminar XI: Lacan's Four Fundamental Concepts of Psychoanalysis*, eds Richard Feldstein, Bruce Fink, Maire Jaanus, Albany: SUNY, pp. 223–232.
7. Colebrook writes: 'We do not apply philosophy to the cinema—asking whether a film or form is "ethical" or "thoughtful"—nor do we simply use cinema for

examples, looking for narratives or images that demonstrate the point we want to make. We ask how cinema is possible—what is life such that it can yield cinematic technology?—and ask what the possibilities of cinema are: how might we perceive and think differently in the face of cinematic images, and what does this tell us about the power of thinking to transform itself?' (2006, 20).

8. Laura Marks notes that 'Deleuze considered any-spaces-whatever to constitute images that arouse an emotional or visceral response, that is, *affection-images*. Yet, whereas it is conventional for these emotional responses to be immediately followed by action (Arnold feels anger and reaches for his gun), in any-spaces-whatever no action is possible. Instead, emotion or feeling opens us to the experience of time (Arnold slips into a reverie)' (2000, 28).

9. The notion of re-coordinating desire comes from Slavoj Žižek's work in *The Pervert's Guide to Cinema* (*Film Four Cinema*, 2006a).

Bibliography

Ahmed, Sara. (2006) 'The Politics of Good Feelings', unpublished paper delivered at the 'Decolonising Affect Theory' Colloquium, University of British Columbia.
——. (2006) *Queer Phenomenology: Orientations, Objects, Others*. Durham: Duke University Press.
——. (2004) *The Cultural Politics of Emotion*. Edinburgh: Edinburgh University Press.
——. (2000) *Strange Encounters: Embodied Others in Post-Coloniality*. London and New York: Routledge.
Akass, Kim and Janet Mccabe, eds. (2004) *Reading Sex and the City*. London: I.B. Tauris.
Alther, Lisa. (1999 [1976]) *Kinflicks*. London: Virago.
Ang, Ien. (1996) *Living Room Wars: Rethinking Media Audiences for a Postmodern World*. London and New York: Routledge.
——. (1985) *Watching "Dallas:" Soap Opera and the Melodramatic Imagination*. London and New York: Routledge.
Appignanesi, Lisa and John Forrester, eds. (1992) *Freud's Women*. London: Weidenfield and Nicolson.
Arthurs, Jane. (2004) *Television and Sexuality: Regulation and the Politics of Taste*. Arthurs: Maidenhead Open University Press.
Austen, Jane. (1996 [1813]) *Pride and Prejudice*. London: Penguin.
Balázs, Béla. (1952) *Theory of the Film (Character and Growth of a New Art)*, translated by Edith Bone. London: Dennis Dobson Ltd.
Barzilai, Shuli. (1995) 'Models of Reflexive Recognition: Wallon's *Origines du Caractére* and Lacan's 'Mirror Stage", *The Psychoanalytical Study of the Child*. New Haven: Yale University Press, 50: 368–82.
Baudry, Jean-Louis. (1974–75 [1970]) 'Ideological Effects of the Basic Cinematographic Apparatus', *Film Quarterly* (Winter 1974–1975) 28 (2): 39–47. Translated by Alan Williams (org. published in *Cinéthique*, 1970, Nos 7–8).
Bauman, Zygmunt. (2001) *The Individualized Society*. Cambridge: Polity Press.
Baumgardner, Jennifer and Amy Richards. (2000) *Manifesta: Young Women, Feminism and the Future*. New York: Farrar, Straus and Giroux.
Beck, Ulrich and Elisabeth Beck-Gernsheim. (2001) *Individualisation: Institutionalized Individualism and Its Social and Political Consequences*. Cambridge: Polity Press.
Beckman, Karen. (2003) *Vanishing Women: Magic, Film, and Feminism*. Durham: Duke University Press.
Bell, David and Gill Valentine. (1995) *Mapping Desire: Geographies of Sexuality*. London: Routledge.
Belsey, Catherine. (1994) *Desire: Love Stories in Western Culture*. Oxford: Blackwell.
Berlant, Lauren. (2004) *Compassion: The Culture and Politics of an Emotion*. New York: Routledge.
——. ed. (2000) *Intimacy*. Chicago: The University of Chicago Press.
——. (1997) *The Queen of America goes to Washington City*. Durham: Duke University Press.

Bernheimer, Charles and Claire Kahane, eds. (1990 [1985]) *In Dora's Case: Freud—Hysteria—Feminism, Second Edition.* New York: Columbia University Press.
Biddle, Jennifer. (1997) 'Shame', *Australian Feminist Studies* 12 (26): 227–37.
Bollas, Christopher. (2000) *Hysteria.* London: Routledge.
Bostic, Heidi. (2002) 'Luce Irigaray and Love', *Cultural Studies* 16 (5): 603–10.
Bowie, Malcolm. (1991) *Lacan.* London: Fontana Press.
Braidotti, Rosi. (2006) *Transpositions: On Nomadic Ethics.* Cambridge: Polity Press.
——. (2003) 'Becoming Woman: or Sexual Difference Revisited', *Theory, Culture & Society*, 20 (3): 43–64.
——. (2002 [repr. 2005]) *Metamorphoses: Towards a Materialist Theory of Becoming.* Cambridge: Polity.
——. (1994) *Nomadic Subjects: Embodiment and Sexual Difference in Contemporary Feminist Theory.* New York: Columbia University Press.
Brennan, Teresa. (2004) *The Transmission of Affect.* Ithaca, NY: Cornell University Press.
——. (1992) *The Interpretation of the Flesh: Freud and Femininity.* London: Routledge.
Breillat, Catherine. (2001) *Pornocratie.* Paris: Éditions Denoël.
——. (1999) *Le Livre du Plaisir.* Paris: Éditions 1.
Breuer, Josef and Sigmund Freud. (1955) *Studies on Hysteria*, translated by James Strachey. London: The Hogarth Press.
Bronfen, Elisabeth. (1998) *The Knotted Subject: Hysteria and Its Discontents.* Princeton: Princeton University Press.
Brooks, Ann. (1997) *Postfeminisms: Feminism, Cultural Theory and Cultural Forms.* London and New York: Routledge.
Brooks, Peter. (2000) 'Introduction', in *Whose Freud? The Place of Psychoanalysis in Contemporary Culture*, edited by Peter Brooks and Alex Woloch. New Haven: Yale University Press, 1–12.
Brooks, Peter. (1995 [1976]) *The Melodramatic Imagination: Balzac, Henry James, Melodrama, and the Mode of Excess.* New Haven: Yale University Press.
Brooks, Peter and Alex Woloch, eds. (2000) *Whose Freud? The Place of Psychoanalysis in Contemporary Culture.* New Haven: Yale University Press.
Brown, Joanne. (2000) 'What is a Psychoanalytic Sociology of Emotion?' *Psychoanalytic Studies* 2 (1): 35–49.
Brown, Wendy. (2003) 'Resisting Left Melancholia', in *Loss: The Politics of Mourning*, edited by David L. Eng and David Kazanjian. Berkeley: University of California Press, 458–66.
Brunsdon, Charlotte. (2006) 'The Feminist in the Kitchen: Martha, Martha and Nigella', in *Feminism in Popular Culture*, edited by Joanne Hollows and Rachel Moseley. Oxford: Berg, 41–56.
——. (1997) *Screen Tastes: From Soap Opera to Satellite Dishes.* London and New York: Routledge.
Buchanan, Ian and Claire Colebrook, eds. (2000) *Deleuze and Feminist Theory.* Edinburgh: Edinburgh University Press.
Buhle, Mari Jo. (1998) *Feminism and Its Discontents: A Century of Struggle with Psychoanalysis.* Cambridge, MA: Harvard University Press.
Bunge, Wiep van. (2005) 'Spinoza on the Politics of the Passions', *Cultural and Social History* 2 (1): 99–111.
Burke, Carolyn. (1994) 'Irigaray Through the Looking Glass', in *Engaging with Irigaray: Feminist Philosophy and Modern European Thought*, edited by Carolyn Burke,

Naomi Schor and Margaret Whitford. New York: Columbia University Press, 37–56.

Butler, Judith. (2003) 'Afterword: After Loss, What Then?' In *Loss: The Politics of Mourning*, edited by David L. Eng and David Kazanjian. Berkeley: University of California Press, 467–74.

———. (1997) *The Psychic Life of Power: Theories in Subjection*. Stanford: Stanford University Press.

———. (1987) *Subjects of Desire: Hegelian Reflections in Twentieth-Century France*. New York: Columbia University Press.

Byars, Jackie. (1991) *All That Hollywood Allows: Re-Reading Gender in 1950s Melodrama*. London: Routledge.

Campbell, Jan. (2005) *Film & Cinema Spectatorship: Melodrama and Mimesis*. Cambridge: Polity Press.

Campbell, Kirsten. (2004) *Jacques Lacan and Feminist Epistemology*. London: Routledge.

Camper, Fred. (1971) 'The Tarnished Angels', *Screen* 12 (2): 68–94.

Carroll, Noël. (1999) 'Film, Emotion, and Genre', in *Passionate Views: Film, Cognition, and Emotion*, edited by Carl Plantinga and Greg M. Smith. Baltimore: John Hopkins University Press, 21–47.

———. (1988) *Mystifying Movies: Fads and Fallacies in Contemporary Film Theory*. New York: Columbia University Press.

Cixous, Hélène. (1994) *The Hélène Cixous Reader*, edited by Susan Sellers. London: Routledge.

———. (1991) 'The Laugh of the Medusa', translated by Keith Cohen and Paula Cohen, in *New French Feminisms: An Anthology*, edited by Elaine Marks and Isabelle de Courtivron. London: Harvester Wheatsheaf, 245–64.

Cixous, Hélène and Catherine Clément. (1986) *The Newly Born Woman*, translated by Betsy Wing. Minneapolis: University of Minnesota Press. (Trans. of *La Jeune Née*. Paris: Union Générale d'Éditions, 1975.)

Clément, Catherine. (1983) *The Lives and Legends of Jacques Lacan*, translated by Arthur Goldhammer. New York: Columbia University Press.

Colebrook, Claire. (2006) *Deleuze: A Guide for the Perplexed*. London: Continuum.

———. (2002) *Gilles Deleuze*, London and New York: Routledge.

———. (2000) 'Introduction', in *Deleuze and Feminist Theory*, edited by Ian Buchanan and Claire Colebrook. Edinburgh: Edinburgh University Press, 1–17.

———. (2000) 'Is Sexual Difference a Problem?' In *Deleuze and Feminist Theory*, edited by Ian Buchanan and Claire Colebrook. Edinburgh: Edinburgh University Press, 110–27.

———. (1999) *Ethics and Representation*. Edinburgh: Edinburgh University Press.

Conley, Verena Andermatt. (2000) 'Becoming-Woman Now', in *Deleuze and Feminist Theory*, edited by Ian Buchanan and Claire Colebrook. Edinburgh: Edinburgh University Press, 18–37.

———. (1992) *Hélène Cixous*. London: Harvester Wheatsheaf.

Constable, Liz. (2004) 'Unbecoming Sexual Desire for Women Becoming Sexual Subjects: Simone de Beauvoir (1949) and Catherine Breillat (1999)' *MLN*, 119: 672–95.

Copjec, Joan. (2002) *Imagine There's No Woman: Ethics and Sublimation*. Cambridge, MA: MIT Press.

———. (1994) *Read My Desire: Lacan Against the Historicists*. Cambridge, MA: MIT Press.

Coward, Rosalind. (1984) *Female Desire: Women's Sexuality Today*. London: Paladin.
Cowie, Elisabeth. (1997) *Representing the Woman: Cinema and Psychoanalysis*. Minneapolis: University of Minnesota Press.
Crews, Frederick. (1995) *The Memory Wars: Freud's Legacy in Dispute*. New York: New York Review of Books.
Cvetkovich, Ann. (2003) *An Archive of Feelings: Trauma, Sexuality and Lesbian Public Cultures*. Durham: Duke University Press.
——. (1992) *Mixed Feelings: Feminism, Mass Culture, and Victorian Sensationalism*. New Brunswick, New Jersey: Rutgers University Press.
David-Ménard, Monique. (1989) *Hysteria from Freud to Lacan: Body and Language in Psychoanalysis*, translated by Catherine Porter. Ithaca, NY: Cornell University Press.
de Lauretis, Teresa. (1990) 'Rethinking Women's Cinema, Aesthetics and Feminist Theory', in *Issues in Feminist Film Criticism*, edited by Patricia Erens. Bloomington: Indiana University Press, 288–308.
Deignan, Alice. (1997) 'Metaphors of Desire', in *Language and Desire: Encoding Sex, Romance and Intimacy*, edited by Keith Harvery and Celia Shalom. London: Routledge, 21–42.
Deleuze, Gilles. (2005) *Cinema 1*, translated by Hugh Tomlinson and Barbara Habberjam. London: Continuum. (Trans. of *Cinéma 1, L'Iamge-Mouvement*, Paris: Les Editions de Minuit, 1983.)
——. (2000) *Cinema 2 The Time-Image*, London: The Athlone Press (org published as *Cinema 2, L'Image-Temps* 1985, Paris: Les Editions de Minuit).
——. (1994) *Difference and Repetition*, translated by Paul Patton. London: The Athlone Press. (Trans. of *Différence et Répétition*, Paris: Presses Universitaires de France, 1968.)
——. (1993) *The Fold: Leibniz and the Baroque*, translated by Tom Conley. Minneapolis: University of Minnesota Press. (Trans. of *Le Pli: Leibniz et le Baroque*. Paris: Les Editions de Minuit, 1988.)
——. (1991) *Bergsonism*, translated by Hugh Tomlinson and Barbara Habberjam. New York: Zone Books. (Trans. of *Le Bergsonisme*. Paris: Presses Universitaires de France, 1966.)
——. (1989) *Cinema 2*, translated by Hugh Tomlinson and Robert Galeta. London: The Athlone Press. (Trans. of *Cinéma 2, L'Image-Temps*, Paris: Les Editions de Minuit, 1985.)
Deleuze, Gilles and Felix Guattari. (1994) *What is Philosophy?* Translated by Graham Burchell and Hugh Tomlinson. London: Verso.
——. (1988) *A Thousand Plateaus: Capitalism and Schizophrenia*, translated by Brian Massumi. London: Athlone Press. (Trans. of *Mille Plateaux*, vol. 2 of *Capitalisme et Schizophrénie*. Paris: Les Editions de Minuit, 1980.)
——. (1983) *Anti-Oedipus: Capitalism and Schizophrenia*, translated by Robert Hurley, Mark Seem and Helen R. Lane. London: Athlone Press. (Trans. of *L'Anti-Oedipe*. Paris: Les Editions de Minuit, 1972.)
Deutsch, Felix. (1990 [1985]) 'A Footnote to Freud's "Fragment of an Analysis of a Case of Hysteria"', in *In Dora's Case: Freud—Hysteria—Feminism*, edited by Charles Bernheimer and Claire Kahane. New York: Columbia University Press, 35–43.
Didi-Huberman, Georges. (2003) *Invention of Hysteria: Charcot and the Photographic Iconography of the Salpêtrière*, translated by Alisa Hartz. Cambridge, MA: MIT Press. (Originally published in 1982 by Paris: Éditions Macula.)

Doane, Mary Ann. (2004) 'Pathos and Pathology: The Cinema of Todd Haynes', *Camera Obscura* 57: 1–22.

———. (1996) 'The Economy of Desire: The Commodity Form in/of the Cinema', in *Movies and Mass Culture*, edited by John Belton. London: Athlone Press, 119–34.

———. (1991) *Femmes Fatales: Feminism, Film Theory, Psychoanalysis*. New York: Routledge.

———. (1987) *The Desire to Desire: The Woman's Film of the 1940s*. Bloomington: Indiana University Press.

Doherty, Thomas. (2002) 'Douglas Sirk: Magnificent Obsession', *The Chronicle of Higher Education*, http://chronicle.com/weekly/v49/i12/12b01601.htm, accessed 4 May 2007.

Dolar, Mladen. (1996) 'At First Sight', in *Gaze and Voice and Love Objects*, edited by Renata Salecl and Slavoj Žižek. Durham: Duke University Press, 129–53.

Duras, Marguerite. (1997) *Moderato Cantabile*, translated by Richard Seaver. London: Calder Publications. (Trans. of *Moderato Cantabile*. Paris: Les Editions de Minuit, 1958.)

———. (1986) *The Malady of Death*, translated by Barbara Bray. New York: Grove Press. (Trans. of *La Maladie de la Morte*. Paris: Les Editions de Minuit, 1982.)

———. (1985) 'Marguerite Duras', The South Bank Show, ITV, 17th November.

———. (1976) *India Song*, translated by Barbara Bray. New York: Grove Press. (Trans. of *India Song*. Paris, Editions Gallimard, 1973.)

———. (1966) *The Ravishing of Lol V. Stein*, translated by Richard Seaver. New York: Pantheon Books and Grove Press.

———. (1961) *Hiroshima Mon Amour*, translated by Richard Seaver. New York: Grove Press.

———. (1960) *Moderato Cantabile*, Paramount (written by Marguerite Duras, directed by Peter Brook).

Eagleton, Terry. (2003) *Sweet Violence: The Idea of the Tragic*. Oxford: Blackwell.

———. (1983) *Literary Theory: An Introduction*. Oxford: Blackwell.

Easthope, Anthony. (1999) *The Unconscious*. London: Routledge.

Elliott, Anthony and Charles Lemert. (2006) *The New Individualism: The Emotional Costs of Globalisation*. London: Routledge.

———. (1999) 'Rethinking Psychoanalysis in the Postmodern Era', *Psychoanalytic Studies* 1 (1): 27–33.

Elliott, Anthony and Charles Spezzano, eds. (2000) *Psychoanalysis at its Limits: Navigating the Postmodern Turn*. London: Free Association Books.

Elsaesser, Thomas. (1992) 'Broadcast Television and the Social Contract', Lecture given at the University of Hamburg, 23rd October, http://home.hum.uva.nl/oz/elsaesser/essay-television.pdf, accessed 2 March 2007.

Eng, David L. and David Kazanjian, eds. (2003) *Loss: The Politics of Mourning*. Berkeley, University of California Press.

Erens, Patricia, ed. (1990) *Issues in Feminist Film Criticism*. Bloomington: Indiana University Press.

Erikson, Erik H. (1990 [1985]) 'Reality and Actuality: An Address', in *In Doras's Case*, edited by Charles Bernheimer and Claire Kahane. New York: Columbia University Press, 44–55.

Faludi, Susan. (1991) *Backlash: The Undeclared War Against Women*. London: Chatto & Windus.

Felman, Shoshana. (1987) *Jacques Lacan and the Adventure of Insight: Psychoanalysis in Contemporary Culture.* Cambridge, MA: Harvard University Press.

——. (1977) 'Turning the Screw of Interpretation', in *Literature and Psychoanalysis The Question of Reading: Otherwise,* edited by Shoshana Felman. Baltimore: Johns Hopkins University Press, 94–207.

Fielding, Helen. (1997) *Bridget Jones's Diary.* London: Picador.

Fink, Bruce. (2002) 'Knowledge and Jouissance', in *Reading Seminar XX: Lacan's Major Work on Love, Knowledge, and Feminine Sexuality,* edited by Suzanne Barnard and Bruce Fink. Albany: State University of New York Press, 21–46.

——. (1995) 'The Real Cause of Repetition', in *Reading Seminar XI: Lacan's Four Fundamental Concepts of Psychoanalysis,* edited by Richard Feldstein, Bruce Fink and Maire Jaanus. Albany: State University of New York Press, 223–32.

Firestone, Shulamith. (1979 [1971]) *The Dialectic of Sex: The Case for Feminist Revolution.* London: The Women's Press Ltd.

Flaubert, Gustave. (2004 [1964]) *Sentimental Education.* London: Penguin Books.

Flaxman, Gregory, ed. (2000) *The Brain is the Screen: Deleuze and the Philosophy of Cinema.* Minneapolis: University of Minnesota Press.

Flieger, Jerry Aline. (2005) *Is Oedipus Online? Siting Freud After Freud.* Cambridge, MA: The MIT Press.

Forrester, John. (1998) *Dispatches from the Freud Wars: Psychoanalysis and Its Passions.* Cambridge, MA: Harvard University Press.

Foucault, Michel. (1996) 'Preface', in *Anti-Oedipus: Capitalism and Schizophrenia,* Gilles Deleuze and Félix Guattari, translated by Robert Hurley, Mark Seem, Helen R. Lane. London: Athlone Press, xi–xiv. (Trans. of *L'Anti-Oedipe.* Paris: Les Editions de Minuit, 1972.)

——. (1986) *The History of Sexuality, Volume Three, The Care of the Self,* translated by Robert Hurley. New York: Penguin Books. (Trans. of *Le Souci de soi.* Paris: Editions Gallimard, 1984.)

——. (1978) *The History of Sexuality,* translated by Robert Hurley. New York: Vintage Books. (Trans. of *La Volenté de savoir.* Paris: Editions Gallimard, 1976.)

Fraser, Nancy and Bartky, Sandra Lee, eds. (1992) *Revaluing French Feminism: Critical Essays on Difference, Agency and Culture.* Bloomington: Indiana University Press.

Freud, Sigmund. (2001 [1974]) *Indexes and Bibliographies,* volume XXIV, The Standard Edition of the Complete Psychological Works of Sigmund Freud, translated by James Strachey. London: Vintage.

——. (2001 [1966]) *Pre-Psychoanalytic Publications and Unpublished Drafts,* volume I, The Standard Edition of the Complete Psychological Works of Sigmund Freud, translated by James Strachey. London: Vintage.

——. (2001 [1964]) *New Introductory Lectures on Psycho-Analysis and Other Works,* volume XXII, The Standard Edition of the Complete Psychological Works of Sigmund Freud, translated by James Strachey. London: Vintage.

——. (2001 [1962]) *Early Psychoanalytic Publications,* volume III, The Standard Edition of the Complete Psychological Works of Sigmund Freud, translated by James Strachey. London: Vintage.

——. (2001 [1961]) *The Ego and the Id and Other Works,* volume XIX, The Standard Edition of the Complete Psychological Works of Sigmund Freud, translated by James Strachey. London: Vintage.

——. (2001 [1958]) *Case History of Schreber, Papers on Technique and Other Works*, volume XII, The Standard Edition of the Complete Psychological Works of Sigmund Freud, translated by James Strachey. London: Vintage.

——. (2001 [1957]) *On the History of the Psycho-Analytic Movement, Papers on Metapsychology and Other Works*, volume XIV, The Standard Edition of the Complete Psychological Works of Sigmund Freud, translated by James Strachey. London: Vintage.

——. (2001 [1955]) *Studies on Hysteria by Josef Breuer and Sigmund Freud*. volume II, The Standard Edition of the Complete Psychological Works of Sigmund Freud, translated by James Strachey. London: Vintage.

——. (2001 [1955]) *Two Case Histories: "Little Hans" and the "Rat Man"*, volume X, The Standard Edition of the Complete Psychological Works of Sigmund Freud, translated by James Strachey. London: Vintage.

——. (2001 [1955]) *Beyond the Pleasure Principle, Group Psychology and Other Works*, volume XVIII, The Standard Edition of the Complete Psychological Works of Sigmund Freud, translated by James Strachey. London: Vintage.

——. (2001 [1953]) *A Case of Hysteria, Three Essays on Sexuality and Other Works*, volume VII, The Standard Edition of the Complete Psychological Works of Sigmund Freud, translated by James Strachey. London: Vintage.

——. (2001 [1953]) *The Interpretation of Dreams (Second Part) and On Dreams*, volume V, The Standard Edition of the Complete Psychological Works of Sigmund Freud, translated by James Strachey. London: Vintage.

——. (1999) *The Interpretation of Dreams*, translated by Joyce Crick. Oxford: Oxford University Press.

——. (1995) *The Freud Reader*, edited by Peter Gay. London: Vintage.

——. (1991) *Case Histories II: The 'Rat' Man, Schreber, A Case of Female Homosexuality*, edited by Angela Richards. London: Penguin Books.

——. (1991 [1977]) *Sigmund Freud: On Sexuality, Three Essays on the Theory of Sexuality and Other Works*, edited by Angela Richards, translated by James Strachey. London: Penguin.

——. (1976 [1914]) *The Psychopathology of Everyday Life*, trans by Alan Tyson, London: Penguin Books.

Friedan, Betty. (1992 [1963]) *The Feminine Mystique*. London: Penguin.

Friedberg, Anne. (1990) 'A Denial of Difference: Theories of Cinematic Identification', in *Psychoanalysis and Cinema*, edited by E. Ann Kaplan. London: Routledge, 36–45.

Fuery, Patrick. (2004) *Madness and Cinema: Psychoanalysis, Spectatorship and Culture*. Houndmills: Palgrave Macmillan.

——. (1995) *Theories of Desire*. Melbourne: Melbourne University Press.

——. (1995) *The Theory of Absence: Subjectivity, Signification and Desire*. Westport: Greenwood Press.

Fuss, Diana. (1989) *Essentially Speaking: Feminism, Nature and Difference*. London and New York: Routledge.

Fuss, Diana and Sanders, Joel. (1996) 'Bergasse 19: Freud's Office', in *Stud: Architectures of Masculinity*, edited by Joel Sanders. New York: Princeton Architectural Press, 112–37.

Gallop, Jane. (1985) *Reading Lacan*. Ithaca, NY: Cornell University Press.

——. (1983) 'Lacan's "Mirror Stage": Where to Begin?' *SubStance*, 37/38: 118–28.

——. (1982) *The Daughter's Seduction: Feminism and Psychoanalysis*. Ithaca, NY: Cornell University Press.

Gamman, Lorraine and Marshment, Margaret, eds. (1989) *The Female Gaze: Women as Viewers of Popular Culture*. Seattle: The Real Comet Press.

Gay, Peter, ed. (1995) *The Freud Reader*. London: Vintage (originally published by W.W. Norton & Co in 1989).

Giddens, Anthony. (1991) *Modernity and Self-Identity*. Polity Press, Cambridge.

——. (1990) *The Consequences of Modernity*. Polity Press, Cambridge.

Gledhill, Christine, ed. (1987) *Home is Where the Heart Is: Studies in Melodrama and the Woman's Film*. London: BFI.

Goodchild, Philip. (1996) *Deleuze and Guattari: An Introduction to the Politics of Desire*. London: Sage Publications.

Gorton, Kristyn. (2008a) *Media Audiences: Television, Meaning and Emotion*. Edinburgh: Edinburgh University Press.

——. (2008b) 'Domestic Desire: Framing Representations of Older Women's Sexuality in Hanif Kureishi's *The Mother* (2003) and *Six Feet Under* (HBO)', in *Homes Fires: Representations of Domesticity in Popular Culture*, edited by Stacy Gillis and Joanne Hollows. London: Routledge.

——. (2007) *Psychoanalysis and the Portrayal of Desire in Twentieth-Century Fiction: A Feminist Critique*. New York: The Edwin Mellen Press.

——. (2006) 'A Sentimental Journey: Television, Meaning and Emotion', *Journal of British Cinema and Television*, 3 (1): 72–81.

——. (2004) '(Un)Fashionable Feminists: The Media and *Ally McBeal*', in *Third Wave Feminism: A Critical Exploration*, edited by Stacy Gillis, Gillian Howie and Rebecca Munford. Houndmills: Palgrave Macmillan, 154–63.

——. (2003) 'Critical Scenes of Desire: Marguerite Duras's *Le Ravissement de Lol V Stein* and *Moderato cantabile*', *Dalhousie French Studies* 53, Summer: 100–19.

Greer, Germaine. (1971 [1970]) *The Female Eunuch*. London: Flamingo Press.

Grosz, Dave. (1971) 'The First Legion: Vision and Perception in Sirk', *Screen* 12 (2): 99–120.

Grosz, Elizabeth. (2004) *In the Nick of Time: Politics, Evolution, and the Untimely*. Durham: Duke University Press.

——. ed. (1999) *Becomings: Explorations in Time, Memory and Futures*. Ithaca, NY: Cornell University Press.

——. (1998) 'Of Being Two – Introduction', *Diacritics* 28 (1): 3–18.

——. (1994a) *Volatile Bodies: Toward a Corporeal Feminism*. London: Routledge.

——. (1994b) 'Refiguring Lesbian Desire', in *The Lesbian Postmodern*, edited by Laura Doan. New York: Columbia University Press, 67–84.

——. (1994) 'A Thousand Tiny Sexes: Feminism and Rhizomatics', in *Gilles Deleuze and the Theater of Philosophy*, edited by Constantin V. Boundas and Dorothea Olkowski. New York: Routledge, 187–212.

——. (1990a) *Jacques Lacan: A Feminist Introduction*. London: Routledge.

——. (1990b) 'Contemporary Theories of Power and Subjectivity', in *Feminist Knowledge: Critique and Construct*, edited by Sneja Gunew. London: Routledge, 59–120.

——. (1989) *Sexual Subversions: Three French Feminists*. St Leonards, Australia: Allen and Unwin.

——Grosz, Elizabeth and Pheng Cheah. (1998) 'The Future of Sexual Difference: An Interview with Judith Butler and Drucilla Cornell', *Diacritics* 28 (1): 19–42.

Ha, Marie-Paule. (2000) 'Durasie: Women, Natives and Other', in *Revisioning Duras: Film, Race, Sex*, edited by James S. Williams. Liverpool: Liverpool University Press, 95–112.

166   *Bibliography*

Halliday, Jon. (1971) *Sirk on Sirk*, London: Secker & Warburg (BFI).

Hallstein, Lynn O'Brien. (1996) 'Feminist Assessment of Emancipatory Potential and Madonna's Contradictory Gender Practices', *The Quarterly Journal of Speech* 82 (2): 125–41.

Hayward, Susan. (2000) *Cinema Studies: The Key Concepts*. London and New York: Routledge.

Henry, Astrid. (2004) 'Orgasms and Empowerment: *Sex and the City* and the Third Wave Feminism', in *Reading Sex and the City*, edited by Kim Akass and Janet Mccabe. London: I.B. Tauris, 65–82.

Hermes, Joke. (2006) '"*Ally McBeal*", "*Sex in the City*" and the Tragic Success of Feminism', in *Feminism in Popular Culture*, edited by Joanne Hollows and Rachel Moseley. Oxford: Berg, 79–96.

———. (2005) *Re-Reading Popular Culture*. Oxford: Blackwell Publishing.

Hill, John and Pamela Church Gibson, eds. (2000) *Film Studies: Critical Approaches*. Oxford: Oxford University Press.

Hollows, Joanne and Rachel Moseley, eds. (2006) *Feminism and Popular Culture*. Oxford: Berg.

Homer, Sean. (2005) *Jacques Lacan*. London: Routledge.

Innes, Sherrie A. (2004) *Action Chicks: New Images of Tough Women in Popular Culture*. Houndmills: Palgrave Macmillan.

Irigaray, Luce. (1996) *I Love to You: Sketch of a Possible Felicity in History*, translated by Alison Martin. New York: Routledge.

———. (1993) *An Ethics of Sexual Difference*, translated by Gillian Gill and Carolyn Burke. Ithaca, NY: Cornell University Press. (Trans. of *Ethique de la Différence Sexuelle*. Paris: Les Editions de Minuit, 1984.)

———. (1990) '"Women's Exile": Interview with Luce Irigaray', in *The Feminist Critique of Language: A Reader*, edited by Deborah Cameron, translated by Couze Venn. London: Routledge, 80–96.

———. (1985) *Speculum of the Other Woman*, translated by Gillian C. Gill. Ithaca, NY: Cornell University Press. (Trans. of *Speculum de l'autre Femme*. Paris: Les Editions de Minuit, 1974.)

———. (1985) *This Sex Which is Not One*, translated by Catherine Potter. Ithaca, NY: Cornell University Press. (Trans. of *Ce Sexe qui n'en pas un*. Paris: Les Editions de Minuit, 1977.)

Irvine, William B. (2006) *On Desire: Why We Want What We Want*. Oxford: Oxford University Press.

Jacobus, Mary. (1986) *Reading Woman: Essays in Feminist Criticism*. London: Methuen & Co Ltd.

Jay, Martin. (1994) *Downcast Eyes: The Denigration of Vision in Twentieth-Century French Thought*. Berkeley: University of California Press.

Johnson, Merri Lisa. (2002) *Jane Sexes It Up: True Confessions of Feminist Desire*. New York: Four Walls Eight Windows.

Jong, Erica. (1998 [1973]) *Fear of Flying*. London: Vintage.

Judith, Feher, Gurewich. (1999) 'Preface' in *Does the Woman Exist? From Freud's Hysteric to Lacan's Feminine* by Paul Verhaeghe, trans by Marc du Ry, London: Rebus Press, vii–ix.

Kaplan, E. Ann. (2000) *Feminism and Film*, Oxford: Oxford University Press.

———. (1997) *Looking for the Other: Feminism, Film and the Imperial Gaze*. New York & London: Routledge.

———. (1990) *Psychoanalysis and Cinema*. London: Routledge.
Kennedy, Barbara M. (2000) *Deleuze and Cinema: The Aesthetics of Sensation*. Edinburgh: Edinburgh University Press.
Khalfa, Jean. (1999) 'An Impersonal Consciousness', in *An Introduction to the Philosophy of Gilles Deleuze*, edited by Jean Khalfa. London: Continuum, 64–82.
Khanna, Ranjanna. (2004) *Dark Continents: Psychoanalysis and Colonialism*, Durham: Duke University Press.
———. (2003) *Dark Continents: Psychoanalysis and Colonialism*. Durham: Duke University Press.
Kintz, Erika. (2006) 'Is Hysteria Real? Brain Images Say Yes', *New York Times*, 26 September, D1.
Kirby, Vicki. (1997) *Telling Flesh: The Substance of the Corporeal*. New York: Routledge.
Klinger, Barbara. (1994) *Melodrama and Meaning: History, Culture and the Films of Douglas Sirk*. Bloomington: Indiana University Press.
Kristeva, Julia. (1989) *Black Sun: Depression and Melancholia*, translated by Leon S. Roudiez. New York: Columbia University Press.
———. (1980) *Desire in Language*, edited by Leon S. Roudiez. New York: Columbia University Press.
Kuhn, Annette. (1982) *Women's Pictures: Feminism and Cinema*, 2nd ed. London: Verso.
Lacan, Jacques. (2007) *The Other Side of Psychoanalysis, The Seminar of Jacques Lacan, Book XVII*, edited by Jacques-Alain Miller, translated by Russell Grigg. New York and London: W.W. Norton & Co. (Trans. of *Le Séminaire de Jacques Lacan, Livre XVII, L'Envers de la Psychanalyse, 1969–1970*. Paris: Les Editions du Seuil, 1991.)
———. (2006) *Écrits: The First Complete Edition in English*, translated by Bruce Fink. London and New York: W.W. Norton & Co.
———. (1998) *The Seminar of Jacques Lacan: On Feminine Sexuality, the Limits of Love and Knowledge Book XX, Encore 1972–73*, edited by Jacques-Alain Miller, translated by Bruce Fink. New York: W.W. Norton and Co. (Trans. of *Le Séminaire, Livre XX, Encore, 1972–1973*. Paris: Éditions du Seuil, 1975.)
———. (1994) *The Four Fundamental Concepts of Psychoanalysis*, edited by Jacques-Alain Miller, translated by Alan Sheridan. London: Penguin Books. (Trans. of *Le Séminaire de Jacques Lacan, Livre XI, 'Les Quatre Concepts Fondamentaux de la Psychanalyse.'* Paris: Éditions du Seuil, 1973.)
———. (1993) *The Psychoses 1955–56: The Seminar of Jacques Lacan, Book III*, edited by Jacques-Alain Miller, translated by Russell Grigg. New York: W.W. Norton and Co. (Trans. of *Le Seminaire, Livre III, Les Psychoses*. Paris: Editions du Seuil, 1981.)
———. (1992) *The Ethics of Psychoanalysis 1959–1960: The Seminar of Jacques Lacan, Book VII*, edited by Jacques-Alain Miller, translated by Dennis Porter. London: Routledge. (Trans. of *Le Séminaire, Livre VII, L'ethique de la Psychanalyse, 1959–1960*. Paris: Les Editions du Seuil, 1986.)
———. (1991 [1975]) *Freud's Papers on Technique 1953–1954: The Seminar of Jacques Lacan, Book 1*, edited by Jacques-Alain Miller, translated by John Forrester. New York and London: W.W. Norton & Company. (Trans. of *Le Séminaire I*. Paris: Les Editions du Seuil, 1975.)
———. (1991 [1978]) *The Ego in Freud's Theory and in the Technique of Psychoanalysis 1954–1955, The Seminar of Jacques Lacan, Book II*, edited by Jacques-Alain Miller,

translated by Sylvana Tomaselli. New York and London: W.W. Norton & Company. (Trans. of *Le Séminaire. Livre II. Le moi dans la théorie de Freud et dans la technique de la psychanalyse, 1954–1955*. Paris: Les Editions du Seuil, 1978.)

——. (1987) 'The case of Aimée, or self-punitive paranoia', in *The Clinical Roots of the Schizophrenia Concept: Translations of Seminal European Contributions on Schizophrenia*, edited by John Cutting and Michael Shepherd. Cambridge: Cambridge University Press, 213–26.

——. (1982) 'Desire and the Interpretation of Desire in *Hamlet*', in *Literature and Psychoanalysis: The Question of Reading: Otherwise*, edited by Shoshana Felman. Baltimore: Johns Hopkins University Press, 11–52.

——. (1977) *Ecrits: A Selection*, translated by Alan Sheridan. London: Routledge. (Selected trans. of *Ecrits*. Paris: Editions du Seuil, 1966.)

——. (1968) *The Language of the Self: The Function of Language in Psychoanalysis*, translated by Anthony Wilden. Baltimore: Johns Hopkins University Press. (Trans. of 'Fonction et champ de la parole et du langage en psychanalyse', in *La Psychanalyse*, vol. 1. Paris: Editions du Seuil, 1956; later published in *Ecrits* [Paris: Editions du Seuil, 1966].)

——. (1965). 'Hommage Fait a Marguerite Duras, Du *Ravissement de Lol V Stein*', *Cahiers de la Compagnie Madeleine* 52: 7–15.

Leavy, Patricia. (2006) 'Ally McBeal as a Site of Postmodern Bodily Boundaries and Struggles Over Cultural Interpretation: The Hysteric as a Site of Feminist Resistance',in *Searching the Soul of Ally McBeal: Critical Essays*, edited by Elwood Watson. Jefferson: McFarland & Co. 19–35.

Lotz, Amanda D. (2001) 'Postfeminist Television Criticism: Rehabilitating Critical Terms and Identifying Postfeminist Attributes', *Feminist Media Studies* 1 (1): 105–122.

MacCannell, Juliet Flower. (2000) *The Hysteric's Guide to the Future Female Subject*. Minneapolis: University of Minnesota Press.

——. (1994) 'Things to Come: A Hysteric's Guide to the Future Female Subject', in *Supposing the Subject*, edited by Joan Copjec. London: Verso, 106–32.

Macey, David. (1988) *Lacan in Context*. London: Verso.

Madison, D. Soyini. (2000) 'Oedipus Rex at *Eve's Bayou* or The Little Black Girl who Left Sigmund Freud in the Swamp', *Cultural Studies*, 14 (2): 311–40.

Mahony, Patrick J. (1996) *Freud's Dora: A Psychoanalytic, Historical, and Textual Study*. New Haven: Yale University Press.

Malkin, Elisabeth. (2007) 'At a School for the Poor, a Mysterious, Crippling Illness', *The New York Times*, 16th April, A4.

Marcus, Steven. (1990 [1985]) 'Freud and Dora: Story, History, Case History', in *In Dora's Case: Freud—Hysteria—Feminism*, edited by Charles Bernheimer and Claire Kahane. New York: Columbia University Press, 56–91.

Mark, John. (1998) *Gilles Deleuze: Vitalism and Multiplicity*. London: Pluto Press.

Marks, Laura U. (2000) *The Skin of the Film: Intercultural Cinema, Embodiment, and the Senses*. Durham: Duke University Press.

Massumi, Brian. (2002) *Parables for the Virtual: Movement, Affect, Sensation*. Durham: Duke University Press.

——. (1992) *A User's Guide to Capitalism and Schizophrenia: Deviations from Deleuze and Guattari*. Cambridge, MA: MIT Press.

Mazdon, Lucy, ed. (2001) 'Introduction', in *France on Film: Reflections on Popular French Cinema*. London: Wallflower Press, 1–10.

McGowan, Todd. (2003) *The End of Dissatisfaction: Jacques Lacan and the Emerging Society of Enjoyment*. New York: State University of New York Press.

McGowan, Todd and Sheila Kunkle. (2004) *Lacan and Contemporary Film*. New York: Other Press.

McHugh, Kathleen and Vivian Sobchack, eds. (2004) 'Introduction', 'Beyond the Gaze: Recent Approaches to Film Feminisms' *Signs* 30 (1): 1205–8.

McNair, Brian. (2002) *Striptease Culture: Sex, Media and the Democratisation of Desire*. London: Routledge.

Mercer, John and Martin Shingler, eds. (2004) *Melodrama: Genre, Style, Sensibility*. London: Wallflower.

Metz, Christian. (1975) 'The Imaginary Signifier', *Screen* 16 (2): 14–76, translated by Ben Brewster.

Micale, Mark S. (1995) *Approaching Hysteria: Disease and Its Interpretations*. Princeton: Princeton University Press.

Miller, Jacques-Alain. (1991) 'The Analytic Experience: Means, Ends, and Results', in *Lacan and the Subject of Language*, edited by Ellie Ragland-Sullivan and Mark Bracher. New York: Routledge, 83–99.

Millet, Kate. (1970) *Sexual Politics*. London: Virago.

Mitchell, Juliet. (2000) *Mad Men and Medusas: Reclaiming Hysteria and the Effects of Sibling Relations on the Human Condition*. London: Allen Lane, The Penguin Press.

——. (2000 [1974]) *Psychoanalysis and Feminism: A Radical Reassessment of Freudian Psychoanalysis*. London: Penguin.

Mitchell, Juliet and Jacqueline Rose, eds. (1982) *Feminine Sexuality: Jacques Lacan and the école freudienne*, translated by Jacqueline Rose. New York: W.W. Norton and Co.

Modelski, Tania. (1988) *The Women Who Knew Too Much: Hitchcock and Feminist Theory*, New York: Methuen.

——. (1987) 'Time and Desire in the Women's Film', in *Home is Where the Heart is: Studies in Melodrama and the Woman's Film*, edited by Christine Gledhill. London: BFI Publishing, 326–38.

Moi, Toril. (1990 [1985]) 'Representation of Patriarchy: Sexuality and Epistemology in Freud's Dora', in *In Dora's Case: Freud—Hysteria—Feminism*, edited by Charles Bernheimer and Claire Kahane. New York: Columbia University Press, 181–99.

Moore, Suzanne. (1989) 'Here's Looking at You, Kid!', in *The Female Gaze: Women as Viewers of Popular Culture*, edited by Lorraine Gamman and Margaret Marshment. London: The Real Comet Press, 44–59.

Morrison, James, ed. (2007) *The Cinema of Todd Haynes: All That Heaven Allows*. London & New York: Wallflower Press.

Mulvey, Laura. (1989) *Visual and Other Pleasures*. Houndmills: Palgrave Macmillan.

Mulvey, Laura. (1975) 'Visual Pleasure and Narrative Cinema', *Screen* 16 (3): 6–18.

Nasio, Juan-David. (1998) *Five Lessons on the Psychoanalytic Theory of Jacques Lacan*, translated by David Pettigrew and Francois Raffoul. Albany, New York: State University of New York Press.

——. (1998) *Hysteria From Freud to Lacan: The Splendid Child of Psychoanalysis*, translated and edited by Susan Fairfield. New York: The Other Press.

Neale, Steve. (1986) 'Melodrama and Tears', *Screen* 27 (6): 6–22.

Nowell-Smith, Geoffrey. (1977) 'Minnelli and Melodrama', in 'Report on the Weekend School', *Screen* 18 (2): 113–18.

Osgerby, Bill and Anna Gough-Yates, eds. (2001) *Action TV: Tough Guys, Smooth Operators and Foxy Chicks.* London and New York: Routledge.

Parisi, Luciana. (2004) *Abstract Sex: Philosophy, Bio-technology and the Mutations of Desire,* London: Continuum.

Pence, Jeffrey. (2004) 'Cinema of the Sublime: Theorizing the Ineffable', *Poetics Today* 25 (1): 29–66.

Petro, Patrice. (2002) *Aftershocks of the New: Feminism and Film History,* New Brunswick: Rutgers University Press.

——. (1989) *Joyless Streets: Women and Melodramatic Representation in Weimar Germany.* Princeton: Princeton University Press.

Philips, Adam. (2005) *Going Sane.* London: Penguin Books.

Phoca, Sophia and Rebecca Wright. (1999) *Introducing Postfeminism.* Cambridge: Icon Books.

Plantinga, Carl. (1997) 'Notes on Spectator Emotion and Ideological Film Criticism', in *Film Theory and Philosophy,* edited by Richard Allen and Murray Smith. Oxford: Clarendon Press, 372–93.

Pollock, Griselda. (1988) *Vision and Difference: Femininity, Feminism and the Histories of Art.* London: Routledge.

Probyn, Elspeth. (2005) *Blush: Faces of Shame.* Minneapolis: University of Minnesota Press.

——. (1996) *Outside Belongings.* New York & London: Routledge.

Projansky, Sarah. (2001) *Watching Rape: Film and Television in Postfeminist Culture.* New York: New York University Press.

Rabaté, Jean-Michel. (2001) *Jacques Lacan: Psychoanalysis and the Subject of Literature.* Houndmills: Palgrave Macmillan.

Ramanathan, Geetha. (2006) *Feminist Auteurs: Reading Women's Films,* London & New York: Wallflower Press.

Rhodes, John David. (2007) 'Allegory, Mise-en-Scène, AIDS: Interpreting *Safe*', in *The Cinema of Todd Haynes,* edited by James Morrison. London: Wallflower Press, 68–78.

Rich, B. Ruby. (1998) *Chick Flicks: Theories and Memories of the Feminist Film Movement.* Durham: Duke University Press.

Rose, Jacqueline. (2005 [1986]) *Sexuality in the Field of Vision.* London: Verso.

——. (1990 [1985]) 'Dora: Fragment of an Analysis', in *In Dora's Case: Freud— Hysteria—Feminism,* edited by Charles Bernheimer and Claire Kahane. New York: Columbia University Press, 128–48.

——. (1982) 'Introduction II' in Juliet Mitchell and Jacqueline Rose (eds) *Feminine Sexuality: Jacques Lacan and the école freudienne,* trans by Jacqueline Rose, New York and London: W.W. Norton & Co, 27–57.

Roudinesco, Elisabeth. (1990) *Jacques Lacan and Co.: A History of Psychoanalysis in France 1925–1985,* translated by Jeffery Mehlman. London: Free Association Books.

Rouse, Joseph. (1994) 'Power/Knowledge', in *The Cambridge Companion to Foucault,* edited by Gary Gutting. Cambridge: Cambridge University Press, 92–114.

Rowbotham, Sheila. (1989) *The Past is Before Us: Feminism in Action Since the 1960s.* London: Penguin.

Ruddock, Andy. (2007) *Investigating Audiences*. London: Sage.
——. (2006) 'Objectionable content: Sex, violence and audiences', unpublished chapter.
Ruddy, Karen. (2006) 'The Ambivalence of Colonial Desire in Marguerite Duras's *The Lover*', *Feminist Review* 82 (1): 76–95.
Sabbadini, Andrea, ed. (2003) *The Couch and the Silver Screen: Psychoanalytic Reflections on European Cinema*. Hove & New York: Brunner-Routledge.
Safouan, Moustafa. (2004) *Four Lessons in Psychoanalysis*, edited by Anna Shane. New York: Other Press.
Sartre, Jean-Paul. (1956) *Being and Nothingness: An Essay on Phenomenological Ontology*, translated by Hazel E. Barnes. New York: Philosophical Library.
Schor, Naomi. (1994) 'This Essentialism Which is Not One: Coming to Grips with Irigaray', in *The Essential Difference*, edited by Naomi Schor and Elizabeth Weed. Bloomington: Indiana University Press, 40–62.
Schulte-Sasse, Linda. (1998) 'Douglas Sirk's *Schlußakkord* and the Question of Aesthetic Resistance', *The Germanic Review* 73 (1): 2–31.
Sedgwick, Eve Kosofsky. (2003) *Touching Feeling: Affect, Pedagogy, Performativity*, Durham: Duke University Press.
Sedgwick, Eve Kosofsky and Adam Frank, eds. (1995) *Shame and Its Sisters: A Silvan Tompkins Reader*. Durham: Duke University Press.
Shattuc, Jane. (1998) '"Go Ricki": Politics, Perversion and Pleasure in the 1990s', in *The Television Studies Book*, edited by Christine Geraghty and David Lusted. London: Arnold, 212–25.
——. (1995) *Television, Tabloids and Tears: Fassbinder and Popular Culture*. Minneapolis: The University of Minnesota Press.
——. (1994) 'Having a Good Cry Over the Color Purple', in *Melodrama: Stage, Picture, Screen*, edited by Jacky Bratton, Jim Cork, Christine Gledhill. London: BFI, 147–56.
Showalter, Elaine. (1997) *Hystories: Hysterical Epidemics and Modern Culture*. London: Picador.
——. (1985) The Female Malady: Women, Madness and English Culture 1830–1980. London: Virago.
Silverman, Kaja. (2000) 'The Language of Care', in *Whose Freud? The Place of Psychoanalysis in Contemporary Culture*, edited by Peter Brooks and Alex Woloch. New Haven: Yale University Press, 150–153.
——. (1988) *The Acoustic Mirror: The Female Voice in Psychoanalysis and Cinema*. Bloomington: Indiana University Press.
Simont, Juliette. (1992) 'Sartrean Ethics', in *The Cambridge Companion to Sartre*, edited by Christina Howells. Cambridge: Cambridge University Press, 178–212.
Sklar, Robert. (2000) 'A Woman's Vision of Shame and Desire: An Interview with Catherine Breillat' in *Cineaste* 25 (1): 24–26.
Smelik, Annette. (1998) *And the Mirror Cracked: Feminist Cinema and Film Theory*. London: Palgrave Macmillan.
Smith, Murray. (1995) *Engaging Characters: Fiction, Emotion and the Cinema*. Oxford: Clarendon Press.
Smith-Rosenberg, Carroll. (1985) *Disorderly Conduct: Visions of Gender in Victorian America*. Oxford: Oxford University Press.
Sobchack, Vivian. (2004) *Carnal Thoughts: Embodiment and Moving Image Culture*, Berkeley: University of California Press.

Sophocles. (1972) *Oedipus the King*, translated by Anthony Burgess. Minneapolis: University of Minnesota Press.

Stacey, Jackie. (2006) 'Transparency, Immediacy and the Legibility of Affect: Reading the Racialised Bodies of Genetic Cinema', paper delivered at the 'Decolonising Affect Theory' Colloquium, University of British Columbia (unpublished).

——. (1989 [1987]) 'Desperately Seeking Difference', in *The Female Gaze: Women as Viewers of Popular Culture*, edited by Margaret Marshment and Lorraine Gamman. Seattle: The Real Comet Press, 112–29.

Stern, Michael. (1979) *Douglas Sirk*. Boston: Twayne Publishers.

Thornham, Sue, ed. (1999) *Feminist Film Theory: A Reader*. Edinburgh: Edinburgh University Press.

Thrift, Nigel. (2004) 'Intensities of Feeling: Towards a Spatial Politics of Affect', *Geografiska Annaler* 86 (1): 57–78.

Tolman, Deborah L. (2002) *Dilemmas of Desire: Teenage Girls Talk about Sexuality*. Cambridge, MA: Harvard University Press.

Tompkins, Silvan. (1995) *Shame and Its Sisters*, edited by Eve Kosofsky Sedgwick and Adam Frank. Durham: Duke University Press.

Tudor, Andrew. (1999) *Decoding Culture: Theory and Method in Cultural Studies*. London: Sage.

Ussher, Jane. (1991) *Women's Madness: Misogyny or Mental Illness?* Hemel Hempstead: Harvester Wheatsheaf.

Verhaeghe, Paul. (1999a [1977]) *Does the Woman Exist? From Freud's Hysteric to Lacan's Feminine*, translated by Marc du Ry. London: Rebus Press.

——. (1999b) *Love in a Time of Loneliness*, translated by Plym Peters. London: Rebus Press.

Walter, Natasha. (1998) *The New Feminism*. London: Virago.

Warhol, Robyn. (2003) *Having a Good Cry: Effeminate Feelings and Pop-Culture Forms*. Columbus: The Ohio State University Press.

Webster, Paul. (1995) *Why Freud Was Wrong: Sin, Science and Psychoanalysis*. London: Fontana Press.

Whelehan, Imelda. (2005) *The Feminist Bestseller*. Houndmills: Palgrave Macmillan.

Whitford, Margaret. (1994) 'Reading Irigaray in the Nineties', in *Engaging with Irigaray: Feminist Philosophy and Modern European Thought*, edited by Carolyn Burke, Naomi Schor and Margaret Whitford. New York: Columbia University Press, 15–36.

——. (1991) *Luce Irigaray: Philosophy in the Feminine*. London: Routledge.

Willemen, Paul. (1971) 'Distanciation and Douglas Sirk', *Screen* 12 (2): 63–7.

Williams, Linda. (1999) *Hard Core: Power, Pleasure and the "Frenzy of the Visible"*. Berkeley: University of California Press.

——. (1991) 'Film Bodies, Genre, and Excess', *Film Quarterly* 44 (4): 2–13.

——. (1981) *Figures of Desire: A Theory and Analysis of Surrealist Films*. Urbana: University of Illinois Press.

Williams, Linda Ruth. (1995) *Critical Desire: Psychoanalysis and the Literary Subject*. London: Edward Arnold.

Wilson, Elizabeth A. (2004) *Psychosomatic: Feminism and the Neurological Body*. Durham: Duke University Press.

——. (1998) 'Post-dated: A Review *Freud 2000*, edited by Anthony Elliott', *Australian Humanities Review*, http://www.lib.latrobe.edu.au/AHR/archive/Issue-December-1998/wilson2.html, accessed 2 May 2007.

Wilson, Emma. (2001) 'Deforming Femininity: Catherine Breillat's *Romance*', in *France on Film*, edited by Lucy Mazdon. London: Wallflower Press, 145–158.

——. (2000) *Memory and Survival: The French Cinema of Krzysztof Kieslowski*. Oxford: Legenda.

——. (1999) *French Cinema Since 1950s: Personal Histories*. London: Duckworth.

Woodward, Kathleen. (1996) 'Global Cooling and Academic Warming: Long-Term Shifts in Emotional Weather', *American Literary History* 8 (4): 759–79.

Wright, Elizabeth. (1999) *Speaking Desires Can Be Dangerous: The Poetics of the Unconscious*. Cambridge: Polity Press.

Wurtzel, Elizabeth. (1998) *Bitch: In Praise of Difficult Women*. London: Quartet Books.

Young, Iris Marion. (2005) *On Female Body Experience: "Throwing Like a Girl" and Other Essays*. Oxford: Oxford University Press.

Young, Robert J.C. (1995) *Colonial Desire: Hybridity in Theory, Culture and Race*. London and New York: Routledge.

Žižek, Slavoj. (2006a) *The Perverts Guide to Cinema*, dir Sophie Fiennes, Film Four Cinema.

——. ed. (2006b) *Lacan: The Silent Partners*. London: Verso.

——. (2001 [1992]) *Enjoy Your Symptom! Jacques Lacan in Hollywood and Out*, 2nd ed. New York: Routledge.

——. (2000) *The Ticklish Subject: The Absent Centre of Political Ontology*. London: Verso.

——. (1999) *The Ticklish Subject: The Absent Centre of Political Ontology*. London: Verso.

——. (1998) 'Whither Oedipus', *Analysis* 8: 146–60.

——. (1994) *The Metastases of Enjoyment: Six Essays on Woman and Causality*. London: Verso.

——. (1991) *Looking Awry: An Introduction to Jacques Lacan through Popular Culture*. Cambridge, MA: MIT Press.

——. (1989) *The Sublime Object of Ideology*. London: Verso.

Filmography

A Streetcar Named Desire (Elia Kazan, 1951)
Code 46 (Michael Winterbottom, 2003)
Safe (Todd Haynes, 2003)
Far from Heaven (Todd Haynes, 2002)
Ali: Fear Eats the Soul (Angst Essen Seele Auf) (Rainer Werner Fassbinder, 1974)
Sex and the City (HBO, 1998–2004)
Ally McBeal (20th Century Fox, 1997–2002)
Bridget Jones's Diary (Sharon Maguire, 2001)
Bridget Jones 2: The Edge of Reason (Beeban Kidron, 2004)
Fire (Deepa Mehta, 1996)
Blackpool (Peter Bowker, 2004)
Dr Zhivago (David Lean, 1965)
Home Stories (Matthias Müller, 1990)
Hiroshima Mon Amour (Alain Resnais, 1959)
Happy Together (Chun Gwong Cha Sit) (Kar Wai Wong, 1997)
In the Mood for Love (Fa Yeung Nin Wa) (Kar Wai Wong, 2000)
India Song (Marguerite Duras, 1975)
Moderato Cantabile (Marguerite Duras, 1960)
Bowling for Columbine (Michael Moore, 2002)
Farenheit 9/11 (Michael Moore, 2004)
Letter from an Unknown Woman (Max Olphüs, 1948)
Pretty Woman (Garry Marshall, 1990)
My Best Friend's Wedding (P.J. Hogan, 1997)
Edward Scissorhands (Tim Burton, 1990)
You've Got Mail (Nora Ephron, 1998)
Casablanca (Michael Curtiz, 1942)
Titanic (James Cameron, 1997)
Solaris (Steven Soderbergh, 2002)
All I Desire (Douglas Sirk, 1953)
Magnificent Obsession (Douglas Sirk, 1954)
All That Heaven Allows (Douglas Sirk, 1955)
Written on the Wind (Douglas Sirk, 1956)
There's Always Tomorrow (Douglas Sirk, 1957)
Time to Die (Douglas Sirk, 1958)
Imitation of Life (Douglas Sirk, 1959)
Anatomy of Hell (Catherine Breillat, 2004)
Romance (Catherine Breillat, 1999)
Dirty Dreams (Rocco Siffredi, 2005)
Nasty Trails (Rocco Siffredi, 2005)
Rocco Ravishes Ibiza (Rocco Siffredi, 2005)
Solyaris (Andrei Tarkovsky, 1972)

Index

References to notes are indicated by 'n' following the page number and preceding the note number